THE WORLD OF
MONSIEUR VINCENT

Mary Purcell

The World of Monsieur Vincent

LOYOLA UNIVERSITY PRESS
Chicago

© 1989 Mary Purcell
A Loyola Request Reprint*

BX
4700
·V6
P8
1989

ISBN 0-8294-0606-9

Loyola University Press
3441 North Ashland Avenue
Chicago, Illinois 60657

*Originally published in 1963 by the Harvill Press
Limited, London, and Charles Scribner's Sons, New
York, this book is a newly revised edition especially
prepared for re-issuance by Loyola University Press
by Mary Purcell. All rights reserved.*

Library of Congress Cataloging-in-Publication Data

Purcell, Mary, 1906-
    The World of Monsieur Vincent.

    Bibliography: p.
    Includes index.
    1. Vincent de Paul, Saint, 1581-1660.   2. Christian
saints—France—Biography. I. Title.
BX4700.V6P8   1989   271'.77'024 [B]   88-27217
ISBN 0-8294-0606-9

*Reprinted by arrangement with the author and/or
the original publisher.

by the same author

THE PILGRIM CAME LATE
THE HALO ON THE SWORD
DON FRANCISCO
MATT TALBOT AND HIS TIMES
THE FIRST JESUIT
ST ANTHONY AND HIS TIMES
THE GREAT CAPTAIN

CONTENTS

ILLUSTRATIONS

PREFACE

Since his death in 1660 the charitable works initiated by St. Vincent de Paul have multiplied throughout the world. Social and humane reforms introduced by him have benefited millions of the poor, the afflicted, and the underprivileged. His prodigious energy and influence had its wellsprings in his love for God; from that inner fount, continually brimming over, flowed his care for the poor, his longing to comfort the troubled and to alleviate human misery.

Popular religious art depicts him as a benevolent old priest carrying an infant in a fold of his cloak and surrounded by ragged waifs. Writers present him as a dear old saint, a shrewd Gascon peasant without a trace of humbug in his makeup, a saint whose good works enclose him like a forest while his humility envelops him like a fog. Such portrayals diminish Vincent, either by oversimplifying his complex character or by underestimating the intellectual and spiritual stature of a truly remarkable man.

His degrees from the universities of Paris and Toulouse, his fluency in Spanish and Italian, his understanding of the Arab world and of the branches of knowledge in which its peoples excelled, are indications of his ability and attainments. Of the 30,000 letters and documents he wrote, only about three thousand have been preserved; but these reveal a keen intelligence, sound judgment, and a profound knowledge of human nature. There is also a rare delicacy of feeling that enables him to strike exactly the right note no matter to whom he is writing or on what subject.

Questions are still being argued by Vincentian and other historians about the exact date of St. Vincent's birth and about his two-year captivity in North Africa. In the most recent life of the saint, published in Madrid in 1981, the author, Fr. José María Roman, C.M., lists 24 arguments decrying and 24 arguments affirming the authenticity of a letter in which Vincent described his capture by pirates and life as a slave. As neither side has been able to unearth any clue to the saint's whereabouts between 1605 and 1607, and as he was always a truthful man, I have given the letter penned in 1607 by himself.

St. Vincent was gifted with a winning manner. In later life he had a tendency towards irony in speech and mimicry in gesture, with a fondness for 'making haste slowly'; but his warm, generous heart and outgoing personality endeared him to people of all classes and creeds. Though an exemplar of true Christian charity, he was equally inflamed with a passion for justice. Injustice sent this normally mild man to confront and upbraid its perpetrators, whether prince or pauper. Who but he had dared Richelieu's anger and gone unscathed? More than once he reproached the Cardinal-Minister for prolonging devastating wars. When Richelieu was on the point of unjustly expelling a young Visitation nun from France, Vincent intervened, departing from his usual humble way of acting to invoke his powers as ecclesiastical Superior of the Visitandines. The nun was not banished.

Though he helped thousands, he never saw them as crowds; for him they were other Christs; he called the destitute "Our Lords, the poor." He recruited women for his first charitable association, seeing in them his own practical qualities, attention to detail, and the ability to organize, to improvise, and make-do. When sending them to serve the sick poor in their homes, he laid down strict rules and gave minute directions; all was to be done in a Christlike manner and with respect for human dignity. Through the manifold works he set in motion, he literally covered France with a network of care and charity in a long period of war, famine, and plague. Thus, he not only rendered service to his *patria,* but also bequeathed to posterity a blueprint for future relief and social welfare work.

The poor, prisoners and galley-slaves, orphans, the aged, war victims and refugees, the mentally ill, and foreign missions were but part of his concern. He also made efforts to revive religion, then at a low ebb in France. His flair for identifying the root of a problem convinced him that the real remedy lay in the proper formation and education of priests, an aim that could not be achieved without good bishops. A Concordat of the previous century had permitted French kings to appoint bishops, with lamentable results. During the minority of Louis XIII, Vincent was appointed to the Council that advised the Queen-Mother. He exerted himself to ensure that only worthy candidates were appointed to vacant sees.

His times and contemporaries mirrored the saint, just as he mirrored them. Meeting a preacher renowned for his learning, but whose pompous sermons were understood only by those as learned as himself, Vincent said, "In the name of God, will you try and use simple language in the pulpit." To another who thundered while his congregations quailed, he wrote begging him to moderate his voice and his sentiments. It was the era of Molière, and Vincent had been talking to an actor who told him that the popular comedians "now speak in normal tones, neither too high nor too low, as in familiar conversation." Vincentian fathers in Poland wrote telling their Founder that an eclipse there had been interpreted "as a sure sign of coming catastrophe, maybe the end of the world." The saint replied: "I met a famous astronomer who says that there are eclipses every year and if things were as bad as the Poles think, the world would have been destroyed long ago."

Of the many charitable works founded under his patronage, one—founded long after his death—is the best known. In 1833 Frederick Ozanam and six fellow law students at the Sorbonne took part in a university debate. A man in the audience asked, "but what are you fellows doing for the poor of Paris." Their reply was not in words but in the formation of the St. Vincent de Paul Society, an apostolate to provide for the material and other needs of the poor. Animated by St. Vincent's ideals, they gave the society his name. From that small nucleus of seven young men it has grown to become a world-wide organization. Through its devoted members many a poor person, in Dublin and elsewhere, has had reason to bless the name of St. Vincent de Paul.

Vincent took life as he found it. There was no event, no aspect of Parisian life during his 53 years in the city, with which he was not familiar. His heart beat in unison with the pulse of Paris, the heart of France. Yet he yearned for more than the poor and unfortunate of one city, one realm. The charity of Christ urged him so strongly that he longed for the peoples of the entire world to belong to that kingdom of justice, love, and peace—the kingdom of God.

Mary Purcell.
Dublin 1988

THE WORLD OF
MONSIEUR VINCENT

Chapter One

OUT OF GASCONY

DURING the spring term of 1598 a student of Toulouse University got word of his father's death. He was a young Gascon, almost eighteen, a first-year student reading theology. Observant, intelligent, imaginative, gifted with an excellent memory, he was also hardheaded and circumspect, too much so perhaps for one still in the impulsive years between boyhood and manhood.

If he visualized the deathbed scene, the grief of the family, the simple funeral, the lately covered grave, he hardly allowed himself to dwell on such thoughts. The initial shock of the bad news absorbed, his characteristic reaction would have been to estimate, in terms of crops and livestock, of sowing and reaping, of shearing and vintage, of prices and taxes and tithes, the reduced circumstances to which the de Pauls must henceforth fit themselves. His practical mind, realizing what the loss of the sower at that season of the year meant to a family living on a few hectares of land, would consider the financial problems raised by the death of his father, and his own future prospects, now in jeopardy. Always alive to contrasts, Vincent de Paul was the kind of student to note the incongruity of the thought of death at a time when spring, moving inland on the Mediterranean air, was bringing Provence and all the Languedoc to life once more.

He had come to the university the previous Michaelmas from his home near Dax, a walled town some two hundred miles to the west. Ranquine, the farmstead where he was born, is no more, but a replica of it stands close to the original site and has been renamed *Le Berceau*, The Cradle. Only an ancient oak, so old that its branches have to be propped up, yet so retentive of vitality that every summer sees it grow green again, remains—the one authentic link with the saint's early years.

It is a measure of the stature of St Vincent de Paul that two great nations contend to possess him, France claiming him as a Gascon, Spain insisting that he was born in Aragon.[1] The French claim is incontestable as regards Vincent himself. The Spaniards may be right in their assertions that his parents were natives of Aragon. Whether the worthy Jean de Paul and his wife, Bertrande de Moras, had their origins north or south of the Pyrenees is now immaterial. They were hardworking and thrifty, typical of a peasantry that had survived a generation of war, uncertainty and hardship. They owned two small farms, pigs, sheep, cows and a horse or two. Like their counterparts in most countries before the era of mechanized farming they lived frugally, spending as little money as possible. By unremitting toil and economy they managed to provide a living for themselves and their six children and to meet the demands of the tax collectors whose visits became more and more frequent as taxes mounted higher and higher.

Vincent spent most of his early years herding. Diversions were few. He and his brothers and companions used to ride races on the farmers' nags. These hungry overworked brutes, left to fend for themselves in the barren country between the Adour and the ocean, were usually vicious, and it took courage and determination to stay astride one of them. Horsemanship was a useful accomplishment for the lad who was later to find himself frequently in the saddle, travelling on the errands of God. In his seventieth year, when he rode posthaste from Paris to Saint-Germain-en-Laye to persuade Mazarin and the Queen-Mother to return to the capital, the sight of submerged bridges did not deter Vincent de Paul from forcing his mount to swim the Seine in flood. He was older still when he won, all unknown to himself, a race that was the talk of Paris. The Prince of Condé and a band of the young bloods of the court were out riding one day in the country when they spied 'Monsieur Vincent' in the distance on his white horse. They could think of no better sport than to pretend to be highwaymen and give chase to the old priest, some of them laying heavy wagers that if he reached the city safely his first act would be to enter a church and thank God. Whooping wildly and discharging their pistols in the direction of their quarry, they put their horses to the gallop and spurred hard to overtake him. But Monsieur Vincent beat them to the gates of Paris. Later they spotted the white horse tethered outside a church. One look inside and a good deal of money changed hands.

During his childhood, however, riding was a recreation Vincent enjoyed only when more serious tasks were done. He was responsible for herding the family livestock. At first he seldom took his charges—cattle, sheep and pigs—out of sight of familiar landmarks, but when he grew older and could balance himself on stilts, he covered considerable distances, sometimes going as far as thirty miles from home. Perched aloft, it was easier to watch rooting pigs and nibbling sheep, to spot a straying cow or nag; easier too, to keep a wary eye on roads and riding tracks. Brigands and hungry soldiers had been known to seize farm animals, so it was wise to keep out of their way. Usually he set out at sunrise and returned at sunset; but in summer and autumn when he found good grazing far from Ranquine he often remained where he was, sleeping in the midst of his beasts. Having said the prayers with which the de Paul family always ended the day, he slept huddled beneath a tree in the oak woods, his pigs, replete with truffles or acorns, grunting and snoring contentedly nearby. The part of Jean de Paul's holding situated in the Landes was poor soil, but, fortunately for the family, most of his land bordered on the Chalosse, a loamy, fertile plain stretching north and east of Dax. South of Ranquine the Adour wound its lazy way, flooding twice a year when swollen by the streams that joined it in its long course from the Pyrenees. The twelve-mile strip of lowland extending along the French coast from Cap Breton almost to Bordeaux and known as the Landes has long ago lost the desolate aspect it presented in Vincent's boyhood. The forest belts since planted to take the force and moisture of

Atlantic winds were then unthought of. Here and there, where the demands of industry and the forest fires of later years have denuded large areas of timber, stretches of the forlorn landscape Vincent knew may be glimpsed, but such patches are few and far between.

Wandering barefoot with his charges, the boy learned a good deal in his open-air life. He knew how to read approaching weather changes in the skies, in the wind, in the behaviour of wild things. For clock, calendar and map he had the sun and stars. This solitary outdoor life played its part in his development:

> To dry and warm himself he had to build shelters against wind and rain, to practise the patient art of lighting fires with flint and tinder, to learn to kindle even the green wood into flame. As submissive to nature as a bird, a tree, a blade of grass, he wandered thus with his shepherd's pouch, his crook and his livestock, crossing and re-crossing the sun-drenched Landes . . . sometimes glimpsing far away to the south the vague, indistinct line of the Pyrenees. . . . This loneliness in-grained in him the habit of recollection and solitude. In the future he will be found reserving a considerable portion of each day for that silence which he so magnificently defines as a conversation with God. . . . 'To keep silence is simply to listen to God and to speak to Him . . . alone, secluded where none may eavesdrop. . . . In silence one hears God more clearly.' A life like his bred resoluteness and confidence. He had no overseer, no supervisor in his task of herding. But he took pleasure in doing it well, each day extending the limits of his pastures a little further afield, in proportion to his developing powers. [2]

Vincent was born in 1580 or 1581. He had three brothers and two sisters. All the family worked hard. Their staple food, that of most Gascon households of the period, was millet potage and bread; they had cider from their own apples and occasionally wine. Natives of Gascony fared well compared to the people of neighbouring provinces such as the Limousin where the only available bread was an unappetizing loaf made from pounded chestnuts. In Vincent's sympathetic references to the hard lives of the countrywomen he had known we may see his own mother and sisters.

I often saw them return from the fields quite worn out, their clothes muddy and bedraggled. Yet, if the weather took up or they were told to return to their tasks, they were off again at once, silent and uncomplaining. [3]

Contemporary French artists, notably the Le Nain brothers, give a true picture of the background to Vincent de Paul's first twelve years. The countrymen of the Le Nain canvases are almost all dejected and careworn, the women patient-faced and retiring, the children ragged and lethargic. The housewife, pouring a measure of wine for guests, or doling out—ever so sparingly— wine or cider for her husband, is careful not to part with flagon or jug, and she never allows herself or the watchful children the luxury of a sip. There is usually one boy, more alert than the others, practising tunes on a home-made violin or flute. Fowl, pigs and other animals are tended with care, representing as they do the family's working capital. The cat is accepted as a household necessity, likewise the dog used for herding, hunting, and maybe poaching. A mongrel pup, the children's only plaything, is barely tolerated; past experience has seemingly taught this creature his proper place and station; he cowers in a corner or beneath a table, keeping well out of range of kicks and blows. To study a farmhouse interior as portrayed by a Le Nain is to gain admittance to a home like that in which Vincent de Paul was reared.

Once, towards the end of his life, Monsieur Vincent was at his door in Paris seeing off some important guests when a beggar-woman approached him asking for alms. To strengthen her plea she added, 'Monsieur, I was at one time a servant to Madame your mother.' Rather brusquely, for he was not easily fooled, much less the kind of man who could stomach lies or flattery, he replied in the hearing of all, 'My dear woman, you must be mistaking me for someone else. My mother never had a servant. She was once a servant herself. She was the wife, as I am the son, of a poor countryman.'

But he had not always openly proclaimed his origins. When the boy Vincent accompanied his father to their local town, Dax, he often felt overwhelmed with shame. Jean de Paul limped, being a little lame. Like other farmers of his time and district he dressed shabbily: baggy trousers buttoned below the knee; a ragged smock in summer, a foul-smelling sheepskin in winter; a broad-brimmed home-woven hat that kept off sun and rain; clogs in wet weather, rope-soled sandals in dry, no footgear in summer; lengths of faded cloth twisted around the legs, puttee-fashion, in lieu of hose. He might turn out in better clothes on special occasions, but to go well clad at all times was to draw attention to himself and run the risk of having the tax gatherers add to his already heavy burden. Vincent used to fall back a few paces when they went to Dax together, hoping that passers-by would not take them for father and son. A couple of years later when he was at college he refused to see his father when that good man called to visit him.

These incidents were probably no more than the usual impatience of the young with the preceding generation. It is not uncommon for an intelligent lad, full of unreasoning anger with his elders for accepting living conditions from which he, vaguely aware of his own latent powers, hopes to emancipate himself, to react in like manner. Vincent's behaviour towards his father caused him remorse in later life and more than once he spoke of it with regret. 'It was a great sin for me,' he declared once, speaking about his early vanity.

Traces of this snobbishness remained and he had to make valiant efforts before finally overcoming the tendency. When in charge of the *Bons-Enfants* college in Paris, word was brought to him one day that a man dressed as a peasant and with a Gascony accent was at the gate asking for admission; the stranger claimed to be Monsieur Vincent's nephew from Dax. At first the uncle was decidedly put out and told the porter to bring the visitor up to his room by the back stairs; but the order was hardly given when it was countermanded; the old temptation was recognized and resisted with that characteristic impulse which carried him almost too much to the other extreme. Hurrying down to the gate himself he gave his nephew a hearty welcome, kissed and hugged the young man and insisted that all the community come and be introduced to the 'most honourable person of my family'. The bewildered nephew was also presented to some notable personages who called at the same time. At the next *culpa* of the community, the superior publicly accused himself of having felt ashamed of his nephew because he was countrified and ill-dressed, and of having wished to hide him on his arrival from Dax. His strong efforts at self-conquest on this occasion seem to have rid him of his weakness, for soon afterwards, when a distant connection of his was condemned to the galleys, he broadcast the news, letting people infer that the convicted criminal was a near relative.

Though he made no secret of the vanity that beset his youth, he left it to others to record the virtues of his early years. As might be expected, in view of his later apostolate, he showed unusual understanding of human affliction and a generosity out of all proportion to his slender resources. If he met beggars on his return journeys from the local mill, he would open his sack of millet or flour, as he had seen his parents do at home, and give fistfuls of the contents to the needy. On at least one occasion he parted with something that was not his parents' property but his own. He carried with him on his daily wanderings with his sheep and pigs a small bag containing thirty *sous*, about fifteen shillings. For a lad in his circumstances it was a large sum and represented his savings over a long period. One day, touched by the wretchedness of a poor tramp he met, he gave all his money to the man, 'not keeping even a *sou*'.

Noting Vincent's intelligence and vivacity Jean de Paul felt sure 'that the boy was destined for greater things than herding'. When M. de Comet, a Dax attorney, commented on the lad's brightness, the Ranquine farmer knew that his estimate of his son had been correct, and he decided to have him educated and prepared for the priesthood. At that time the Church was the one institution in France in which a gifted boy might hope to rise. Only in ecclesiastical circles did intelligence give its possessor an advantage equal if not superior to that which noble birth and influential connections gave others. The de Pauls had a relative, prior of a neighbouring monastery, whose family had hitherto been quite poor. Now, thanks to the revenues his benefices yielded and to his influence, which extended far beyond the priory, they were poor no longer. Jean de Paul, looking to the future, probably saw *his* son doing likewise. It was a time for optimism. The wars of religion were over. Henri of Navarre was King of France and seemed likely to rule wisely and for a long period. With high hopes Vincent's father sent him to the Franciscan college in Dax, agreeing to pay a pension of sixty *livres* a year, roughly seventy-five pounds in present currency.

The college, a struggling one, was no better or no worse than many similar institutions throughout France:

> It was in a far from flourishing condition and the rules were neither enforced nor obeyed. . . . Masters came and went, for often it was just a wandering life of adventure that brought them there at all; they were like so many birds of passage and no one asked to see their qualifications, if they had any. Sometimes lay teachers were employed, sometimes clerics; there was no freedom of choice; those who came that way were taken on if they offered themselves as teachers. [4]

The planned syllabus, the orderly, well-graded systems of progress, the training of teachers and the organization of studies on a rational basis had not yet been perfected by the Jesuits who, in the following century, were to earn for themselves the title 'schoolmasters of Europe', and whose successful methods were to be widely followed, thus raising educational standards all around. In Vincent's time there were almost as many methods as teachers and since there was no set syllabus the masters, most of them ignorant of the basic rules of their profession, taught what they would and as best they could. But a bright pupil needs little teaching. Though hitherto he spoke only the local dialect, a derivative of Low Latin, Vincent was well-equipped for fast learning. He had brains, the ability to concentrate, and the self-confidence of a true Gascon.

M. de Comet evidently got good accounts of him from the Franciscans, for he took him to live in his own home; in return Vincent taught the attorney's two sons what he himself learned. A deep mutual respect and affection sprang up between the lawyer and young de Paul. 'He treated me with fatherly affection and care,' said Monsieur Vincent, speaking of M. de Comet, 'and I loved him as a son his own father.' The Ranquine lad learned to speak, read and write both French and Latin. Though he himself speaks deprecatingly of his schooling, saying that he went 'only to fourth year' in Dax, he was ready for the matriculation test of Toulouse University in 1597.

In the third week of Advent, 1596, the young student set off for Bidache, a fortified town some twenty miles away, where he received Tonsure and Minor Orders from the Bishop of Tarbes.[5] The See of Dax was then vacant and youths of that diocese had to go elsewhere for the conferring of the Orders that marked them as aspirants preparing to ascend the remaining steps to the priesthood and the altar. Vincent could have gone to Aire, but the Bishop of Aire, 'a perfect alchemist . . . and very expert with firearms, who was reputed to have found the philosopher's stone', was more given to experimenting than ordaining. The following summer the question of the boy's theological studies came up. His father, who had been relieved of paying the sixty *livres* pension for all but the first year his son spent in Dax, now decided to invest something really valuable in Vincent's future. He sold a yoke of oxen, representing to him what a tractor or combine-harvester would to a small farmer of today, gave the proceeds to his son and sent him off to Toulouse and its university.

His first biographer, Abelly, tells us that Vincent studied for seven years at Toulouse, but adds that he also went to Saragossa in Spain and spent some time at the university there.[6] Some writers dismiss Saragossa without a mention, regarding the idea of St Vincent's stay there as just as untenable as the Spanish claim that he was born in Aragon. But if France is in an impregnable position in claiming him as a Frenchman, the Spaniards are on solid ground as regards his sojourn in the Aragon capital. Witnesses for beatification and canonization, the Roman breviary, the Jesuits of San Carlos College, Saragossa, with whom he lodged, all state that he was there. References in the saint's own writings confirm the fact: he defends stoutly and explains as one having practical experience of it the manner of teaching in the universities of Spain. He praises the Spanish theologians of the time, showing intimate acquaintance with the teachings of the doctors of theology in Saragossa and quoting them frequently.[7] He speaks of the Carmels of Spain as one who has visited them, for he knows customs peculiar to the Carmelites in that country.[8] He remarks the esteem in which the king was held 'in a certain realm where I once lived'; it requires no great mental effort, considering the countries he lived in and the circumstances in which he made this remark, to deduce that he spoke of Philip II and the Spain of his time.[9]

Saragossa had attractions for impecunious students in the provision made for them there. The university had a special fund which aided foreign and poor scholars, and they got free treatment in the hospital under the care of the faculty of medicine. More than likely his journey to Spain took place in 1598 when, as will be seen, the University of Toulouse was at a low ebb, and when his father's death and his own dwindling funds would have spurred him to seek some means of completing his studies in the shortest possible time and at the lowest possible expense. It is tempting to think that he might have had relatives in Aragon who helped him on his way, and the Aragon de Pauls and their supporters are very positive that he had, but there is no conclusive evidence that such was the case.

He would have had to travel 'between the snows', for the tracks across the High Pyrenees can be used only for a short period each summer. The passes were unfrequented and dangerous. Wolves and bears, eagles and vultures, lay in wait for lone travellers, as did bands of robbers and criminals who had broken French or Spanish laws. It is a memorable experience to penetrate one of the crevices in that vast Pyrenean wall which cuts the Peninsula off from Europe, and to emerge through the waterfalls and mists and shadows of the lofty cols on to flat shelves of highland overlooking further hills and plains. When mountains and hills are left behind, nothing lies ahead but copper-coloured expanses of country, the sunbaked land of Aragon where Pompey and Caesar, Charlemagne and Roland, the Emirs and the Cid wove the stuff of history and trailed the imagery of a thousand legends. This was the country Vincent traversed on his way through Upper Aragon, past villages with dark churches, houses with wrought-iron gates and balconies and with coats-of-arms carved above their doors. One wonders did he note any house bearing the shield of the de Pauls of that area, with its threefold device: a castle, a crowned head, and Our Lady of Pilar supported on a flame-coloured cloud.

Our student was not in Spain in the autumn of 1598. In September and again in December that year he was in Tarbes at Quarter Tense, receiving first the subdiaconate, then the diaconate. His route from Saragossa to Tarbes should have taken him either by the Roncesvalles Pass where the legendary horn of Roland sounded its last despairing blast, or along the highway to Pamplona and north to the Bidassoa river, then as now marking the frontier. When he sighted the Atlantic he turned north for the Pass of Béhobie, a few miles from the present international bridge at Irun-Hendaye. It is not likely that he had any trouble there or at Roncesvalles or at any other sentinelled pass.[10]

When the Bishop of Tarbes raised him to the subdiaconate in the third week of September, Europe was ringing with the news of the death of Philip II of Spain. Nine years previously the last Valois king had been assassinated in Paris. In England the Tudor line was dying in the person of the aged Elizabeth. With Philip's death power would begin to slip from the Hapsburgs until the last of his three incompetent successors would let the Spanish sceptre fall to the French side of the Pyrenees, the crown and the throne to the Bourbons. Though Vincent the subdeacon, trudging steadily from Tarbes to Toulouse to begin the Michaelmas term there, was probably unaware of it, he was a witness to the end of an era.

Chapter Two

TOWN AND GOWN

TOULOUSE, the city where Vincent de Paul spent most of the seven years between 1597 and 1604, was and is still sometimes called the Queen of the Midi. Its regal and affluent air must have been somewhat bewildering at first for a lad coming from a small farm on the western seaboard. Refinements and luxuries were not the monopoly of the wealthier citizens; humbler folk shared in the prosperity brought by a boom in trade, enjoying amenities unknown to artisans and labourers elsewhere. The Toulousains lived well. Fruit, cheese, fish and game were plentiful. Good wine was cheap. Needy students of the various colleges fared better than their fellows at other seats of learning. The varied and abundant food must have been welcome to Vincent, accustomed for most of his eighteen years to the monotonous, meagre menu of the de Paul household.

The Languedoc capital was then on the crest of a trade wave which had kept rising right through, and in spite of, thirty years of religious wars. While these wars, with seven breathing-spaces euphemistically called truces, ravaged France, fortunes were made in Toulouse through a little blue weed known in Provence as *guède* and in England as woad. This plant, native to the Toulousain plains, yielded six crops a year and was the basis of a vast if ephemeral industry. Great numbers found employment as pickers in the fields; in the city vats the *guède* was boiled, pounded to a stiff paste and rolled into egg-sized lumps; these blue dye 'pastels' were thèn exported. Assézat, the Huguenot merchant prince who was the initiator and chief exporter of this profitable trade, was one of the richest men in France. His magnificent residence, the Hôtel Assézat, designed by a French pupil of Michelangelo, is today the headquarters of several learned and cultural societies. In Vincent de Paul's time it was new and the owner could ascend the lantern tower and look right across the Garonne to the plains where flourished the humble weed that had made his fortune.

In the streets so often traversed by the students, other merchants, following Assézat's example, built themselves noble houses of the local brick, the colourful effect of which has been enhanced and mellowed by the years. Toulouse changes hue with the passing hours, flaming fiercely at noon, paling through all the shades from magenta to mauve at sunset, and greeting each dawn anew, 'a rose-red city, half as old as time'. The lords of commerce did well to enrich their town by raising so many fine mansions in the years of plenty. Sooner than they thought, indigo would oust their woad product from the market and Toulouse's period of prominence as the world centre for blue dye come to an end.

The Toulousains were uppish and gave themselves airs extremely disconcerting to the country lads who each year made their way to the Midi city in quest of learning. Contemporary travellers recorded the citizens' traits:

> They are curious and insolent and given to staring fixedly at strangers, their behaviour rather resembling that of wild beasts brought over from Africa in that they will interrupt their meals to turn and gape at passers-by. . . . They are very volatile; when accompanying funerals they utter loud cries and lamentations. Right in the middle of the city streets their young girls may be seen dancing, making the most astounding gestures as they do so.[1]

The students came from the slopes of the Auvergnes, from Velay and Périgord, from Béarn, Gascony and Guyenne, from Navarre on the French and Navarre on the Spanish side of the Pyrenees. Some were from further afield, from Champagne, Lorraine and Burgundy, from Spain, the Spanish Netherlands and the Germanies.

Young students of Gascon origin received more than the

usual measure of that disdain which the Toulousains showed to strangers within their gates. In the opinion of the haughty and cultured citizens of the southern capital Vincent's compatriots were among the least of the lesser breeds beyond the law. Apart from the Gascon patois, a mixture of French, Spanish and Basque, 'all *higue, hogue, hagasset*', they were given to mimicry, waggishness, and the broader type of practical joke. Their braggart speech was proverbial, fighting their favourite occupation and recreation. Henri III, last king of the Valois line, would have none but Gascons for his personal bodyguard; yet, for all their mighty oaths of *Cap de Dieu*, the famous Forty-Five had been unable to save him from the assassin's steel. Before he was many weeks in Toulouse Vincent de Paul would have learned how he and his like were rated there. Within the university and without there were free lessons in 'the proud man's contumely . . . the spurns that patient merit of the unworthy takes'.

For many years Toulouse University, 'nursing-mother of jurisprudence', had provided France with her leading judges and statesmen. In its heyday it was no place for dilettantes. The students of civil and canon law were up at 4 a.m. After an hour's prayer they trooped into the lecture halls, 'our bulky books under our arms, our writing materials and candle sconces in our hands'. Magistrates of the Toulouse Parlement were obliged to attend the opening of classes at 5 a.m. in summer, an hour later in winter. 'More than once, when they were late, not arriving till seven of the clock, they were admonished by the Masters of the University.' [2] But by Vincent's time there a decline had set in. A complaint sent by the French clergy to the Paris government shows the pitiable state into which most of the French universities had then fallen:

The abuses are so great in the universities of this realm that there is no longer any need to have studied or answered publicly nor even to be present to receive degrees. . . . It suffices . . . to send the money and the name . . . from which it happens that the universities are deserted and the bar and

31

judiciary full of persons little versed in the knowledge of civil law. [3]

Charlatanism was the order of the day. The religious wars had affected most of the seats of learning in France, Toulouse not excepted. Students were fewer in number. The professors in consequence received less fees and demanded subsidiary payments from the Parlement and the Town, from the bishops and the King. In 1598 the Rector, Cabot, painted a sorry picture of conditions then obtaining and drew up what he deemed to be an ideal charter for the university. But Henri IV was not greatly interested in universities or learning; he had more than enough to do to manage his double teams, north and south, Huguenot and Catholic. The Parlement of the Languedoc, sitting in Toulouse, took some notice of the plight of the university and raised the salt tax from three farthings to fourpence halfpenny in an effort to hold the regents who were being attracted to other fields. With the increase in salaries the legislature handed out a warning to those of the Law faculty who were having their lectures read by substitutes. In his spirited defence of the censured professors the Rector pointed out that to eke out their wretched stipends and to save their wives and families from starvation they were obliged to engage in public trials and plead in law courts. The King had reduced the royal grants; the bishops were in arrears with pensions promised from their dioceses; the Rector was not surprised that some of the best regents had left Toulouse University for that of Cahors, or that no one had been found to fill chairs vacant for years.

Such was the state of affairs when Vincent left for Saragossa. On his return things were little better. The university beadles had seized Church revenues in one diocese and the bishop's horses in another in lieu of the unpaid pensions. The regents were at loggerheads regarding the allocation of the moneys that the increase in salt tax had brought their way. The Parlement was issuing further reprimands:

The regents must be more attentive to their duty of lecturing and see to it that the University of Toulouse be restored to its pristine glory and splendour, and its scholars withdrawn from the debaucheries all too common among them.

Degrees are to be refused to persons not of the requisite quality.

Students of the various 'Nations', especially the Burgundians and the Gascons, are to be strictly prohibited from carrying arms and intimidating the citizens. [4]

Vincent attended the Collège de Foix, founded by the fifteenth century Cardinal of that name and better endowed, culturally and materially, than the other colleges. The founder, Pierre de Foix, entered the Franciscan Order in his youth. In later life he was raised to the Cardinalate. He became the confidant of eight Popes and acquired wealth and possessions, partly through inheritance, partly through Papal favour, as when a reigning Pontiff, knowing his passion for books, presented him with the library of a dead anti-Pope. Cardinal Foix was a patron of learning and art and his library, the envy of Europe, comprised a collection of manuscripts and another of printed works. His entire fortune went on the purchase of rare items to add to it, and he bequeathed it to the college he had founded. That magnificent bequest was the pride of the college during Vincent's time there and helped in part to make up for the scarcity and negligence of the professors as far as the Dax scholar was concerned. During the following century the library's contents were shamelessly appropriated, the worst plunderer being an official of Louis XIV who visited the college and took away more than three hundred manuscripts, legalizing his raid by leaving a paltry sum in payment. [5]

The Collège de Foix was in the centre of the university quarter, where its buildings occupied a quadrangle. The enclosing walls boasted four watch-towers and the main entrance was on the Street of the Dry Holm Tree. The Cardinal had placed his foundation under the patronage of two saints of very different temperaments, the fiery Jerome and the gentle Francis of Assisi.

Vincent de Paul was in his second term at Toulouse when he got word of his father's death. In his will Jean de Paul stipulated that the family should assist Vincent and pay his way until his studies were completed. But the de Foix scholar did not wish to burden his mother, brother and sisters. For most of two years and while yet only a boy, he had managed to support himself in Dax. If that town, with little to commend it save its hot, therapeutic springs and baths, could yield him a livelihood in his off-school hours, surely wealthy, populous Toulouse could do likewise. He opened a school at Buzet-sur-Tarn, about twelve miles from the city, and in a short time was doing so well that he transferred the thriving academy to Toulouse, taking the pupils along as boarders. That there were no objections from parents suggests that the venture was a decided success. Two of his charges were of the Valette family, nephews or close relations of the Duc d'Épernon, the powerful noble and commander who rose to be *demi-roi* of France.

In September, 1600, armed with certificates requested and obtained from the Vicar-General of Dax, Vincent set off for Périgueux. The roads were infested with brigands. The notorious Captain Caravelle, who had once seized Buzet-sur-Tarn, making it his headquarters while he raided the plains of Toulouse, was at large again. The three sons of the Baron d'Entraigues, fugitives from Dauphiné because of their crimes, were ranging the lands between the Garonne and the Lot. Though they successfully evaded capture in 1600, the days of these desperadoes were numbered; not long afterwards they were all beheaded in the Place du Capitole, that site at the heart of Toulouse where St Sernin's martyrdom and the city's Christian history began.[6] Vincent's journey to Périgueux being too important for him to take the risk of encountering highwaymen on the road, he would have chosen the safest mode of travel, the water-coaches that plied the reaches of the Garonne and other rivers between Toulouse and his destination. He was on his way to ordination.[7]

If passers-by noted the young stranger in the streets of sleepy Périgueux they would have described him as a typical Gascon, of middle height but with broad, powerful shoulders. He carried no spare flesh and was well-built, walking with quick and supple movements. A contemporary says that St Vincent had a large head with a broad and majestic forehead and a face neither too full nor too narrow. His habitual expression was mild, though he had a keen, penetrating glance and acute hearing. The portraits show us the heavy eyebrows, the large nose and ears, the strong jaw of Vincent the old man; but even age has not obliterated the lurking, quizzical smile, the mobile mouth, the suggestion of determination tempered with kindness and compassion, the warm humanity that won Vincent de Paul so many friends.

Seven miles north of Périgueux the bishop of that diocese had a summer château. He was an old man, infirm, almost blind, but very holy. When Vincent de Paul presented himself for ordination at the September Quarter Tense he was hardly asked his age. If he were he would have had to answer 'nineteen or twenty,' an age four or five years short of that prescribed for ordinands by the Council of Trent. But the Council's decrees were not enforced in France until 1615 and it is doubtful whether the Tridentine regulations had by 1600 reached the French bishops, many of whom were endeavouring to administer several dioceses in addition to their own. Many bishoprics, Dax among them, were vacant since the religious wars and large areas were without priests. Bishops were glad to ordain candidates offering themselves for the priesthood without making very rigorous inquiries as to age or proficiency in studies. There were then no seminaries in France and anyone, without vocation or preparation, could and did enter the ecclesiastical state with results lamentable and discreditable to religion and disastrous for souls.[8]

The young man ordained at Château l'Évêque in September, 1600, was—thanks to the grace of God, and to his upbringing, intelligence and application—less unworthy and better educated than most ordinands of his time and country. But he was not the Vincent who would yet proclaim, 'If I had known, when I had the rashness to present myself for ordination, as I know since, what it means to be a priest, I would far rather have spent my life tilling the soil than undertake the formidable obligations of the priestly state. . . .' He was not the Vincent who in his latter years would warn parents against pushing their sons into the priesthood from no other motive than that of getting ahead in the world and enriching their families.

The ordination took place in the Bishop's private chapel, since incorporated into the village church. A statuary group, showing St Vincent carrying a foundling infant and consoling an orphan boy, is now above the altar where he was ordained. Château l'Évêque is pleasantly situated in Périgord, the verdant province where a century and more later the child Talleyrand was reared by that domineering lady, his great-grandmother, the Princesse de Chalais. From the tower of the château adjoining the church one can get a fine view of the rolling country Vincent traversed when he set off, a priest of God, on his way back to Toulouse. It was six days before Michaelmas and the commencement of the autumn term, and he had to say his first Mass. Overcome with awe at the thought of this tremendous occasion, he chose a little frequented place, the chapel of Our Lady of Graces in the woods near Buzet, for his initial exercising of the powers just conferred on him. He had no congregation. He invited no relatives or friends. An acolyte and a priest whom he asked to accompany him were the only ones present.

There was little if any change in his life; he had yet four years of study to complete before obtaining his degree, so he continued as before attending his lectures and teaching his school. Between 1600 and 1604 some exciting events took place in Toulouse, not least the adventure which befell a former Rector who left the city about 1596 as one of a delegation bound for Rome. He and those travelling with him never arrived at their destination. They were heard of no more from the day they left, and had been presumed dead—lost at sea, or killed while traversing war-torn Provence, or murdered by brigands. After an absence of almost seven years the ex-Rector returned, in a pitiable condition and with an amazing story to tell. The delegation had been captured by pirates and taken to the slave-marts of Barbary; he alone had escaped and made his way home. Again and again he had to relate his experiences and 'the untold hardships he had suffered'. One wonders whether Vincent de Paul, present no doubt in the crowd of students who flocked to hear the Rector tell his tale of misadventure, had any premonition that at a not too distant date he himself would undergo a similar ordeal.

Such a trial did not befall him on the road to Rome, which he took in 1601, the year following his ordination. Through the influence of his friend, M. de Comet, he had been nominated to a parish in the Dax diocese; but another priest contested the appointment and took the matter to the appropriate Roman court. Vincent, determined to stand up for his rights, set off for Rome. As far as his claim was concerned his journey was fruitless, the decision being given in favour of his opponent, but it was not without profit to his soul. Thirty years later, in a letter to a friend, he recalled his first visit to the Eternal City, when he had been 'moved to tears, so great was the happiness I felt . . . at walking on that ground hallowed by the footsteps of so many apostles, martyrs and holy people'.

He returned to Toulouse and continued with his studies and his teaching. During 1602 a gallows was erected on the rue de la Pomme, 'on which students caught carrying arms were to be hanged or strangled'. In the same year heretical pamphlets printed in Nîmes were found circulating among students and citizens. The authorities of state, town and university, having collected as many of the publications as they could find, summoned all the students and citizens to the Place du Sellin where the offending theses were condemned and then burned in public by the hand of the executioner.

That year, also, the university and the town came into conflict more than once. Some German gentlemen visiting Toulouse were held up by Burgundian and Languedoc students and forced to 'pay for their welcome'. The foreigners lodged a complaint and a councillor, accompanied by the city watch, was sent by the Parlement to demand restitution of the amounts extorted from the strangers. But 'the new Rector and a few hundred armed scholars were all waiting in the Great Hall', and the detachment sent by the town authorities beat a hasty retreat. The Parlement then ordered the arrest of the student leaders, and preparations were afoot to waylay them when a worse hold-up took place. The Seneschal of Puy, returning from Vespers at Saint-Sernin, was held up to pay *his* welcome. The Canons, told of his plight, rushed out to rescue him and a battle-royal ensued in the streets. A runner was sent for the city watch, which came at the gallop. Although most of the students made their escape the ringleaders had been recognized and were soon afterwards arrested. Most of them were from Gascony and Bordeaux.

Other visitors to Toulouse during those years reported that the students waylaid strangers at every turn, extorting from them 'on the excuse of almsgiving and Masses which had to be said, sums of money which they spent on feasts called *morsles*'. One traveller complained not only of the exactions practised but of how the students' conduct was allowed to go unpunished by the various authorities.

Perhaps no one suffered more than the Toulousains themselves from the unruly, high-spirited youths. Vincent was in Toulouse when a climax in the relations between the citizens and the scholars was reached. Two students from Champagne murdered M. Céléry, a councillor who tried to break up a riot between groups from different colleges. The guilty pair were condemned to death, but later reprieved because of their youth. Before being banished from city and university for five years they were made to sue for pardon publicly in the council chamber, on bended knees, clad in their shirts and with the noose they had so narrowly escaped dangling from their necks.

Toulouse, between 1597 and 1604, was not lacking in grand spectacles and moving scenes. There were the state processions when the États de Languedoc met in plenary session, the Constable Montmorency riding into the city at the head of the lords and maréchals, the *Te Deum* in St Étienne's, the Cardinal de Joyeuse receiving the Constable and taking him to lodge with him in his palace. There was the day when Henri de Joyeuse,

Duke, Peer and Marshal of France, the Cardinal's brother whom the King had made Governor of the Languedoc, left armour, rank and honours to resume the Capuchin habit and cowl which he had for a time laid aside to rule a people who would have no other leader:

> When it became known in the city that he was coming back, wearing once more the brown serge of a friar, the whole populace turned out to acclaim him. The City Magistrate, the Parlement, the Capitouls were all for having a big procession to lead him in triumph to the Capuchins' convent. But, getting word of what was afoot, he entered the town secretly at dawn from the neighbouring village where he had slept, and went to the friary. The news spread like wildfire that he was there and the Magistrates with the assembled citizenry came to the Capuchins and found Père Ange in the garden, tending on the masons and carrying hods of mortar on his shoulder. He thanked them all kindly and said that being now in the state in which he wished to spend the remainder of his life he could offer them nothing but his prayers. . . . One could not after that travel any road of the Luraguais or Narbonne, those roads which he had previously ridden at the head of armies, without meeting him on his errands of mercy to the poor, whose wants he cared for, sharing with them his last crust of bread. [9]

Vincent de Paul could well have met this famous Capuchin in 1604, when he journeyed over the very roads where Père Ange was engaged in his apostolate of charity. Having obtained his degree as bachelor of theology in that year, Vincent was considering his next move when he got a message summoning him to Bordeaux. His business there has never come to light but the general opinion is that the Duc d'Épernon, whose nephews were among Vincent's pupils, was trying to get him a bishopric. The young Abbé de Paul had yet a long way to go before his voice would echo throughout France, crying, 'I tremble lest this damnable traffic in bishoprics draws down God's curse upon this realm.' His father had started him on an ecclesiastical career from rather worldly motives; he himself, whether he shared his father's ideas or not, was a Gascon through and through and therefore likely to be both ambitious and optimistic. For the journey to Bordeaux he hired a horse and went to the expense of buying new clothes and staying at reputable inns. Later he referred to 'the high costs which this Bordeaux business, the nature of which I dare not even mention, made me incur'. But the episcopal mitre, if that was the purpose of his journey and expenditure, did not materialize.*

Returning to Toulouse a poorer and disappointed man, he was somewhat compensated by an unexpected stroke of luck. An old lady who had died during his absence left him three or four hundred *écus* (about £200), a tidy fortune in those days. Unfortunately, this sum was not in ready cash but in debts owed the deceased by 'a useless rogue, who, to get out of paying me, decamped to Marseilles' (the description is Vincent's). The situation was intolerable to the Abbé de Paul, he himself penniless and dunned by his creditors for the expenses of his Bordeaux journey while his rightful inheritance was being squandered in Marseilles. Having first obtained legal advice as to the propriety in law of such a course, he resolved to go hot-foot after the spendthrift and make him pay up. He still had the horse hired for the trip to Bordeaux. It was not his property but, calculating that when he got back from Marseilles he would be in a position to recoup the owner, he sold the animal to defray the expenses of his second journey. The main thing was to waste no time and to reach Marseilles before the runaway had spent all the legacy.

He was then about twenty-four. He had had six years' teaching experience and had finished his seven-year university course with a baccalauréat in theology. The picture we get of him is of an efficient, self-reliant, hard-working young man, a little snobbish perhaps, attractive in manner, somewhat easily

*The Duc d'Épernon had just installed himself in a magnificent new château; though sacked during the Revolution it still draws tourists, and an American car has been named after it—Cadillac.

moved, fundamentally generous but with no outstanding virtues or vices. Though his reputation as a man of honour and good conduct was beyond question, though he was a good priest in a land where good priests were few, he showed no signs of being on the highroad to sanctity. A saint interprets the Gospel in the letter as well as in the spirit. Not so the Abbé de Paul. He was one who defended his rights. He had no intention of letting the man who took his coat take also his cloak, of letting the ne'er-do-well who had absconded with his money spend any more of it than he could help.

Speed being as essential on this journey as safety was on the journey to Périgord, or a good mount and a costly outfit on the trip to Bordeaux, he would have done the first stage at least by water-coach, leaving Toulouse at sunset from the quay near the Pont Saint-Michel. Silhouetted against the western sky were the four towers of the Collège de Foix, beyond them the great bulk of Saint-Sernin. The law students usually came to watch the packet pull out, and to exchange quips with the girls living in the *guède*-workers' houses on the Ile de Tonnis, St Anthony's island in the river. When the boat passed under the old bridge where the cage used for ducking blasphemers in the Garonne was kept the girls and students joined in the chorus of the boatmen. A firm favourite, then as now, was the troubadour song, *La Fontaine de Nîmes*. That refrain, which has haunted many a visitor to Toulouse-la-Rose, may well have been the city's last farewell to Vincent de Paul:

Sé can-to, qué can-to Can-to pas per you Can-to
per ma mio Ques al-lein dé you.

Chapter Three

BY THE WATERS OF BABYLON

IN THE summer of 1607 Vincent de Paul wrote to his old patron and friend, M. de Comet of Dax, describing the adventures that befell him after he left Toulouse two years previously:

. . . I got to Marseilles, caught up with my man and had him jailed. He then agreed to pay up and settled on the spot, paying three hundred crowns in hard cash. I was making ready to return [to Toulouse] when a gentleman who had shared my lodgings in Marseilles persuaded me, the weather being so fine, to go by sea with him as far as Narbonne. Thinking that by so doing I would get back sooner and at less cost, I agreed; but the outcome was that I did not get back at all and lost everything I had into the bargain.

The wind was with us and we should have made Narbonne . . . that same day, had not God permitted three Turkish brigantines . . . to bear down upon us, attacking us with such violence that a few of our men were killed and the rest, myself included, wounded; indeed, the arrow-wound I got will serve me as a clock for the remainder of my days. We had to surrender to these blackguards, these worse than tigers, whose fury was such that they slashed our pilot to little pieces in revenge for the loss of one of their leaders and four or five of their galley-slaves at the hands of our men.

The butchering finished, they bandaged our wounds roughly, put us in irons and continued their course. . . . Finally, laden with booty, they set sail for Barbary, a real den of pirates and thieves. Having first proclaimed that we had been captured from a Spanish ship, they put us up for sale, their lie ensuring that the Consul whom our King maintains there to keep trade open between Barbary and France would not intervene to demand our release.

I must tell you how they sold us; we were stripped naked, given each a pair of trews, a linen doublet and a cap; in this rig and with heavy chains around our necks, we were paraded through the streets of Tunis . . . five or six times. Then they took us back to the ship where the slave-dealers came to inspect us; they noted who could eat heartily and who had no appetite. . . . The inspection over, we were trotted off to the market-place again, the buyers examining us much in the same way as cattle or horses are examined at a livestock fair, making us open our mouths and show our teeth, feeling our muscles, poking at our wounds, forcing us to walk, trot, run, shoulder packs and wrestle one another; aye, and a thousand other brutalities besides.

I was sold to a fisherman but, as the sea and myself never get on well together, he had to get rid of me and was glad to do so soon. My next owner was an old Spagirite (alchemist), an expert at distilling perfumes and essences. He was very kind and humane; for fifty years, he told me, he had been trying to discover the philosophers' stone. Though he had not succeeded in this he had found a method of transmuting metals.[1]

Vincent goes on to describe how his owner 'changed silver into gold . . . and congealed quicksilver into real silver, selling this gold and silver for the benefit of the poor'. Compassion for the needy was but one of the virtues common to master and slave. The only fault the alchemist could find in his helper was his Christian faith and he tried hard to win him to Mohammedanism, promising to leave him his entire property and all his scientific secrets if he became a follower of Mohammed. But Vincent was not to be moved. He had a conviction that for him, as for the Rector of Toulouse, some day a way of escape would present itself. Meanwhile he prayed daily to God and Our Blessed Lady for deliverance. Among the useful things he learned from his master were remedies for various ailments. He later sent one prescription 'guaranteed to work miracles for those suffering from stone' to M. de Comet. This was the recipe:

Take two ounces of Venetian turpentine, two ounces of white turbith, half an ounce each of resin, galanga, cloves and bark of cinnamon, and one ounce of powdered aloes. Mix all to a paste with half a pound of white honey and a pint of the strongest brandy. Let the mixture settle for some time, then distil. Quarter of a spoonful to be taken, fasting, each morning, diluted in water in which borage or buglose leaves have been boiled. As it causes no harmful effects it may be taken as often as one pleases. Indeed, as well as being a remedy for kidney disorders, it will be found beneficial to general health. [2]

In August, 1606, the Sultan, Achmet I, hearing of the alchemist who could change mercury to silver and silver to gold, ordered the useful man to be brought to work for him in Constantinople. Tunis being then under Turkish rule, the transmuter of metals had no option but to obey. Vincent, apart from his anxiety concerning his own future, felt real regret at the loss of the upright and wise Muslim from whom he had learned 'beautiful and useful secrets . . . among them the beginning but not the full perfection of the mirror of Archimedes; and an artificial spring by means of which a skull can be made to speak . . . as well as a thousand geometrical wonders'.

The old man, heartbroken at having to leave home and friends and the den where he and his slave worked so happily together, died on the way to Constantinople. He must have had a premonition of his end for, before leaving Tunis, he made a will bequeathing Vincent to his nephew. This man, neither a Mohammedan nor a Christian, was a type Vincent de Paul had not hitherto encountered, a complete atheist. Fortunately for the slave a rumour got abroad that the French Ambassador at Constantinople was coming to Tunis with letters from the Sultan ordering the release of Christian captives. Tunisian slave-holders, the alchemist's nephew included, hastened to dispose of their human merchandise, and Vincent found himself again up for sale. He was bought by a compatriot, a Frenchman who, like other weak-kneed Christians captured and sold, had discovered that captivity could be alleviated by conforming to Muslim law and practices. 'Having accommodated himself to the law of the Prophet he consoled himself for his lost religion and *patria* in the company of three wives two of whom at least were gentle, compassionate, and of superior character.'

Vincent's new owner lived, as did several of his kind, in the hill country beyond Tunis. As the Turks seldom bothered to cultivate conquered lands they tolerated and even welcomed any conformist Europeans who agreed to work a *metayer* or tenant farm, the profits of which were evenly divided between landlord and tenant-employee. The enslaved priest was set to dig in the fields. Years before, in Ranquine, he had seen the de Paul fields dug to drain off excess water; on these desert plains of the Tunis hinterland the parched earth always needed water, so Vincent worked from dawn to dark making and freeing the network of channels and water-courses that irrigated the land.

His former masters did not encourage their women folk to speak to such as he. But Vincent's French owner, though he had adopted other Muslim customs, did not believe in keeping his wives in seclusion and the three ladies seem to have enjoyed as much liberty as Frenchwomen of that time. Each in turn went to see her husband's new slave. One, a Christian of the schismatic Greek Church, a highly intelligent woman, found Vincent interesting to talk to. Another, a Turkish woman, curious to know how Christians really lived and finding her husband naturally reluctant to enlighten her, often went to the fields where the slave was working and questioned him about his beliefs.

On one occasion she asked Vincent to sing some Christian hymn praising God. Remembering the plaint of the Israelites, *How shall we sing the songs of the Lord in an alien land?*, Vincent felt the tears stinging his eyes. It was a far cry from his home in Gascony, from Toulouse and the Collège de Foix, from his little school, and from high-vaulted Saint-Sernin's where he and the scholars had so often joined the canons in singing the Hours. Leaving his spade aside he intoned the 136th Psalm, *Super flumina Babylonis*:

> Upon the rivers of Babylon,
> there we sat and wept:
> > when we remembered Sion.
> On the willows in the midst thereof
> we hung up our instruments
> For there they that led us into captivity
> required of us the words of songs.
> And they that carried us away, said:
> Sing ye to us a hymn
> > of the songs of Sion.
> How shall we sing the song of the Lord
> > in a strange land?

The familiar words, the rise and fall of the chant, filled the slave with a yearning for France. He sang well, so well that his listener begged for more Christian hymns. He obliged with the *Salve Regina*.

> After the *Salve* I sang many other canticles which pleased her greatly and left her marvelling. That night she ceased not to say to her husband that he had erred in forsaking his religion, a religion she believed to be very good, to judge by the things I had told her of our God and His praises which I had sung for her.

The Turkish woman's praises of the faith he had denied so moved the renegade that next day he was a changed man and told Vincent that he would plan some way of escape for them both. Ten months later the two Frenchmen, risking the recapture that meant certain death, made their way to the coast where they boarded the 'little skiff' that brought them back to their native land. In June, 1607, they stepped ashore beneath the magnificent ramparts of Aigues-Mortes, and at once set out for Avignon, some fifty miles away. That the Abbé de Paul had exercised his sacerdotal zeal to good effect during the previous months was evident on their arrival at the 'City of the Popes'.

There Monseigneur the Vice-Legate, with tears in his eyes and a catch in his voice, publicly reconciled the renegade in the church of St-Pierre, to the glory of God and the edification of all around. Monseigneur has kept us both with him, intending to bring us to Rome with him on June 24th, when his term of office here expires. He has promised the penitent entrance to the austere monastery of the *Fate bene fratelli*** which he has made a vow to enter. Monseigneur has also promised to obtain a good benefice for me.[3]

The Vice-Legate took an instant liking to Vincent who was evidently a very likable person. His pupils and their parents, M. de Comet, the old Toulouse lady who left him the legacy, the Tunis alchemist, the Turkish wife of the renegade, the renegade himself, the high Church dignitary—all seem to have been drawn to him. The Vice-Legate was completely won over when he found that the Abbé de Paul had brought back from captivity the wonderful knowledge of the Berbers and Arabs.

I taught him some of the secrets of alchemy I learned in Tunis. He thought more of this than if I had given him a mountain of gold, for he has been always devoted to the study of alchemy and nothing gives him greater pleasure.

Concluding the long letter in which he tells M. de Comet all this, Vincent asks him to forward his ordination certificate and his Bachelor of Theology diploma from Toulouse, documents he now needs. He encloses a gift of a turquoise for the Dax lawyer and says that although the renegade, his former owner, has presented him with 120 crowns, money he admits should go to meet the demands of the creditors left behind in Toulouse in 1605, he has been advised to hold the money until he returns from Rome to Dax, in case further misfortunes befall him. He

---

* The Brothers of St John of God founded in Granada in the previous century, and today known universally as the Hospitaller Brothers of St John of God.

also mentions letters he has sent to his mother by another messenger.

Seven months later, in a second letter to the lawyer, Vincent states that he is in Rome, pursuing his studies and supported by the Vice-Legate, who is still keen on learning all the ex-slave knows of alchemy. 'My Lord is so jealous about this, that he does not even want me to meet anyone, for fear I should teach them. He wishes to reserve to himself the reputation of knowing such things, which he sometimes demonstrates for His Holiness [Pope Paul V] and the Cardinals.' The required documents had been sent to Rome on receipt of Vincent's first letter but the ordination papers needed the seal and signature of the Bishop of Dax and a form had to be completed. If the decrees of the Council of Trent were not yet in force throughout France they were elsewhere, and proofs of ordination and education were required in Rome before there could be any question of a benefice. Vincent begs M. de Comet to have the forms correctly completed and returned immediately. Though he assures him that the Vice-Legate's promise still holds good, one senses a certain anxiety in this second letter. Possibly the secrets of alchemy learned in Tunis were dwindling in number; when the last of these had been passed on the chances of a benefice might vanish too. [4]

He was in Rome for a year and some months. He does not say what he studied there, but he acquired a fair knowledge of Italian. He also had an opportunity of seeing at first-hand how the Church is governed. 'For the rest of his life he was to know how business was transacted in Rome, and the proper way to introduce a question for consideration in this Roman atmosphere; how, without being discouraged at a rebuff, the matter should be raised again and again until at last, with time, whatever God wills is granted.' [5] He visited the one-time renegade, his former owner, in the St John of God monastery on the isle of St Bartholomew in the Tiber. He saw the great hospital for the poor there and watched the *fratelli* going about their works of charity in the spirit of their Founder, John of God. He came to know something of the quiet exemplary lives of the priests of the

Oratory. He heard of the recently deceased Archbishop of Milan, Charles Borromeo, and his great reform work. There were several Frenchmen in Rome at the time. One he would have known by sight: Cardinal de Joyeuse, brother of the famous Père Ange, the Maréchal who had returned to the Capuchins during Vincent's years in Toulouse. Another compatriot had left Rome shortly before Vincent arrived there, but the Eternal City still rang with stories about him. He was a young French cleric named Armand du Plessis of Richelieu, for whom the Pope had waived the Tridentine regulations, allowing him to be ordained and consecrated bishop in his twenty-second year. A famous preacher, who had held a large and fashionable congregation spellbound for more than an hour at Easter, was somewhat put out to find that Richelieu had repeated the entire sermon, word-perfect, for some learned doctors on the way home from church. Hearing of this feat Paul V sent for du Plessis and asked if he still remembered the discourse. Not only did Richelieu recite the sermon again, but he then preached impromptu on the same theme 'giving another sermon so teeming with ideas and quotations and delivered in so splendid a manner and with such choice sentiments and words that everyone cried out "A miracle!"' When granting the brilliant young man permission to be ordained and consecrated while yet under canonical age Paul V —according to Richelieu's friends—remarked '*Aequum est ut qui supra aetatem sapis infra aetatem ordineris*. It is but just that he whose knowledge is above his age should be ordained while under age.' But Richelieu's enemies, and he had them even then, said that he had brought a faked baptismal certificate from France and that when he was ordained and consecrated and in the Pope's good graces following the demonstration of his powers of memory and rhetoric he had confessed to the deception, 'which the Pope took in good part, merely calling the young man a great rogue'. While Vincent was in Rome Richelieu was back in Paris immersed in his studies preparatory to taking his final degree and gaining a place of honour among the doctors of the Sorbonne. It was typical of his ambition, intellectual gifts and capacity for driving himself that he completed the courses of higher study in half the usual time and astounded all by his answering.

Before Vincent left Rome he saw three Tartar families, who had visited the city, baptized 'and received by the Pope with tears in his eyes'. He also witnessed the return to Catholicism of a bishop sent to Rome as ambassador by the Greek schismatics.

He left for Paris towards the end of 1608. His first biographer states that Paul V sent him on a secret mission to Henri IV, but nothing has ever been discovered in Vatican or French archives to prove that this was so. King Henri, the *Béarnais*, and the Gascon priest were natives of adjoining provinces and had for mother-tongue a *patois* more or less common to both Gascony and Béarn. But it is hardly likely that an unknown priest would be entrusted with a confidential message while Papal officials, accustomed to going on similar missions, were available. Besides, during his stay in Rome, the Abbé de Paul had not blown his own trumpet loudly, effectively, and into the right ears, as Richelieu had done. He is not mentioned in Papal or Roman chronicles of 1607 and 1608. His best claims to public notice, 'the secrets of alchemy, the talking skull and the thousand geometrical wonders', he had given to another who passed them off as his own.

Travellers from Rome to Paris found the going hard until they reached Lyons. From then on the journey was completed by water-coach, a popular and cheap service which was fairly regular and less dangerous than road travel. Vincent, with the countryman's eye for land, would have noted the fertile plains of Burgundy, the verdant hills of the Charollais, the bared vinestalks blackening in the first frosts in the vineyards of Beaune and the Nivernais. He saw fine cities: Dijon, clinging like Toulouse to its ancient independence, with its own Parlement which assembled every three years and vigorously defended Burgundian privileges, especially in the matter of taxes; Autun, half in ruins since the wars; Auxerre, withdrawn and austere; Sens, with its cathedral and marvellous chanters; Montereau, proud of its strong walls and castle. Occasionally the waterways ran parallel to stretches of paved road where the King's posts might be seen galloping madly to outpass the other users of the highway: some country squires, accompanied by a couple of lackeys armed to the teeth, riding to court to seek their fortune; great ladies or prelates travelling in carriages, the mule-carts with their baggage lumbering along behind; troupes of clowns and comedians; students, French and foreign; porters, soldiers, wagoners, cattle, horse and sheep dealers; those 'Egyptians', the gypsies, birds of passage then as now, regarded by the country folk with suspicion and dread as they roved the roads of Europe—

Poor folk, all full of *bonadventure*
Carrying naught but a glimpse of the future.

When they neared Paris barges and smaller craft multiplied and the captain and boatmen on the coaches swore as they manoeuvred to avoid the piles of logs being floated from forest to town. Navigation was still more hazardous on the final five-league reach between Villejuif and the city where the Seine was crowded with huge flat-bottomed boats laden with hay, charcoal, wine, wheat and other provisions for the Paris markets.

Finally the passengers saw, rising from the flat country through which the river wound its way, the towers of Notre Dame, mother of all the churches of Paris. The water-coaches had their termini in the very heart of the city at the Place de Grève (now the Place de l'Hôtel de Ville), where there was a sandy bank that made a suitable landing stage. There, too, was a gibbet and more than likely the first sight to meet Vincent's gaze at journey's end was the corpse of some criminal, a ghastly pendulum swinging heavily to and fro in the chill breeze that heralded winter.

Chapter Four

FLAGSTONES OF THE GREAT

VINCENT DE PAUL had come to the city where he was to spend almost all of the next fifty-two years, the city where he was to become a saint. Though strong in the faith and imbued with a certain zeal for straying souls, though free from the vices then bringing discredit on so many of the French clergy, he was as yet—and he was in his late twenties when he arrived in Paris— a man with an eye on the main chance. In a letter written more than a year later to his mother he laments having to remain so long away from home and his inability to help pay for a nephew's education, 'not having been fortunate enough to obtain the advancement I had hoped for'. He inquires after his brothers and sisters, some married, some single.[1] The note of depression and gloom in this letter was due not merely to his failure to obtain a benefice but to a heavy trial that befell him some months previously.

He lodged in the Faubourg Saint-Germain, sharing a room with a compatriot named Dulou, judge of a district near Bordeaux. One day Vincent, who took care of his health, felt ill and remained in bed. He sent to an apothecary to have a mixture prepared—doubtless one of the prescriptions collected from the Tunis alchemist. The messenger who brought the medicine, searching in a cupboard for a spoon or glass, saw the judge's purse there, bulging with money. It was a simple matter to slip it up his sleeve while Vincent was taking the draught. When Dulou returned and missed the purse, which contained four hundred crowns, he accused Vincent of having stolen it, refused to listen to his protestations of innocence and turned him out of the room that very evening. Worse still, he went around Paris telling the Abbé de Paul's acquaintances and friends what a thief the man was. [2] Mortified and distressed, Vincent had to seek lodging elsewhere; he found it in the rue de Seine 'at the Sign of St Nicholas'.

About this time he came under the influence of a saintly priest five or six years his senior, Pierre de Bérulle. Bérulle, later to become Cardinal, was of aristocratic birth. A few years before Vincent met him he had brought St Teresa's Carmelites of the Reform from Salamanca to Paris and he was now endeavouring to introduce St Philip Neri's Oratorians into France. Other priests were eager to assist Bérulle in his plans for reform and Vincent de Paul found himself drawn more and more towards this group. One day while he was speaking to them Judge Dulou passed by and began to abuse his former room-mate, calling him a thief and a hypocrite. 'God knows the truth,' was Vincent's only reply. Not long afterwards the real thief, arrested in Bordeaux and brought before Dulou on various charges, confessed to the judge that he had stolen four hundred crowns from his room in Paris the preceding year. The magistrate at once wrote to ask Vincent's pardon, offering to come to Paris and ask forgiveness in person.

The clouds were beginning to lift. The Abbé de Paul's character was cleared. In the spring of 1610, a few weeks after his doleful letter to his mother telling her how badly things were going, he was assigned to his first post as a priest. Although it brought him into wealthy and influential circles the tasks it entailed made him a servant of the poor. He was appointed almoner to Queen Marguerite of Valois, that most royal of royal ladies, grand-daughter of Francis I, daughter of Henri II, sister to the next three Kings of France whose combined reigns had totalled only thirty years, and ex-wife of the reigning monarch, Henri IV, formerly Henri of Navarre. Her marriage was annulled in 1599 when the King married Marie de Medici, a princess of the Florentine banking family.*

* Marie de Medici brought to France the biggest dowry of any Queen before or after, a dowry that included the cancellation of the French debt to the Grand Duchy of Tuscany, an enormous sum going back over three reigns.

How Vincent supported himself from the time of his arrival in Paris until his appointment to Queen Marguerite's household we do not know. With his experience of school teaching and private tutoring in Dax, Toulouse and Rome he could have started a small academy or given tuition. In the French capital interest in higher learning did not preclude curiosity about the bizarre and unusual. There would have been no lack of students eager for instruction on talking skulls and the processes whereby base metals could be changed into gold and silver. Such fascinating subjects were not taught in the Sorbonne.

During the last decade of the sixteenth and the first decade of the seventeenth century Henri IV and his able minister, Sully, had made many improvements in the capital. New bridges spanned the Seine; palaces and public buildings were erected, while projects begun in previous reigns, but abandoned because of the wars and lack of money, were completed. When Vincent de Paul first came to Paris there was open country, with meadows and market gardens, beyond that bend of the river near which the Eiffel Tower now stands. Even within the city walls there were fields; donkeys grazed between the Tuileries and the river, and thrifty citizens set snares for the rabbits and hares that played there. High-gabled houses shut off the sun from the narrow streets where carriages, wagons, horsemen, chair-bearers and pedestrians milled and slithered about on the cobblestones carpeted with the overflow from the open channels that served as sewers. Signs and streets bore quaint names: *The Fishing Cat*, *The Spancelled Cow*, *The Street Too-Fast-to-Last*.

The Seine was polluted with ordure, carcases, offal and the wash from dye-shops and tanneries. Those whose employment depended on the river were a people to themselves: measurers of grain and timber; counters of beasts, fowl and hides; dealers of all kinds; onion, wine, grain and salt merchants; bridge winders, boatmen, unloaders and porters; fishwives and water vendors and street criers. They had their corporations, their own laws and customs and lingo, their special saints, festivals, signs and banners. They formed 'a populace within a populace before whom in troubled times even Kings quailed'.

On the left bank the various colleges of the university clustered about the Sorbonne, and in the adjacent streets were many churches and religious houses. The university students, turbulent as ever, carried arms and indulged in brutal games and pleasantries at the expense of the citizens who often retaliated. Public fairs and pilgrimages were sometimes marred by riots and violence, students of rival colleges or 'nations' profiting by such gatherings to settle old scores with one another and usually managing to escape recognition and arrest by mingling with the crowds.

The hub of Paris in 1609 was the Pont Neuf, then really new, and La Samaritaine, the hydraulic pump near the bridge, an invention King Henri had installed to supply the city with clean drinking water. On the bridge charlatans, fortune tellers, hawkers of charms and love-potions, sellers of gingerbread, falcons and rabbit skins had their booths. At the fountain tooth-pullers, dog-clippers, clowns, lottery-ticket sellers, ballad singers and sellers of broadsheets shouted one another down; among the loungers who hung around were pickpockets and layabouts of every description watching a chance to ply their trades. The carriages of the great rumbled by to the Place Dauphine where the ladies bought finery and jewels and their escorts ransacked the bookshops for the latest pamphlets and satires. To stand on the Pont Neuf was to hear the heart of Paris beat, people said. Vincent de Paul, always interested in his fellow men and in the places where he found himself, always keenly observant, had his lodging a few minutes' walk from the bridge, the fountain and the Place Dauphine. When he became the ex-Queen's almoner he moved nearer still to this focal point upon which Paris life, high and low, converged. So, from his first years in the city, he was at the very centre of things.

Marguerite, 'last of the Valois', was fifty-seven when Vincent was appointed to her household. At twenty she had been in love with the Duc de Guise but was forced to marry Henri of Navarre.* Political intrigue, sensational love affairs and scandals so filled Marguerite's life that her husband, himself no paragon of virtue, had her confined to a fortress for eighteen years. Even there the erring lady found opportunity to stray from the paths of rectitude. Henri, a Bourbon and a Huguenot, eventually became King of France, though if Salic law had not been in force Marguerite would have had a far stronger claim to the throne. To ensure his acceptance as King the new monarch turned Catholic and to ensure the succession he had his marriage annulled and married a Medici princess, a close relative of Catherine de Medici, Marguerite's mother. Henri, not Marguerite, was the one who wept when the annulment papers were signed. In 1605 the ex-Queen moved to Paris to occupy the palace built for her at the end of the rue de Seine nearest the Pont Neuf. Those of the older generation of courtiers who remembered her as the beautiful princess who spoke faultless Latin and Greek, who read the Italian Renaissance poets and loved music and dancing, hastened to call upon her. They found her sadly changed:

> She who was once so svelte and supple, made for dancing the latest gaillardes and branles, was now stout and ungainly, her heavy, bulky shoulders made larger still by the great amplitude of her skirts. Instead of the abundant ebony locks which she had prematurely lost she had a blond wig of grass-bleached tow which she wore half a foot higher than the coiffures other ladies were then wearing.

Sainte-Beuve says that she kept several tall, fair-haired footmen who were shaved from time to time to improve the appearance of the blond wig. She was forever trying to restore her once lovely complexion with washes and cosmetics that caused rashes

---

* Henri being then a Protestant and Marguerite a Catholic, the ceremony took place on a platform erected outside the west façade of Notre Dame. When the bride refused to answer 'I will' her brother King Charles IX, who was standing behind her, held her head and made her nod her consent. In 1599 the fact that she had been forced into marriage was pleaded as one of the reasons why the annulment should be granted.

and eruptions. To hide these she 'painted and bedaubed her comely face' until she was like a circus clown. She could never forget that she was a descendant of the Valois and the de Medici. 'Indeed, she lived in the past, and before long men of distinction deserted her court; needy adventurers and cadgers played upon her weaknesses and flattered her for what they could get out of her. She was an antiquity, a kind of fetish that could be preserved as a curiosity to show what departed elegance was like.'

With all her faults Marguerite had a generous heart and Vincent de Paul was but one of the almoners she employed to dispense money and food to the poor. When Henri IV, who had granted her an ample allowance, begged her 'to be a better manager' she replied that prodigality and spending was in the blood of the Medici. 'She mixed loose living and piety, love and learning, vanity and injustice and Christian charity.' Some of her eccentric acts of charity were the talk of Paris:

> On Saturday, September 10 . . . as Queen Marguerite entered the Jacobins to gain the indulgence, she found a poor Irishwoman at the door of the church about to give birth. Scarcely was the poor woman delivered, of a boy, than the Queen wanted to keep him; and having discovered that M. de Montpensier was present she made him godfather and had the infant baptized then and there, giving him the name Henri.

As Marguerite stepped from her carriage on a spring morning in 1606 one of her blond footmen, in a fit of jealousy, stabbed and killed before her eyes his rival for her affections, a young equerry of her suite. She swore she would neither eat nor drink until justice was done and, having obtained the requisite authority, stood by next morning to see the footman beheaded. After that she prayed a little more, hearing three Masses daily. She resumed once again the studies that had been the passion of her youth. When the Abbé de Paul came to serve her her palace was a magnet that drew men of letters, artists and musicians every evening, so that King Henri had to write asking her to stop 'turning night into day and day into night'.

The new almoner could not have been ignorant of her past and of the scandals associated with her name since her return to Paris. The fair-haired footman's end was the theme of a popular ballad. Since that affair she had a terror of death and 'wished to have on hand at all times priests and monks to sing Psalms by day and by night; learned men to distract her with their discourses; musicians to calm her; and always lovers and admirers, such as they were, to prolong the illusion of youth and her lost beauty'. [3]

If Vincent was now moving in high society he was also in contact with the lowest. Each day he went to the Charity Hospital of the Brothers of St John of God, distributing the Queen's alms to the sick poor and helping to tend the afflicted. He was not many weeks in his new post when a terrible occurrence threw Paris into consternation. On May 14th, 1610, Queen Marguerite and her household were celebrating her birthday when they got news that Henri IV had been assassinated by a fanatic. It was typical of the Queen in whose veins coursed Valois and Medici blood to cease from weeping to insist that investigations be started to discover the conspirators who she felt sure were behind the wretch whose hand had driven the dagger home.

That very week Vincent de Paul got word that the long hoped-for benefice was his at last. The Cistercian Abbey of St Léonard de Chaumes, in a diocese north of Bordeaux, with its revenue of 1,200 *livres* annually, was granted to him. But there was an occupant in St Léonard's drawing the revenues; as in the case of many other French benefices a Huguenot official had been granted the Abbey during the religious wars and was in possession. Soon Vincent was involved in a complicated lawsuit. The character of this priest in his thirtieth year, a year that was destined to mark the turning point in his life, presents some strange contrasts. He goes to law, still adamant when it is a question of his rights. On the other hand, when a wealthy man gives him a gift of 15,000 livres he hurries to the Charity Hospital and hands the entire sum to the Brothers for the poor. If the young man who trudged to Rome nine years before to represent his case for a parish he thought should be his is not yet dead, neither is the shepherd lad who handed over all his savings to a beggar on the road near Dax.

Among the priests attached to Marguerite's household was a noted theologian who suffered violent temptations against the faith, 'being unable to continue preaching or teaching catechism any longer, by reason of his distress of mind and despair of soul'. He confided his troubles to Vincent, who besought God to allow him to suffer in the other's stead. The theologian soon recovered peace of soul while the Abbé de Paul found himself assailed by the most terrible doubts and temptations, a trial he was to endure for four years.

Chapter Five

HUNGRY FLOCKS AND
FALLOW FIELDS

THE CAREER his father had dreamed of for him seemed assured, provided that the lawsuit ended satisfactorily. Yet, just when his father's ambitions and his own were in sight of realization, Vincent de Paul's life took a different direction. Any one of a combination of causes could have been responsible for this change of course. The protracted lawsuit in which the long hoped-for benefice involved him. The conviction, daily made clearer to him in the court of a Queen who feared for her soul while continuing to expose it to danger, of the nothingness of earthly grandeur. His meetings with Francis de Sales, Adrian Bourdoise, Madame Acarie and the others active in the promotion of the Counter-Reformation in France. The influence of Bérulle who had become his spiritual guide. His own charity to the sick and poor and the graces their prayers won for him. His even greater hidden charity which impelled him to take upon himself the doubts and anguish of the theologian suffering from temptations against the faith.

During 1610 and the following years he was in constant contact with Bérulle. In later life he could never speak of that great priest without praising his sanctity: 'He was one of the holiest men I have ever known. His equal could hardly be found for solid piety and learning.' St Francis de Sales described Pierre de Bérulle as 'one of the clearest and purest intellects ever'. Bérulle, who came of an influential and aristocratic family, spent himself in prayer, charitable works and plans for reform. He was responsible for introducing into France Orders whose worth had been proved in other countries. Having installed St Teresa's Carmelites in Paris in 1604, in 1611 he brought the first Oratorians to the capital and found them a house there. From this saintly guide Vincent received not only a training in the spiritual life, in which Bérulle was already far advanced, but also an awareness of the grave problems confronting the Church in the France of that time. Ecclesiastical organization and discipline, overthrown during the Religious Wars, had never been restored. Churches, especially in country parishes, were in ruins or crudely and inadequately repaired: 'If a pagan from faraway Japan were to come here,' wrote Adrian Bourdoise, the zealous curé of the church of Saint-Nicholas in Paris, 'and saw a French country church, poor, badly kept, half in ruins, he would think it fit only to lodge beasts, not a place where sacrifice is offered to the Living God.'

The decrees of the Council of Trent, accepted and bearing fruit elsewhere, were not in force in France where their promulgation was opposed not merely by Crown and nobility but by the greater majority of the French clergy. Bérulle, heart and soul in the movement for Catholic reform, made the position clear to Vincent de Paul. In their country the priesthood had become a profession into which men lacking in vocation, morals, preparation and ability, could and did easily insinuate themselves. Such unworthy, unschooled and undisciplined priests could not give their people what they themselves had not got. Religion was neither taught, practised nor held in honour.

Speaking to a conference of clergy in 1659, Vincent de Paul, then near the end of his life, could say:

Ah, if you only saw the ugly ways and the different ways Mass was celebrated forty years ago, you would have felt ashamed. There was nothing more ugly in the world. . . . Some started off Mass with the *Pater Noster*; others, taking the chasuble in their hands, would say the *Introibo* before putting on the chasuble. Once when I was at St-Germain I noticed seven or eight priests, all saying Mass differently; one did it one way, another in another way; there was such diversity that you would have wept to see it.[1]

The Abbé Courtin tells us that ecclesiastical dress or a soutane was unheard of at the beginning of the 17th century in France, much less worn. Priests stood at the altar wearing practically the same clothes they wore in the street. 'Many priests . . . celebrated Mass with the vestments put on over their jerkins and sometimes over a footman's overcoat.'

The vestments do not make the priest, but in fact the French clergy of that age from the highest to the lowest presented a sad picture. The bishop was a temporal lord with fiefs and revenues, his mitre and crozier no longer the symbols of the shepherding of souls but of worldly authority, power and glory.

> Abbeys, priories, and canonries represented a source of opulence and honours which parents coveted and sought for their children—children who, as the Bishop of Lisieux stated in 1614, 'were either still in their nurses' arms or under their teachers at school'. . . . The ecclesiastical or religious state offered to youths of good family an excellent opening, a secure livelihood and, to crown all, one that made little demands on the paternal purse. That, too, was a very important consideration. [2]

The nobility regarded the Church as a field to be exploited. Rich convents and abbeys could restore fortunes lost in gambling or war, or serve as country houses and summer residences; all that was needed was to install a child as Prior or Prioress, Abbot or Abbess. The ill-favoured, the deformed, the one who would be a misfit in court, army or professions could be shoved willy-nilly into a religious house—as its superior. Parents who themselves had had no say in their choice of a marriage partner could not see why their children should be free to choose their path in life. A son of the family who employed Vincent de Paul as tutor was made a bishop at eleven as the bishopric had to be kept in the family. He was not a very exemplary bishop; later, when he became Cardinal de Retz, succeeding his uncle as Archbishop of Paris, this pupil of a saint could write:

I do not believe that there was on earth a better-hearted man than my father and I can certainly say that he was the very essence of virtue. . . . Yet, though he saw that my love of duelling and gallantries unfitted me for it, he never ceased his efforts to push me—me, the least ecclesiastically-minded soul in the whole world perhaps—into the church. [3]

Saint-Simon tells of his friend who ended up as an archbishop, 'his mother having beaten him into the priesthood with a stick'; and of that character hailed by all as *le bon Langres*, a Bishop of Langres, who was one of the most popular men in Paris, 'he had nothing really bad in him, as regards his morals, but he had not what goes to make a Bishop'. This churchman loved gambling for high stakes and once allowed three courtiers, all good billiard players, to coax him into playing with them. He lost heavily. 'He said never a word but betook himself to Langres where he set himself to study the addresses of billiards, locking himself up well so that no one would know. On his return to Paris these gentlemen pressed him to come and play billiards, but he demurred saying that he was as good as beaten before he began, having spent six months in Langres seeing no one, only canons and curés. Finally he gave in to their importunities. At first he played a mediocre game, then better, and let the wagers increase. Finally he won all, and had a good laugh at them, having gained much more than he lost to them six months previously.' [4]

Many prelates spent most of their time at court where, by keeping themselves constantly in the royal eye, they could hope for honours and benefices as these became available. Their vices were the vices of the courts of Henri IV and Marie de Medici, of Louis XIII and Richelieu, of Anne of Austria and Mazarin and of Louis Quatorze. A Concordat of 1516 having given the French Crown the right to appoint archbishops, bishops, abbots and other church dignitaries, the King could appoint those he knew would be subservient to him, or those whose services he wished to reward, or members of families he wished to favour. This pernicious practice meant that the monarch could bribe in advance men prominent in state affairs, key figures in the judiciary, the army, the treasury, the court, by promising them recompense through their children—a recompense that cost nothing as it did not come from the royal coffers. It is easy to see why the Tridentine reform regulations, which forbade these abuses, found no welcome in France.

Not only were abbeys and priories ruled by lay Catholics, men, women and children, but sometimes by Protestants, as Vincent de Paul discovered to his cost when granted the Abbey of St Léonard de Chaumes in 1610. Sully, Henri IV's financier, a well known Huguenot, held four abbeys which brought him in 45,000 livres a year, one of the perquisites of his post as Minister for Finance.

Vincent de Paul's own early motives for becoming a priest show how widespread was the conception of the ecclesiastical state as an avenue of worldly betterment. His benefice, granted by the boy king, Louis XIII, in the first days of his accession, was probably due to Queen Marguerite. She would have at once put forward clerics in her household for the consideration of Louis, who was greatly attached to her and visited her often. But Vincent could not have been long under the influence of Bérulle and his circle without hearing denunciations of what these earnest men considered to be the source from which all the ills of the Church in France stemmed: the Concordat that enabled the temporal power to delegate spiritual power, the law that authorized the hand that held the sceptre to give the crozier. Until the reforms of Trent were introduced it seemed likely that hirelings would continue to be appointed and the flock lack true shepherds. Daily, Vincent could see at Marguerite's court and the court of the Queen-Regent, Marie de Medici, bishops like *le bon Langres* and others whose lives gave even greater scandal. As yet Vincent de Paul was but an observer, but a time would come when his voice, grown powerful and sure of a hearing throughout France, would cry warnings wrung from his own terrible anxiety for his country's soul. A day would dawn when

Monsieur Vincent would refuse to sign the nomination papers of a priest put forward for a bishopric, even though a reigning Queen demanded his signature. When Anne of Austria asked him to confirm her nominee for the Diocese of Poitiers he replied:

> Madame, this abbé, whom you propose as bishop, spends his days drinking in the cabarets; he is such a drunkard that each evening he is found lying dead drunk at street corners, so fuddled that he often cannot remember his own name. His family are quite well aware of his conduct and they want, not without good reason, to see him far removed from Paris. But an episcopal see is not the place to which he should be retired.*

The gap between the nobility and the commoners was paralleled by the chasm between the higher and lower clergy. Wealthy prelates and canons looked down upon the country curés and vicars who, as often as not, had offered themselves for ordination and were ordained without preparatory study or spiritual formation, with little appreciation of the sacredness of the calling they presumed to follow, and with no tests of their ability, morals, or suitability. 'It is a great thing nowadays,' wrote a famous Frenchman of that time, 'to find a priest who can read or write.' Priests heard confessions without knowing the words of absolution. Madame de Gondi, whose sons Vincent was to teach, was a devout Christian who confessed regularly. To be sure of validly receiving absolution she used to carry a written copy of the form of absolution and get the confessor to read it.

* It is on record that Queen Anne, dreading the anger of the duchess who had asked this bishopric for her son, sent Vincent to tell the lady that her request had been turned down. The furious duchess threw a footstool at the bearer of the bad news, wounding him on the temple. When the Brother who had been waiting for the aged priest saw him coming out, his forehead and face covered with blood, and heard the abuse the *grande dame* hurled after him, he wanted to protest. But Vincent firmly pushed his young confrère through the hall door before him, assuring him that there was nothing to be gained by making a fuss. After mopping his bleeding forehead they returned the way they had come, Vincent commenting in his sardonic Gascon fashion, 'Well! Well! What a wonderful thing it is to see the lengths to which a mother's tenderness and love for her son will go!'[5]

Speaking of the need for good priests, well prepared for their high office, Vincent de Paul said:

> The Church is facing ruin in many places because of the bad lives led by priests. . . . A Canon wrote to me saying, 'In this diocese the clergy know no discipline, the people know no fear, the priests know neither piety nor charity. The pulpits have no preachers, learning is not honoured, vice is not chastised. Virtue is persecuted and the Church's authority is either hated or despised. Self-interest is the customary measure in the sanctuary. The most scandalous are the most powerful and flesh and blood have taken the place of the Gospel and the spirit of Jesus Christ.'[6]

Vincent did not resign his benefice until 1616, but the six years during which it had been at least nominally his covered the period in which, unknown to himself perhaps, he changed. The change did not come suddenly, but so slowly as to be almost imperceptible. He was oftener in the Charity Hospital and in the poorer quarters of the city. He went through agonies of doubt when the temptations against faith swept across his soul, at times being unable to do more than touch with his hand the *Credo* he had written on a piece of paper and wore folded over his heart. He put himself completely into Bérulle's hands, even to the extent of going to live at the Oratory and making a retreat there.

During his retreat he would have looked back over the thirty years behind him before deciding what to do for the future. He must have admitted to himself that his life thus far had been packed with varied and enriching experience. He knew the hardships of those who farmed the soil of France: their endless toil and frugal living, the taxation that had become unbearable. He had had experience of student life and its problems. He had known the misfortune of enforced exile, the slavery and the indignities and sufferings man bears from his fellow men. He had seen life in Rome and gained some knowledge of ecclesiastical procedure and protocol. In Paris he had observed a great cross-section of life, moving as he did among the rich, the poor, the great, the lowly, the intellectuals, the place-hunters, the holy, the sinful. Even if he had confined himself to the ex-Queen's palace and the Charity Hospital he would have learned as much about human nature in a year as most men would in a lifetime—at least he would know that *les misérables* were as plentiful in the palace as in the hospital. Having reviewed his life he could not but ask himself if all this experience had been vouchsafed him merely to spend his life as a worldly abbé, a collector of benefices. And if he did not do so, Bérulle was near, ready to suggest and advise at the opportune moment. Finally Vincent de Paul made a promise to God to devote his life to the service of the poor. The very moment he did so the temptations against the faith left him.

One of the first to join the Oratory at its foundation in November, 1611, was the curé of Clichy, a poor village on the site of the present Paris suburb of that name. The curé was somewhat hesitant about leaving his parishioners until Bérulle suggested that Vincent de Paul take his place. Though he still kept his post as court almoner and his room in the rue de Seine 'under the Sign of Saint Nicholas', Vincent was installed in St Medard's, Clichy, in May, 1612. The parish was a large one, extending north of the city walls and covering an area that now extends from the Madeleine practically to Saint-Ouen. The new curé's predecessor, the priest who had gone to join the Oratorians, left behind him excellent parishioners. Vincent was delighted with them and in old age liked to recall how happy he had been with them:

They were good people and most obedient in doing anything I asked them to do. When I told them that they ought to go to Confession on the first Sunday of the month, they never failed to do so, coming to church and going to Confession and seeing for themselves daily the benefit that was for their souls. I felt so consoled and happy that I used to say to myself: 'Mon Dieu! How happy you are to have such good people. The Pope himself is hardly as happy as a parish priest surrounded by kind-hearted people.' One day Cardinal de Retz asked me, 'Well, how are things going with you?' and I replied, 'Your Eminence, I cannot tell you how happy I am, because of my good obedient people. I often think that neither the Pope nor Your Eminence knows happiness like mine.'[7]

At first Vincent felt a bit ashamed to find that his parishioners outdid him at singing the Psalms. Clichy was one of the districts where, since medieval times, parents had passed on their knowledge of the chant. Though their curé had sung the *Salve* and the 136th Psalm in a manner that charmed the Turkish wife of the renegade in Tunis, though he had a good voice and sang well, he found himself at a bit of a disadvantage in his parish:

> To my confusion I must admit that when I became a parish priest I found myself unable to lead the chant. I used to listen to those country folk singing the praises of their God and never missing a note in the psalms. And I used to say to myself: 'And you, their father in God, know nothing whatever of this.' I was very put out. God, who is pleased to hear His praises sung, has allowed His humble poor to keep the chant while we churchmen have, to our shame, lost it.[8]

Vincent taught catechism, preached, heard confessions, set about rebuilding the church and got to know the market gardeners and small farmers who were his parishioners. The church where he was curé may still be seen at 92 boulevard Jean-Jaurés, Clichy, where it forms part of a newer church, its apse opening on to the choir of the present church. The pulpit is said to be the one Vincent preached from and a crucifix to the left of the altar dates from his year there. In the garden is a very old tree planted by the saint, and the baptismal font he erected soon after arriving to take up duty in Clichy is still there. Other relics of St Vincent kept at Clichy include a stole, a piece of a rosary, and a quaint and very tattered period umbrella.

He was little more than a year in Clichy when Bérulle told him to go as tutor to the sons of a very important man. Vincent did not give up his parish work altogether. The family he now served had a town house in the Faubourg Saint-Honoré and

another in the rue des Petits Champs, so when his duties ended
he was able to go to Clichy where he had installed assistant priests
of the highest character to look after his 'good people'. Recorded
reports of the prelate who visited Clichy at intervals during the
next twelve years mention that the church, sacristy, and all therein
were kept clean and in good order. Mass was celebrated in a
worthy manner. Catechism was taught regularly and registers
kept up to date. 'The people have no complaint to make about
their curé or the other priests, and the curé has no fault to find
with his people.' In 1626, when increasing commitments made it
impossible to visit Clichy often, Vincent de Paul resigned the
parish.

The man to whom Vincent was sent as tutor for his sons was
Philippe-Emmanuel de Gondi, General of the Royal Galleys and
nephew of the Cardinal de Retz who not long before had asked
the curé of Clichy how he was getting on in that parish. They
were descended from an Italian banker who had settled in Lyons
but uprooted himself to join Catherine de Medici's entourage as
she journeyed from Florence to wed Henri II in the middle of the
preceding century. The family became immensely wealthy and
two of the highest posts in France were regarded as hereditary
to the house of de Gondi: in each generation the eldest son
became General of the Galleys and the second eldest Archbishop
of Paris. Philippe-Emmanuel's Italian mother had brought up—
very badly indeed—Queen Marguerite, and the ex-Queen
frequently visited de Gondi and his wife who were her intimate
friends.

The General of the Galleys was upright and pious; at least
he practised regularly and even with ostentation the religion
to which he owed his fortune. He was most particular about
his place in church and about the honours he considered his
due, such as benedictions, genuflections and incensings: but
with the commandments themselves he took great liberties.
. . . Very jealous of his prerogatives, he applied himself to
keeping his high position. Though in command of the royal

galleys he never risked his life by going to sea. His main preoccupation was to find out what solemnities were coming off—functions in which he could cut a dash—and the choice of attire appropriate to the occasion. [9]

Yet de Gondi was intent enough on his soul's salvation to become an Oratorian after his wife's death.* Madame de Gondi was vivacious and impetuous, inclined to impatience. She was pious and charitable, highly imaginative and scrupulous, 'destined to become as great a torment to her directors as she was to herself'. Her portraits give the impression of a person who masked her real self; her head is held in a manner that might be caused either by her enormous, stiff, upstanding collar or by an obstinacy of character usually concealed. She used to say that she would rather see her children saints than great noblemen, but in reality they were spoiled. Their paternal aunt described them as young devils; this lady, a Marquise, widowed in her youth when her husband was killed in a duel, was a good deal with the de Gondis, and Vincent would have met her frequently. She thought of nothing but doing good, assisting the condemned in prison and on their way to execution and remaining beside the gibbet till their struggles were over. She spent her considerable fortune in making the lot of women prisoners in Paris less wretched.

Already in 1613 the future of the de Gondi boys had been decided. Thirteen-year-old Pierre was to inherit the family property and succeed to his father's post. Henri, then two, was to be Archbishop of Paris, and the infant Jean-François Paul was to be a knight of Malta. Henri's accidental and early death caused his younger brother to be forced into the episcopate by his father. Even with a future saint for mentor neither boy did much credit to tutor or parents. Pierre was at the centre of every plot against Richelieu and Mazarin. Jean-François, made Bishop at eleven, eventually succeeded to the archbishopric, becoming Cardinal de Retz. He was related to the sprightly Madame de Sévigné, and

* He first applied for admission to the Mission Fathers, but the Founder, Vincent de Paul, turned him down.

probably encouraged her in her letter-writing. His own *Mémoires* show him to have been headstrong, licentious, a more inveterate intriguer than his brother Pierre, and a master at dissimulating his real feelings and intentions. Yet Vincent de Paul seems to have always kept a 'soft spot' for him and when nearing his end wrote to the Cardinal, then banished from France because of his complicity in plots against the Crown.

After St Vincent went to heaven he must have interceded powerfully on behalf of his wayward pupil, for Cardinal de Retz spent his last years in retirement, 'living with exemplary piety, considerably retrenching his expenses, and hardly allowing himself common necessaries in order to save money to pay off a debt of three millions, which he had the happiness to discharge, and to balance all accounts with the world before his death, which occurred in Paris on August 24th, 1679'.

De Gondi, when Vincent first came as tutor to his home, was heavily in debt. Though living in princely style, with mansions in Paris and at least three country châteaux, he had to borrow from his uncle the Cardinal and had sold the Hôtel de Gondi to the Prince de Condé. He was also addicted to duelling, then widespread in France. One morning Vincent found him on his knees a long time after Mass had ended. He was praying before going out to fight a duel with a man who had killed a relative of his. Flinging himself on his knees before the nobleman, Vincent held up a crucifix and implored him, for love of Our Lord, not to engage in the duel, warning him that if he persisted divine justice would fall on him and his. There was no duel. Vincent de Paul, always charitable, speaks highly of M. de Gondi, omitting to mention that he was deeply embroiled in the plots that bedevilled political life in France at that time, his homes both in Paris and the country being used as meeting-places and refuges by partisans.

The de Gondis entertained on a lavish scale, but Vincent did not take part in the social gatherings. His duties done, 'he would retire to his room as a Carthusian to his little cell'. He looked after the household staff, making peace when they quarrelled, comforting those who bore the brunt of Madame's anger—that lady being prone to tantrums. When the family resided on one of their country estates he preached to the local people, heard confessions, and gave instructions on religion.

His example had its effect on Madame de Gondi, who realized that her sons' tutor was no ordinary priest. She was the type of woman who was forever peering into her soul, beset with scruples about the past—one author says that she had a brief and gallant adventure with Bassompierre—and worrying about the future. She asked Vincent to become her confessor and spiritual guide. At first he demurred, but she asked again, this time through Bérulle, and Vincent had to undertake the direction of the pious if self-centred lady. The de Gondis had the granting of certain benefices, and Vincent was not many months with them before he was made a Canon of Écouis in Normandy. He had now fully achieved all his early ambitions: an assured income, a good position where he could live with one foot in both worlds as it were, quietly serving God and his neighbour in his allotted sphere.

But Écouis saw the Canon de Paul only once. He went there in 1616 to occupy his choir stall and receive his appointment as treasurer of the Chapter. He took the customary oath, gave his fellow canons the kiss of peace and entertained them to dinner. Then he asked and obtained permission to name a substitute to take his place. When in the following year he resigned the Priory of St Léonard de Chaumes he probably resigned his Canonry too, for his name appears no more in the Écouis records. During that year he must have become better acquainted with the regulations of the Council of Trent which forbade priests retaining care of a parish to accept benefices, especially benefices like that of Écouis which necessitated residence. As the de Gondis spent much time in Paris he continued to preach and minister in Clichy when occasion offered. His reason for not resigning his parish was probably that he regarded his teaching appointment as a temporary one.

His employers' beautiful country residences were in Picardy, among a hot-headed, brave and industrious people, in Champagne where the people were proverbially 'unwary, submissive, loyal, and good taxpayers', and in Burgundy, where the great role that Duchy had played during the later Middle Ages was never forgotten. Vincent's direction of Madame de Gondi seems to have aimed at making her more self-controlled and less self-centred. The astonished servants now frequently saw their mistress go on her knees and beg their pardon for having lost her temper, or set off carrying on her own arm a hamper laden with food and clothing for the poor.

In the winter of 1617, a winter so bitterly cold that a ballad records its rigours, Madame de Gondi with her household went to spend a few days on estates some twenty miles south of Amiens bequeathed to her by her father. One day word was brought to the château that a tenant on the estate was dying and needed a priest. Vincent hastened to the stricken man, heard his confession and prepared him for death. Later Madame de Gondi visited him and was amazed when the poor fellow said to her, 'Madame, if I had not made the general confession I have just made to Monsieur Vincent, I would have been damned.' Although leading to all appearances a blameless life, the penitent for many years had on his conscience guilt he had never confessed. Madame la Générale immediately began to wonder how many others were in like case. If this man whom everyone respected as upright and good-living had such need of a general confession, she reasoned, many were perhaps being lost through not having a like opportunity, many, perhaps, of her own tenants for whom, as her new confessor had shown her, she bore a certain responsibility before God. She asked Vincent to do something to help the people of that area to realize what a boon for the soul the sacrament of Penance was when worthily received. On the following Sunday, the feast of that most wholly converted man, St Paul, Monsieur Vincent mounted the pulpit in the little church of Folleville and preached:

I told them how important and useful a general confession was and I instructed them how to make a good one. . . . God blessed my sermon and all these good people were so touched by His grace that they came to make general confessions. I continued the instructions and helped them to prepare, but the crowds were so great that even with the assistance of another priest we could not manage and Madame sent for the Jesuit Fathers in Amiens to come and help us.[10]

The Congregation of the Mission had its *fons et origo* in that sermon. A regular crusade of preaching, catechizing and hearing confessions followed in all the neighbouring villages. Madame de Gondi, already showing signs of forgetting herself for others, set aside the first of many generous donations for the maintenance of a community of priests who would give similar missions on her estates every five years. But though the seed had been sown, time had to elapse before it burgeoned.

While Vincent de Paul was slowly discerning the direction his life should take, his contemporary, Armand du Plessis of Richelieu, the brilliant young cleric for whom Paul V had waived the Tridentine rules, was applying himself to his episcopal duties. He rebuilt the cathedral church, the other churches and the Bishop's palace in Luçon, his diocese. He had marshes around Luçon drained, cemeteries enclosed and other works undertaken. He introduced some of the reforms of the Council of Trent, establishing a diocesan seminary and bringing the Oratorians and Capuchins to preach to his people. He settled quarrels among the higher clergy, called a synod fixing feasts and holy days, and issued instructions to his curés. He adopted a conciliatory policy towards the Huguenots and preached the almost unknown virtue of tolerance. But ambition was strong in him. For the seven years following the death of Henri IV he deliberately absented himself from the court, a decision that had the appearance of turning his back on advancement but which was 'wisdom at long range'. While the Abbé de Paul was taking counsel with Bérulle and divesting himself, so slowly that it seems to have been a rather painful process, of his benefices, the Bishop of Luçon was drawing up for himself a rule of conduct against the day when he should return to court.

Having decided that his first visits were to be brief and infrequent, he goes on to count every step, weigh every thought, watch every gesture. Nothing is to be left to chance or improvisation. He is to be always master of himself, his will the ever vigilant guardian of his inner thoughts which must never be permitted to appear in public. His lodging is to be chosen, 'neither too far from God nor from the King'. Concerning the King, it is a great art to know when to visit him; without appearing to be importunate one must, however, be on hand at the propitious moment; once a week at Paris, every second day when His Majesty is relaxing at Fontainebleau. He tells himself not to appear anxious for favours from nobles, never to angle for invitations, but to contrive, however, to frequent great houses, banquets, and other worldly functions, 'without excess but with dignity'. He notes how to listen to people, 'without seeming inattentive, yet showing no eagerness in the eyes or a sad or melancholy air, no matter who the speaker; listening with the keenest attention and graciousness, but more by silence and attention than by word and applause'. Answers to queries must be framed so as 'to avoid blame should a falsehood be discovered and to avoid the perils truthful answers sometimes bring'. Correspondence needs special care: to write as little as possible; to think in advance of the possible consequences a phrase imprudently thrown on paper might have; to keep copies of all important letters; to answer all correspondents whatever their rank; to read and re-read many times letters received and sent: 'The fire should guard letters which the locked drawer keeps only with peril.'

And so the *Instructions and Maxims I Gave Myself for My Conduct at Court* goes on and on. Armed with perseverance, ambition, suppleness of mind, and dissimulation, the Bishop of Luçon prepares for his political career, his immediate aim the favour of the boy King, his field of action the court, the first engagement the winning of the Queen-Regent, Marie de Medici. In 1614 he is elected to Parliament, as a representative of the clergy. In Lent, 1615, he preaches for the court. Bérulle, whose Oratorians he had called to Luçon to found his seminary, is indebted to him. He is friendly towards Père Coton, the Queen's Jesuit confessor, but not too friendly, for he sees ahead the wave of hostility that is mounting against the Company of Jesus. He allies himself with Père Joseph, the Capuchin Provincial for Poitou, an ardent reform priest with an *entrée* everywhere. In 1616 he is appointed almoner to Anne of Austria, the Spanish bride of young Louis, and also State Councillor, and at the end of the year Secretary of State for Foreign Affairs. But in 1617 an unforeseen disaster halted—temporarily—his swift ascent.

Marie de Medici had been for seven years under the sway of two Italians, Concini and his wife, a low-born couple who filled their pockets, demanded and received titles and offices, and exerted such an influence over the Queen-Mother that they even succeeded in having ministers dismissed. The Prince of Condé, Pretender to the Throne, the powerful Guise family, and other nobles chafed and fumed at the ridiculous situation in which they found themselves, subject to a woman who was herself subject to a carpenter's daughter and the latter's insufferable husband. In the last week of April, 1617, a favourite of Louis, de Luynes, conspired with others to murder Concini; the latter's widow, found guilty of sorcery and other crimes, was executed at the Place de Grève. Monseigneur Richelieu, summoned hastily from the Sorbonne to the Louvre by the distracted Queen-Mother, saw from his carriage the cheering mob dragging the naked corpse of the hated Italian along the street. At the Pont Neuf he witnessed the horrible butchery inflicted on the cadaver and, suddenly realizing his own danger, for it was known that he had favoured the Concinis who spoke well of him to the Queen-Regent, began to shout: '*Vive le Roi!* Cry, all of you, *Vive le Roi!*' This secured him a safe passage and escape from the peril of the moment.

When Marie de Medici went into retirement in Blois the following week, the Bishop of Luçon accompanied her in his new role of counsellor to the Queen-Mother and intermediary between her and her son, now on the throne. In the last of the long file of carriages in the ex-Queen's entourage sat the Bishops of Luçon and Chartres. Richelieu saw the people of Paris, their faces contorted with hate, heard their insults hurled at the Queen and her followers, and at himself. Yet, when all the others trembled and wept, he reflected. What mistakes had Concini made that one should avoid? Where had Marie de Medici failed? Concini had underestimated the King. So had Marie de Medici, mother of the heir to the Crown. Only fools fail to learn from the mistakes of others. Richelieu was no fool.

As the Bishop, replanning his future, drove towards Blois, Vincent de Paul, having told Bérulle that 'he felt in his soul that God was urging him to go to some distant province and devote himself to instructing and serving poor country folk there', was also fleeing from the scenes and people he had known. Leaving the de Gondi home by night he set off for a small parish on the confines of Burgundy and the Dombes, in territory ceded to France by the Duke of Savoy sixteen years previously. This parish, Châtillon-les-Dombes, having become vacant, the priests of the Oratory in Lyons and the Archbishop of Lyons had written to Bérulle to ask if he knew any good curé who would come there. The priests already in the parish were careless and parishioners were falling away. There may have been a connection between the eclipse of Marie de Medici and Vincent's flight. De Gondi, of Italian extraction and closely connected with the ex-Queen, would have had that lady's partisans sheltering in one or other of his homes or even meeting there to plot against the new King. At all events, one morning the de Gondi boys were without a tutor and their mother, in tears, without a confessor.

Chapter Six

OUR LORDS, THE POOR

VINCENT DE PAUL left no diary, no spiritual journal that would enable us to trace his progress along the road to God. But his increasing detachment from material good, from dreams of self-advancement, is already apparent in 1617. The man hastening by water-coach to Lyons in the early summer of that year to receive the documents and instructions necessary before presenting himself in Châtillon-les-Dombes had not the ambition, the eagerness for the security an assured income could bring, that sent him so hopefully up the same waterways to Paris ten years before. He was now hurrying to parishioners very unlike his good people in Clichy, to a parish 'large and in great need of a good curé'. No rival candidate contested this appointment, for no one wanted to be curé of Châtillon.

The presbytery in his new parish was uninhabitable and at Lyons he was given a letter of introduction to a prominent man in Châtillon who could be counted upon to give him temporary lodging. He was also briefed on what to expect. Things were not very promising. The churches, as well as the presbytery, were in a ramshackle condition, so was the eighteen-bed hospital and the leper *maladerie*. The six resident priests were all advanced in age but not in virtue; they were negligent and the open scandal of their lives caused them little worry. The people, fallen away from religious beliefs and observances, were indifferent. The Huguenots were numerous and had their own conventicle.

His first sight of Châtillon-les-Dombes, now renamed Châtillon-sur-Chalaronne, must have reminded him of Dax, and its surroundings of the Landes. The town, with a population of a couple of thousand, was set in a fertile valley; all around lay the monotonous melancholy flats of the Dombes country, with vistas resembling the lonely fens he had known in his boyhood. There were two churches: the older, St Martin's, on the outskirts of the town; the principal one, St Andrew's, at the foot of the hill where the old castle stood and from which it was separated by the Chalaronne.

The Lyonnais priest who gave him the letter of introduction to M. Beynier had explained that this man was a Huguenot. Beynier was no model for Huguenot or Catholic. Young and well-to-do, 'he lived in all the libertinage towards which his great wealth, his youth, and the places he frequented impelled him'. Yet he received the new curé hospitably and gave him and Louis Girard, a zealous priest Vincent soon summoned from Lyons to help him, the second floor of his house, thus ensuring them the privacy they needed for their prayers and devotions. They did not, however, have much time to spend in their lodgings. There was too much to do.

Châtillon was a town in rapid decline. Its great fairs and markets held on Saturdays, and vigils of feasts, when the wines of Beaujolais, the fish of the Dombes rivers and streams, the fowl and livestock of the verdant Bresse changed hands, were but a shadow of what they had been. Merchants no longer came from as far away as Geneva to buy the leathers, hemp and linen cloth of the Saône valleys. The taverns, however, had not shut their doors. At the time Vincent arrived there, Châtillon-les-Dombes had the highest wine consumption of any other French town of its size. Already its citizens regretted the day, sixteen years before, when their allegiance had been transferred from the House of Savoy to the French King and government. Since 1600 the Paris authorities had had too much to contend with in the capital to bother about a small remote township whose inhabitants did not even speak proper French.

Vincent wasted no time bemoaning the state of affairs in Châtillon, worse indeed than he anticipated. Having sent for and obtained reinforcements in the shape of Père Girard, he began to learn the local patois, *le bressan*. His accent, which retained the

79

Gascon lilt that is to French what the Welsh or Cork accent is to English, caused some smiles when he stopped to greet people in the street. He set himself out to be 'extra cordial to all', giving alms where he saw it was needed. His preaching, during his first weeks in the parish, was given not in words but by example. He and his assistant rose at five, devoted half an hour to prayer, tidied their rooms and went to the church to recite the Divine Office and say Mass. Their days were spent cleaning the churches, attending the few sick people in the hospital, arranging for and supervising the repair of both St Andrew's and St Martin's. They dressed in 'long clothes', a change from the knee breeches, hunting jackets and military capes of the other priests: 'They kept their hair cut short and their neck-stocks were high, with the frills cut away.'

Curiosity at first drew the people into the churches; they stayed to hear sermons and instructions in simple, down to earth language. They saw the full Catholic ceremonial restored. 'Ceremonies are only shadows,' their pastor told them, 'but they are shadows of the greatest things.' They were taught the meaning of the Mass and how to assist properly at the great sacrifice: 'It is not the priest alone who offers the holy sacrifice of the Mass, but also those who are there present.' They had the significance of the sacramental and liturgical rites explained. They were encouraged to join in the chant when he told them that congregational singing to glorify God as in the *Gloria*, to affirm their beliefs as in the *Credo*, to implore mercy as in the *Agnus Dei*, to adore as in the *Sanctus*, to honour Our Lady and the Saints as in the *Salve* and the Litanies, drew down a special grace of concord and peace on the community taking part.

When he had won them, Vincent, his experience in Folleville still fresh in his memory, urged them to make general confessions. The most urgent need was to reform the clergy already in Châtillon; how this was achieved, we do not know, but within a few months the priests were living in community and giving good example where formerly they had given scandal. One of the earliest and most notable of several Huguenot converts was

Vincent's landlord, M. Beynier, many of whose relatives also followed him into the Church. All his life Vincent inclined to the methods of St Francis de Sales when dealing with those of other faiths. He was convinced, and probably all his experience proved it true, that controversy does not make converts. 'Controversy is of little service and, in most instances, more productive of sound and fury than of good. A good life and the constant exercise of the Christian virtues is the sweet odour that attracts wanderers back.'[1]

Fifty years later, when evidence was being collected for the Beatification of Vincent de Paul, there were many in Châtillon who retained a vivid memory of him:

> It would be impossible to relate all that Monsieur Vincent managed to do in so short a space of time and we could scarcely believe it only that we both saw it for ourselves and heard of it. He was so highly thought of that everyone spoke of him as a saint. We never had and never again will have such a curé. He left us far too soon for our liking. What he accomplished in Châtillon alone would, we believe, be sufficient to canonize him and we have not the slightest doubt that if he acted elsewhere as he did here he will surely be canonized some day. [2]

Others were more emphatic and detailed:

> He was always very modest and recollected in his bearing, whether in the church or elsewhere, and most generous to the poor. He never defended his rights; he was profoundly humble and prudent and his charity went far beyond the ordinary. He loudly condemned the practice of public confession, the payments exacted from penitents, and a debauch known as the *Royaume* that used to take place in the belfry, and many other abuses and scandals. [3]

The abuses referred to had been introduced during the forty years prior to 1617. The first two listed probably accounted for the lapse of so many from the sacraments.

At Châtillon Vincent inaugurated the Association of Charity, a work which had an astounding success and which still functions throughout the Catholic world. He himself described how he came to found the first Charity Confraternity:

> One Sunday as I was vesting for Holy Mass word was brought to me that in an isolated house a quarter of a league away everyone was ill, not one being on his feet to help the others, and that all were in indescribable need. I had only to mention this in the sermon when God touched the hearts of those who heard me and they found themselves deeply moved with compassion for these poor afflicted ones.

The congregation acted at once. That afternoon no less than fifty housewives set off to visit the stricken family, taking chickens, wine and other good things. Monsieur Vincent also went after Vespers to see if any of the sick persons needed confession. At every turn of the road he beheld little groups of ladies, some sauntering along in the broiling August evening, some resting in the shade. All had baskets, full ones being carried to the house of sickness, empty ones returning. When Vincent arrived he found the table and chairs piled high with the gifts of his kind-hearted parishioners. As he walked home he could not help thinking that it would be impossible for a family in the best of health, not to mention a household where all were ill, to consume a fraction of the food provided: and most of the provisions he had seen were perishable. His frugal upbringing had given him a dread and abhorrence of waste and he must have felt like returning to the house he had just left and begging some of the surplus for the poor. But such an action might hurt one of the benefactors. Some plan would have to be devised. 'So I suggested to all these dear kind people whose charity had moved them to visit that family that they should take turns to visit them and cook for them and not only for the family in question but for similar cases that might arise.'

Seven ladies, among them the lady of the château, came to a meeting at Vincent's request the following Wednesday. During the preceding two days he had planned the framework for the association whose members 'should take turns on succeeding days to aid corporally and spiritually all those needing such assistance; corporally, by the provision of food and medicines; spiritually, by disposing the dying to die well and those who were recovering to lead a better life'.

The rules outlined for the Ladies of Charity that day were committed to paper some weeks later; they were carefully thought out, matter-of-fact, practical, precisely worded. Few documents penned by the saint show so clearly his profound knowledge of human nature. Married women and girls living with their parents may not be admitted as members without the permission of husband or parents. If a candidate for membership seems to be the sort of person who will at first give herself enthusiastically to a new enterprise and later grow weary and haphazard, she is on no account to be accepted. The sick poor need visitors who will never weary but continue to visit them; perseverance and a sense of responsibility is an essential quality in a 'Servant of the Poor'.

The member on duty on any particular day is to go to the sick person, 'dealing with him as she would with her own son or indeed with God, who counts as done to Himself what we do to the poor'. She is to cook the meal first—a substantial meal by our modern calorie-conscious standards. 'At midday a quarter of a pound of boiled mutton or veal; on Sundays and feasts a chicken. In the evening some roast beef or a stew with meat and vege-tables.' As much bread as the patient wished was to be provided at each meal and a half-pint of wine—except if the sick person was feverish. Fish and egg dishes were to be supplied on days of abstinence and those on a special diet were to be catered for.

The number of members in each branch was to be limited to twenty and 'as it was unfitting that ladies should be required to see to financial and business affairs', legacies and donations that might be bestowed on them and similar matters were to be entrusted to some devout and able cleric or to 'some virtuous *bourgeois* of the town, someone who loved doing good to the poor and who was not too taken up with temporal affairs'. At Châtillon the procurator chosen for the first Confraternity of Charity was none other than the Huguenot convert, M. Beynier.

Having made clear the type of meal to be prepared, the rule for the member on duty continues:

> She is then to carry the meal herself to the sick person. On entering she is to greet him cheerfully and charitably, arrange a tray on the bed, placing on it a cloth, drinking cup, spoon and bread. She should help the sick man to wash his hands, say grace for him, pour the soup into the drinking cup into which she has broken some bread, place the meat on a plate and arrange everything on the tray. Then she will invite him to eat for love of Jesus and His Holy Mother. . . . She will try to cheer him up if he seems unhappy. Sometimes she will need to cut up the meat and pour the wine for him. Having started him at his meal she will leave him if there is someone in the house to attend to him and go seek another whom she is to deal with in like manner. She is to remember always to begin with one who has somebody with him and finish with one who lives alone, so as to be able to stay a little longer with those who have no one. [4]

Was it in the hospitals of the St John of God Brothers he had seen the little attentions that mean so much to the afflicted? 'Wash the sick person's hands. See does he need clean linen. Cut up the meat and pour the wine for him. If he dies make a shroud for the corpse and have the grave dug for the dead.' Was it the example of the Marquise de Maignelay, the pious sister of the General of the Galleys, he had in mind when he wrote, 'Lead the dying by the hand to God, and attend their funerals, taking the place of mothers who accompany their children to the burial ground'?

Thus a great work of charity had its beginnings. One may wonder what kind was the sermon and what persuasive power had the preacher whose words sent fifty of his hearers hot-foot on their errand of mercy on that August Sunday in 1617.* The only time he himself referred to it he said that the plight of the misfortunate family had deeply moved him and that he spoke from his heart. He never wrote his sermons, so none of them, much less the impromptu one preached to such effect in Châtillon, has come down to us.

Perhaps our best clue to his preaching is to be found in his instructions to other priests on the subject. Referring to the bombastic, flowery pulpit oratory then the vogue in Paris he noted sadly that all this affected speech, pompous display and empty eloquence did not seem to be converting anyone. He denounced as sacrilege the vanity a preacher was guilty of who used the pulpit merely to parade his range of learning, his command of language, his wit, 'his acquaintance with new-fangled words'. Such a one, 'playing the peacock by making beautiful discourses just to win praise and fame', was anathema to Monsieur Vincent.

Setting forth the essentials of good preaching, as he considered it, he, unconsciously perhaps, tells us how he himself preached. The first requisite is simplicity, simplicity of content, simplicity of language and style, simplicity of demeanour and tone. It is interesting to note that Vincent had a talk with a retired actor one day and passed on to others what he learned—that on the Paris stage it was no longer fashionable to speak in a high-pitched, declamatory tone, but familiarly, as man to man. One is irresistibly reminded of Hamlet's advice to the players begging that they use all gently, anything overdone being from the purpose. Having warned against shouting and declaiming in the grand manner Vincent gives a second, no less important, ingredient of good preaching—persuasiveness. To read him on this is to read a little masterpiece on the art of persuasion. We have seen his own powers of persuasion brought into action in Folleville and Châtillon. Those Hidden Persuaders of today, the advertising moguls, who seem to think that they invented the

* If his heart and feelings supplied the motive power on the Sunday, his head took control on Monday when he began to put order into something that might prove ephemeral and of little benefit if not put on a planned and rational basis.

science of persuasion, should read Vincent de Paul on how to persuade people to act in the way one wishes. But Monsieur Vincent was not conducting a course in high-pressure salesmanship nor giving tips on how to cajole people into buying luxury goods. He was showing preachers how to persuade their hearers to seek the one thing necessary and not be satisfied with anything less. To persuade, the preacher must first show the advantages of what he proposes; then he must explain the full nature of the proposal; finally he must point out how his hearer is to go about realizing the matter proposed to him.

He went to sermons himself and knew what he liked: 'We do not believe a preacher because he is very learned, but if we think he is good we love him. The devil is very learned and yet we do not believe anything he says. . . . Our Lord first had to love people whom He wished to believe in Him.' He warned the priests who came to his Tuesday Conferences in Paris to go to the trouble of preparing their sermons carefully. He begged them to lay the foundations of good preaching in a life of prayer. 'Mental prayer is *the* great book for a preacher.' Bossuet, who was present at many of these conferences, wrote to Clement XI about the wonderful benefit the Paris clergy, himself included, derived from the preaching of Vincent de Paul.

When he let his heart run away with him, as at Châtillon and as on one occasion when he pleaded the cause of the Paris foundlings before the great ladies of France who were members of the Confraternity of Charity in the capital, he could rise to magnificent heights. Like all Gascons he was an excellent mimic, but he did not use this gift in the pulpit though he availed himself of it in the intimate family atmosphere of the talks and instructions he gave to the members of his two Orders, the Daughters of Charity and the Priests of the Mission. When four young Sisters volunteer to go to plague-stricken Calais to take the places of others who contracted the fatal contagion while ministering there, Vincent assembles the community for a farewell homily. Having praised their self-sacrifice, which prompts them to offer themselves for what may well mean death, he warns them—as though he fears for their humility—against pride. They are not to say to anyone that the Queen honoured the Daughters of Charity by sending them to Calais in preference to other nursing Sisters. He recommends each to consider herself as the most unworthy and imperfect one in the entire company. He calls them *mes petites*, and then, looking at the four standing quietly there and bearing the brunt of a lecture that they, least of all his followers, deserve, he has to stop, overcome by the sudden lump in his throat and the tears that overflow in spite of him.

The Brother detailed by the Superiors of the Mission to record Monsieur Vincent's instructions registered his gestures as well as his words. Speaking of a possible future decline in fervour within the Order he gave warnings. 'When I am gone you may have Mission priests who will be cowardly unmortified men, libertines in spirit, asking for no more than diversion; men who, provided they have a good dinner, will not bother much about other things. They will be . . . I hate to say it . . . the kind of men who pamper themselves.' And the Brother notes how Vincent put his hands beneath his armpits, hugging himself. Further on in the same discourse the Brother relates how the Founder, when emphasizing certain points, 'gave his voice a contemptuous disdainful inflection', or 'imitated a snail drawing its horns and itself back into its shell', or 'made expressive movements with his hands or head'. Sometimes he feared that he had gone too far, as when he confessed publicly before the community: 'Last Friday I gave a bad example to you when speaking; I cried so loudly and clapped my hands so much it seemed as though I were annoyed with someone. Fathers, I beg your pardon.'

Both his letters and instructions abound in exclamations, seemingly the escape-valve of an overburdened heart. In this context he resembles St Teresa of Avila. A few samples from their letters will show this similarity. St Vincent:

I never met such a woman as you for making a tragedy out of certain things. . . . In the name of God, Mademoiselle, stop it.

Now, that's all the news concerning you. But tell me, when are you coming back? *O Mon Dieu!* I forgot to tell you that I expect Madame Moussot this morning. . . . I thank you for the excellent bread, jam and apples you sent me. . . . Oh, but really, Mademoiselle, it was too much. . . . In the name of God, don't do it again.

You see, Sir, both you and I allow ourselves to be carried away by our own opinions. . . . In the name of God, Sir, will you attend to that. How on earth could you, Sir, with a good conscience, do what you have done? . . . You say X is a fool, that he begged alms along the roads and does next to no work. Granted. But you, Sir, should have considered that I might have had a special reason for doing as I did. . . . Ah, Sir, pay heed to me. Just think, if that were to happen what would become of all these poor people? . . . But, there you are. To whom can I speak more frankly and with more confidence than to you, my second self?

I am rather doubtful about the news (in the letter from Silesia), all the more so as the lady you know of—the one who hears everything—has assured me of the contrary. . . . But I am telling you this on the spur of the moment.

We live according to the spirit of the servants in the Gospel in regard to our Lords the Bishops, who say to us: 'Go' and we go; 'Come' and we come; 'Do this' and we do it. . . . As for your point about displeasing their Lordships, have no doubt, my dear Mother, that however little you may do you will cause them a certain amount of surprising annoyance and stir up a tempest. . . . Ah, My Saviour: What am I saying? Where on earth has my mind been wandering to write as I have just written? In truth my judgment hasn't been keeping up with my will. But, good Heavens! give me a chance to submit both will and judgment to God. . . .

And here is St Teresa:

I can't imagine how you let the muleteer go off without sending me a letter. . . . When sending a packet by someone not a muleteer don't put any money in. You know what generally happens. . . . For the love of God, don't be careless and let that fever run on without taking something for it. . . . Oh, how I envy you hearing the preacher you have, how I wish I were in Seville now. . . . The Agnus Dei and the rings have turned up, thank God. . . . In case I forget it, your letter to Fr M. would have been fine only for the bit of Latin. God preserve my daughters from displaying their knowledge. Don't ever let it happen again.

Oh, Father, how your letter made us laugh about your meals in the hospital! Those dreadful cod patties! . . . As regards that lady, I believe firmly that it is not melancholy she is suffering from but the devil. He's the one who put her up to those deceits. . . . She's a thorough fraud—may God forgive me!—and she likes having dealings with your Reverence. She probably made the whole thing up. . . . I wish you were far away from her. . . . What a malicious one I am! . . . I beg you, Father, to speak very tactfully if you have occasion to complain of anyone. I fear you are careless about this, in fact I know that you have been—you are so outspoken. God grant that what you have said may not get to the Nuncio's ears! . . . I received your letter today. Blessed be God, who has been so good to me in restoring you to health. . . . But I must say it's a nice thing to have you back hearing confessions so soon, and in this weather too! As though you hadn't enough to do already. Will your Reverence please remember that you aren't made of iron. Just think of all the good brains in our Order that have been ruined from overwork. . . . You annoy me, I tell you again, with all your falls. For pity's sake get yourself tied to the mule to keep you from falling off. What sort of brute you ride I cannot imagine or why you think you can do thirty miles a day and on a pack saddle. Sheer suicide!

My daughter, the great thing is not the number of convents but the number of saints living in them. I dread one discontented nun more than a legion of devils. . . . Thanks for what you sent but stop telling me my gratitude is a sign of perfection. It's my nature, I think; anyone could bribe me with a sardine. . . . The orange-flower water was delightful; some of the quinces arrived in good shape; the dogfish was nice; the tunny-fish was left reposing at Malaga—and long may it stay there! [5]

The knack of adding exactly the right dash of vinegar to praise and of topping reproofs with honey came as easily to Vincent de Paul as it did to Teresa of Avila. Though she had the keener sense of humour, his gift for friendship was equal to hers. There is the same refreshing naturalness about the exclamations that escape from both quills, Spanish and French.

In August, 1617, the month the Association of Charity had its beginnings in Châtillon, Vincent wrote to the General of the Galleys, then in Marseilles, explaining and making a belated apology for his departure from the de Gondi household. Not having any of the qualities which a tutor in a family of the higher nobility such as the General's should possess, he had left Paris, he said, secretly, resolved to exercise his priestly ministry in the parish where he now found himself.

Philippe-Emmanuel, whose lady had been inconsolable all summer, wrote to her at once, enclosing the Abbé de Paul's letter. De Gondi himself had by this time been completely won by Vincent. 'I am in despair,' he began, 'over a letter I have just had from Monsieur Vincent. I enclose it herewith. See if you can find any remedy for the disaster of losing him.' The General goes on to speak of the need he had of their former tutor: 'I know he will greatly aid me and my children to save our souls,' (is he implying that Madame's salvation was assured?) 'and that he will help me about those resolutions I mean to take and which you know of.' He implored her to get Bérulle and others to secure Vincent's return; he need not act as tutor, but can supervise a

tutor and will be left absolutely free to live as he pleases, 'but
no matter what, I passionately desire his return to our household
so that, some day or other, I can lead a good life with him nearby'.
Madame de Gondi wept all day on receiving this letter and
wrote to a friend bewailing Vincent's desertion of her and hers:

> I never could have believed he would do the like. . . . He
> who showed such interest in my soul, to abandon me like
> that! . . . He knows my need of him and the confidential
> matters I have to discuss with him. . . . He knows the good
> I wish to do on our estates and which I cannot do without his
> advice. . . . My soul is in a pitiable state, the General in despair,
> my children wasting away daily, and the good he did in this
> household and to the seven or eight thousand souls, our
> tenants, gone for good. As if they were not redeemed by the
> same precious Blood of Our Lord as were the people of
> la Bresse![6]

At least she knew his whereabouts. The thing was to get him
back. Having implored hundreds of holy persons to lay siege
to heaven for her intention she wrote to Vincent. She also got
young Pierre, 'wasting away daily', to write and her uncle-in-law
the Cardinal in Paris and several other people, some of rank, some
of piety, some combining rank and piety.

In her letter Madame de Gondi pleaded and stormed by turns.
If her runaway confessor did not return she would die unshriven
and her damnation would be his fault. No other priest understood
her. She would pine away or lose her reason if he did not come
back. Vincent, who could write to another, less tempestuous,
lady, 'I never met such a one as you for making a tragedy out of
nothing', did not reprove Madame la Générale in like manner.
If, in an exasperated moment, he asked his God why his path and
that of this highly-strung imperious creature had crossed, he
would have at once asked forgiveness and begun to think of the
potentialities for good that lay beneath the troubled surface of her
soul. Did he reflect on the goodness he had encountered in so
many of her sex: his own mother and sisters, patiently toiling in

Ranquine that he might go to school and college; the old Tou-
lousaine who remembered him in her will; the kindly women who
shared the renegade's harem in the Tunis hill country; Queen
Marguerite, 'that unfortunate, above the wreckage of whose
virtue and talent floated her love and pity for the poor'; the
women of Châtillon, compassionate and quick to assist the needy
and ailing? We do not know, but the lead he later gave the women
of France shows that not only had he a profound knowledge of
the workings of the feminine mind, but a conviction that his
country's ills could not all be solved by men, not even by men
as holy as Bérulle and Francis de Sales, not even by men as far-
seeing, as brilliant and as powerful as Sully and Richelieu. To
nurture, to comfort, to cherish, to foster and preserve, to sustain,
to tend and to heal was the function of woman; not merely her
physical organism but her sensibility and thought, her whole
instinct prompted her to do so. For the Catholic Reform France
needed good priests. For moral and social reform she needed good
women. Vincent de Paul was to recruit and train both.

Although he resisted her entreaties at first, he capitulated
when Bérulle, appealed to by the de Gondis, told him to return.
Heavy at heart, he bade farewell to Châtillon, now a model parish.
His parishioners wept to see him go. He was back in Paris by
Christmas.

Chapter Seven

OPENING FURROWS

FOR THE next seven years (1618-25) Vincent remained with the de Gondis, not leaving until after Madame de Gondi's death. He was free to come and go on their estates where he devoted himself to the spiritual and temporal welfare of the tenants. He gave missions, urging those who attended to make general confessions and reform their lives. In areas where there was widespread poverty and sickness he established branches of 'the Charity', the General and his wife giving him, as well as liberal donations, the support of their prestige and authority. He seems to have visited Clichy fairly regularly; although he resigned Châtillon early in 1618 in favour of Père Girard, his co-worker there, he did not resign his Paris parish until 1626.

In the capital he found further scope for his charity and zeal. Being chaplain in the household of the General of the Galleys he knew how the oarsmen on the ships were conscripted. As it was impossible to recruit rowers for that hated task an easy and cheap solution to the problem of supplying man power had been found by sending convicted criminals to the galleys. No wages were paid, food was cut to a minimum and, once chained to his bench, a man could be forced to obey. To meet the demand, for the death rate in that unenviable occupation was high and the fleets were constantly calling for more hands to man the oars, judges sent men to the galleys for comparatively trivial crimes. Once condemned to serve on the Mediterranean or the Atlantic, *galériens*, whether their sentence was long or short, seldom returned. Their full term served, they pleaded in vain for release. Usually they were kept on, 'to write upon the waters with their eighteen-foot pens', until death finally loosened the ankle from the fetter and the hand from the oar.

Most of these unfortunates served their apprenticeship to misery in the prisons of Paris. De Gondi's sister, the Marquise de Maignelay, who spent her life trying to alleviate the lot of the prisoners and urging the authorities to improve prison buildings, had harrowing tales to tell Monsieur Vincent. Early in the New Year following his return from Châtillon he began a round of the city prisons: the Conciergerie, the Grand Châtelet, the Petit Châtelet, Fort l'Évêque, the Bastille, and other, smaller jails. These fortresses may not have equalled, in the number of their inmates or in the bestialities and degradations perpetrated within their walls, the concentration camps of our century; nevertheless, fearful rigours awaited the man unlucky enough to be jailed in any one of them.

The Grand Châtelet, one of the worst of the prisons, stood right in the city centre. It was on the north bank of the Seine near a bridge where the goldsmiths and silversmiths had their booths and not far from the Hôtel de Gondi. Contemporaries of Vincent who suffered incarceration in this grim pile have recorded for us the names of its dungeons: the Butchery; the Prick-and-Sting; the Barbarities; the Chains; the Trap-Dungeon; the Ditch, 'into which prisoners were lowered by a rope like a bucket going down a well-shaft'; the End-of-Ease, ankle deep—sometimes knee deep—in sewage and crawling reptilian creatures. The most dreaded of all was the Dyke of Hypocras where a prisoner could not sit or lie down; he had to stand in or trample wearily the filthy water swishing about him, his body chained and bent over his swollen, rotting feet. Fifteen days in the Dyke was certain to cause death or madness, but not many confined there lasted that long.[1] The majority of the Grand Châtelet prisoners, including those destined for the galleys, were in flagged passages and hallways, chained to the walls like so many cattle, their bedding vermin-infested straw, their food a totally inadequate ration of black bread. The inhumanity Vincent de Paul had witnessed and suffered among the Mediterranean pirates and in the Tunis slave marts was no worse than that prevailing in the Paris prisons.

As might be expected, on his first visits he was met with oaths and blasphemies, the bitterest revilings coming from those who felt that their punishment was out of all proportion to the wrong they had done. Before anything could be done to help them spiritually their physical conditions had to be improved. As chaplain to the General and high in that great man's favour, Vincent was in a particularly advantageous position to effect reforms, but the speed with which he carried them out was extraordinary. Within a month of his return to Paris he had purchased or rented a house in the Saint-Honoré quarter and transferred groups of *galériens* there. Even if there was not then so much red tape as there is nowadays to be untied or cut, still a vast network of officialdom did exist and Monsieur Vincent would have had to wait on and seek interviews with persons in power and with officials in the galley and prison services, not to mention finding the house, equipping it, seeing to the convicts' eating and sleeping arrangements, and satisfying the authorities as to security precautions.

When the most wretched of the prisoners had been transferred to this new place of detention, he installed himself in their midst, remaining for days and weeks on end, seeing to their needs, writing their letters, consoling them as well as he could. When he found an opportune moment he ministered to their souls and promised to follow them as soon as possible to the ports where the fleet lay. Every six months, when a batch of *galériens* left 'on the chain' for Marseilles or Bordeaux, 'a trail of bloodstains marking their journey south', another lot was transferred from the prisons to Monsieur Vincent's house. Cardinal de Retz, approached for help, had an appeal for funds and helpers made in the Paris churches, and money and offers of assistance flowed in so abundantly that Vincent was enabled to extend this work considerably. If he had to absent himself from the city to fulfil his duties to the de Gondis, he left behind two other priests he recruited to act as his assistants. One of them, M. Portail, he had met and befriended at Clichy in 1612, helping him to discover his vocation and encouraging him to persevere. Antoine Portail was a desperately shy, retiring character but his charity and devotion to the galley-prisoners mirrored that of Vincent himself. We shall meet him again.

A year later, Vincent de Paul's apostolate to the *galériens* received recognition from a very high quarter. Louis XIII named him as almoner-general to the galleys, 'with the same honours and rights as those enjoyed by other officers of the Mediterranean fleet'. This appointment enabled him to redeem his promise to the prisoners that he would visit them at the ports. A few days after receiving news of his appointment he set out for Marseilles and there he found his poor felons, two hundred and seventy-five of them to the galley, each pair chained by the ankle to an iron ball. Paintings and films of galley-slaves under the lash, far from exaggerating, understate the cruelties inflicted, cruelties sometimes inflicted merely to provide sport for or settle a wager between the commanding officers on the various ships. The episode in the film, *Monsieur Vincent*, in which Pierre Fresnay, in the name part, unshackles a *galérien* and takes his place, has its foundation in Abelly's *Life of Vincent de Paul*, the biography written within a few years of the saint's death. Later biographers have questioned the incident and expressed doubt that such an exchange would have been permitted on the galleys, but the Mission Fathers living with Vincent in his last years attributed the dropsical condition of his legs and feet to the weight of the ball-and-fetters on his ankles when he accepted servitude and the lash in place of another. He was not the first or last priest to act thus since the Priest of Priests suffered the death of the Cross, offering Himself in place of His brother, man. In the present century priests stepped forward to take the place of other men in the queues for the gas-chambers at Auschwitz, Dachau and Buchenwald. If Vincent took the drastic step of manning an oar, it was because he had failed to obtain humane treatment for the *galériens* by other means and wished to shock the responsible authorities into a realization of the cruelty they ordered or condoned. On his return to Paris he undoubtedly made strong representations to de Gondi. That great lord, never a seafaring man, towards the end of 1619 seems to have been suddenly made aware of his duties as General of the Galleys. For the next six or seven years he was with the galleys constantly, whether they lay to or went to sea. Incidentally, the General was rewarded for his belated attention to the duties of his state. His galleys, having chased a corsair who had been terrorizing the southern coast of France, returned to Marseilles in triumph, towing behind them four captured pirate ships, with many prisoners and guns and large quantities of ammunition. In view of his own early experience at the hands of corsairs Vincent would have rejoiced at this successful chase. But his heart would have bled for the wretches whose skinned hands, strained muscles, sore backs and shoulders told of their part in the victory, and for their comrades who, unable any longer to respond when the pace quickened and whip and whistle signalled 'Double Stroke!', died on the oars. Alas, despite all the efforts of Vincent de Paul to improve the lot of the *galériens*, when Evelyn, the English diarist, visited Marseilles twenty years later, things were as bad as ever:

We then went to visit the galleys, being about twenty-five in number; the Capitaine of the Galley Royal gave us a most courteous entertainment in his cabin . . . then he showed us how he commanded their motions with a nod, and his whistle making them row out. The spectacle was to me new and strange, to see so many hundreds of miserably naked persons, their heads being shaven close and having only high red bonnets, a pair of coarse canvas drawers, their whole backs and legs naked, double chained about their middle and legs, in couples, and made fast to their seats, and all commanded in a trice by an imperious and cruel seaman. . . . The rising-forward and falling-back on their oar is a miserable spectacle, and the noise of their chains, with the roaring of the beaten waters, has something strange and fearful in it to one unaccustomed to it. They are ruled and chastised by strokes on their backs and soles of their feet, on the least disorder, and without the least humanity. . . . [2]

In 1623 when the Mediterranean fleet, then in the Atlantic, put in at Bordeaux, the almoner-general was waiting for the *galériens* and organized a general mission for them. As de Gondi was there in person we may be sure that the officers and overseers and other seamen were rounded up also. A Turk was converted and baptized as a result of the sermons. They named him for the King: Louis.

It was almost twenty years since Vincent had been so near his home—he was less than ninety miles from Dax—and he wondered if he should visit his family. He had scruples about going, for reasons he explained to friends whose advice he asked:

> I had seen good priests who accomplished much good when far away and I noticed that after visiting their relations they came back quite altered and of no use to their flocks. They had become wrapped up in their families and could think of nothing else, though before they went home they had been devoted to their work and quite detached from their relatives. I, too, was afraid of becoming too attached to my family.

His friends advised him to go, saying that they thought his visit would be a great consolation to his relatives who deserved, just as much as strangers, the benefit of his spiritual counsel and prayers. So he set off for Ranquine. He did not, however, sleep at home but in the house of the local curé where his mortification was noted. He slept on straw, ate but little, and spoiled, with liberal dousings of water, the drop of wine he permitted himself.

The de Paul family was proud of him, and with reason. Their Vincent, though slow to improve his prospects in the first decade of his priesthood, had now, in his early forties, risen to be a man of some consequence in national and ecclesiastical circles. How many small farmers of their standing had a brother almoner-general of the Royal Galleys, chaplain to one of the richest noblemen in France, and curé of a Paris parish? They let him see that they were highly pleased at the turn his fortunes had taken, and that they expected even greater things of him. They also expected something *from* him. That yoke of oxen, sold by their father twenty-six years before to start Vincent in Toulouse, still ploughed furrows in the minds of the de Paul brothers and sisters. Vincent's letters, including the one written in 1610 excusing his inability to help them because his hopes of a benefice had not materialized, were remembered if not quoted. But Vincent had by this time another family, far more numerous and needy than his blood brothers and sisters. Besides the *galériens* he had the poor, the poor of Clichy, of Picardy, of Champagne, of the Beauce, of Burgundy. And behind them the vast multitudes of poor in Paris and in all the provinces of France. He had pledged his word to God that he would serve the poor. To his pledged word he would not be untrue.

After spending eight or nine days in his native place he prepared to go. He sat down for his last meal in Ranquine with Jean and Gayon and Bernard and their wives, and his two sisters with their husbands; a crowd of young nephews and nieces hovered hopefully around and neighbours waited outside to bid him Godspeed. He spoke plainly to his brothers and sisters, 'telling them how to save their souls and to put far from them covetousness of earthly riches'. He went further still: 'You must not expect anything from me; and even if I had chests of gold and silver I would not give you anything, for a priest who possesses anything owes it to God and the poor.' They were frugal-living, hard-working people and he must have seen the disappointment showing on their faces. It hurt him to the heart to have to shatter their hopes. They were his own folk and he loved them. If their brother had dedicated himself to the poor they had not done so. Though not destitute they had a constant struggle to make ends meet and regarded themselves as poor. But there was nothing more Vincent could add by way of explanation. Having made his farewells he set out, his tears blinding him, along the paths he had so often traversed in the old days when he drove his cattle and sheep to the pasture and his pigs to the oak woods.

I was so deeply grieved at parting with my poor brothers and sisters and relatives that I did nothing but weep and sob all along the road. When I dried my eyes I was full of ideas of helping them and of settling them in better circumstances, giving this to such a one, that to the other. . . . I walked on, so swayed by my feelings that I kept dividing among them, in my mind, both what I had and what I had not. . . . [3]

Thus he described in later years his final departure from Ranquine. He adds that the temptation to advance his family remained with him for three months. Recognizing it as a temptation he prayed earnestly to be delivered from it, 'and God gave me the grace to leave them in His Fatherly care and to regard them as better off than if they had every comfort, though indeed they have had to receive alms, and still do so'.

During the seven years after his return to Paris at the end of 1617 his chaplaincy, his missions in the country and his work for the *galériens* in the prisons and on the galleys were not his only interests. In the capital his closest friends were Bérulle and the other spearheads of the movement for Church reform. Madame Acarie, whose home had been a favourite rendezvous for the group, was dead but Vincent de Paul, with the English Capuchin, Benet of Canfield, Père Coton the Jesuit, Bourdoise, M. du Val of the Sorbonne, and others, continued to meet Bérulle for discussions on ways and means of promoting throughout France the canons of the Council of Trent. The prisoners' friend, the Marquise de Maignelay, 'always dressed in sombre shades of grey or violet', sometimes came to those gatherings, as did Louise, wife of Antoine Le Gras, Secretary to Marie de Medici, and other ladies interested in seeking solutions to the pressing problems, religious, moral, and social, of the day. Towards the end of 1618 Vincent de Paul, present at a meeting of Bérulle and his circle, made a new friend—Francis de Sales.

The Prince-Bishop of Geneva, one of the leading theologians, writers and preachers of the age, was already known to him by reputation and by his devotional works.* The two could have met during Vincent's months in Châtillon but there is no evidence that they did. When they met in Paris the Savoyard was fifty-one, the Gascon thirty-eight, and they seem to have been mutually attracted. Though Francis de Sales died in 1622 and Vincent knew him for only four years, hardly any other exercised such an influence over him. 'In Bérulle he (Vincent de Paul) found sanctity and bent the knee; in Francis he found a saint and gave him his heart.'⁴ As has been seen, Vincent de Paul's heart was not a cold or unfeeling one, but though he had read of joy and serenity of spirit neither his own experience nor Bérulle's direction had given him any real understanding of these virtues. He saw them personified in St Francis de Sales. Nearly forty years later he wrote to Alexander VII, adding his voice to that of France and other nations then beseeching the Pontiff to canonize 'Monsieur de Genève'. In the course of his letter he says:

As I was on rather familiar terms with this excellent Servant of God who often did me the favour of conversing with me . . . I find it impossible to keep silent now. When so many are petitioning Your Holiness I, unworthy though I am . . . cannot stand by and say nothing.

Faith, hope, charity . . . all the virtues . . . seemed natural to him and, to my mind at least, formed such a source of goodness in him that once when I was ill and remembered a conversation I had had with him a little while before I could not but think of his exquisite kindness and mildness

* The *Introduction to the Devout Life*, published in 1608, became a best-seller in France within a few months and translations into several European languages followed, the work being popular with Calvinists and Protestants as well as with Catholics. Though its author refused payment, being with difficulty persuaded to accept a dowry for a poor girl who wished to enter religion, the printer made a fortune in a few years on the sales. The *Treatise on the Love of God*, written mainly for the Visitandines (founded by St Francis de Sales and St Jeanne de Chantal) and published in 1616, was recommended by Vincent de Paul to his followers, 'as a universal remedy for the weak and a spur to the lazy'. The *Entretiens*, published after the death of Francis de Sales, were a series of conferences on the spiritual life he gave to Mère de Chantal and her nuns.

and say to myself, 'How good God must be, since the Bishop of Geneva is so good.'

Elsewhere he spoke of St Francis de Sales as a preacher and as a conversationalist:

> All who heard him preach hung on his every word. He accommodated himself to the capacity of his hearers by considering himself indebted to each. If a person went to consult him on some important matter or concerning some scruple of conscience he would keep his visitor until he was completely satisfied in mind and consoled in heart. So great was my admiration for him that whenever I recalled his words I used to think of him as the man of our times whose life copied most closely the earthly life of the Son of God. . . . He was so kind, so gracious, so good, that those who had the happiness of having conversations with him felt their hearts overflow with joy. I myself had that delightful experience.

Vincent and his new friend discussed many matters: the dangers to the faith, now that religious conflict was again reviving in France; the education of women; the tremendous need for missions to the people and of systematic religious instruction; the direction of souls. They discussed current politics. Père Coton, their friend, had been dismissed. Chaplain to Henri IV, confessor to both Louis XIII and the Queen-Mother, in his spiritual office the Jesuit could not but reprove his royal penitent if Louis confessed to condoning or instigating the murder of the Italian favourites. It was significant that he was soon dismissed to be replaced by another priest. The courtiers, not sorry to witness the eclipse of one 'respected, loved and feared by all', passed on the joke, 'No cotton (Coton) in the King's ears now'. The Jesuits themselves, from whose ranks the new confessor was chosen, were as certain as Francis de Sales and Vincent de Paul that the King had not gained by the change. Almost the first action of Père Coton's successor was to preach a sermon before the King and the court accusing the Protestants of ignorance of the Bible.

At once learned and able divines put quill to paper and countered with *Defence of the Reformed Churches of France*. Controversy raged as preachers, Huguenot and Catholic, some of whom had been a long while missing from their pulpits, contradicted and fulminated. Francis de Sales, who had converted the Calvinists of the Chablais by thousands and by tens of thousands, deprecated the denunciations and thunderings of those who thought their sermons helped the cause of Catholicism. 'Love,' he had told his Canons, 'will shake the walls of Geneva. By love we must invade and conquer it. Ardent prayer must break down the walls and brotherly love charge them. . . .' His affability towards sinners and those not of his faith scandalized his friends, one of whom said to him, 'Francis de Sales will of course go to Heaven—as Francis de Sales; I am not so sure about him going there as Bishop of Geneva; he may find that his gentleness to some will prevent him entering Paradise.' But Monsieur de Genève replied: 'I would rather answer to the good God for too much gentleness than for too much severity. Is not God all love? The Father is the Father of Mercies; the Son is a lamb—the Lamb of God; the Holy Spirit a dove—the Heavenly Dove. Are you wiser than God?' His advice to all who would win others became a proverb in French and countless other tongues: 'You will catch more flies with a spoonful of honey than with a barrel of vinegar.' Some ascribed this proverb to Henri IV, but that shrewd if loose-living monarch could have taken it from Francis de Sales, of whom he had a high opinion, as his description of him shows:

> Monsieur de Genève is a rare bird indeed: devout, learned and a gentleman into the bargain. . . . He does not know the art of flattery, having a mind too sincere for that. . . . He is the one who is most capable of restoring Church order to its pristine splendour. He is mild, good and humble, intensely pious but without any futile scruples. [5]

Vincent de Paul was of the same mind as the Bishop concerning those outside the Church. He will yet be found writing to one of his priests:

Oh, Father Grimal, my dear brother, what great missionaries we would be, you and I, if we only knew how to animate souls with the spirit of the Gospel. . . . I assure you that that is the most efficacious way of sanctifying Christians and converting heretics . . . and that nothing can make them more determined to cling to vice and error than to adopt the opposite methods.

Now, I can just hear you saying, 'Must I, then, see a Catholic oppressed by a Protestant and not interfere on behalf of the former?' The answer is that such oppression had a reason; you will find it arose either from something the Catholic owes the Huguenot or from some insult or injury he did him. Now, in any of these cases, is the Huguenot not justified in demanding his rights? Is a Catholic less subject to justice because he is a Catholic? (There is, you know, a great deal of difference between being a Catholic and a just man.) 'Yes,' you say, 'but the judges are Huguenots.' They are, but they are also lawyers and they judge according to the laws, customs and ordinances; and, apart from their consciences, they profess to be men of honour. The Governor is much more clearsighted about the duties of his office than you and I.

And again, the echo of Francis de Sales is evident in this letter from Vincent:

Let us labour humbly and with respect for others. Protestant ministers should not be challenged from the pulpit, nor should they be asked to point out this or that article of their faith in Holy Writ, except very rarely and then only in a spirit of humility and sympathy. Otherwise God will not bless our work. The poor will turn against us, concluding that we acted out of vanity, and will no longer believe in us. . . . People will never believe in us if we do not manifest love and sympathy for them. . . . I am not saying this, Sir, because I know you to have been guilty of such a thing, but just to put you on your guard. . . . Bitterness has never served any purpose except to embitter. . . .

At the time Monsieur de Genève and Monsieur Vincent made one another's acquaintance, Armand du Plessis of Richelieu, Bishop of Luçon, was again in the public eye.* While the preachers of different faiths were hurling epithets and invective at one another from their respective pulpits Richelieu was writing. Within three months he completed and published a bulky tome entitled *Principal Points of Catholic Faith Defended*, a masterpiece of tact and tolerance, of theology and logic and literary art, which he dedicated to the King. It would have reinstated him in the royal favour then and there had not his enemies, already numerous, read between its lines further evidence of his formidable ability. False reports concerning his allegiance were circulated and Louis ordered him into exile at Avignon, then Papal territory. Contenting himself with a dignified and calmly worded protest and a request for an open inquiry into his conduct, the Bishop obeyed the King's mandate and, with the sense for timing that was second nature to him, left for Avignon on Good Friday.

There he remained for a year writing, waiting, sometimes hopeful, once so pessimistic about regaining past or attaining to future prominence that he made his will. A letter from Louis recalled him from exile. He was to post with all speed for Angoulême to rejoin the Queen-Mother as her adviser. The word 'adviser' was underlined. Marie de Medici had played into the hands of a group of disaffected nobles led by the *demi-roi*, the Duc d'Épernon whose nephews Vincent de Paul had taught at Toulouse, by allowing herself to be inveigled into an escapade as unwise as it was 'difficult and unbecoming for a woman of the Queen's *embonpoint*'. Making a midnight escape, complete with pass words, rope ladders, and all the trappings of melodrama, from Blois Castle, she was met by d'Épernon who escorted her to Angoulême where a court more brilliant than that of the Louvre had assembled. Nobles and governors of a dozen provinces were

* Having received warning that the King intended ordering him from Blois, where he acted as confidant to the Queen-Mother since her banishment from court, to his diocese, Richelieu forestalled the monarch by leaving for Luçon where he lived quietly, deaf to Marie de Medici's tearful appeals to return.

flocking to her aid and civil war could erupt at any moment. The only one to whom the indiscreet, rather stupid woman might listen was Richelieu. Though the Auvergne country was frost-bound and snow falling heavily he was in his carriage within hours of the royal courier's arrival at Avignon. Not many days after his meeting with the rebel Queen, mother and son were reconciled, temporarily. The Duc d'Épernon, beaten for the moment, retired gracefully and with a full pardon to his estates. Richelieu was on the road to power.

As Bérulle had a leading part in the negotiations, having spent three months coming and going between Paris and Angoulême, bearing the King's instructions to Richelieu and giving spiritual counsel to the Queen-Mother, Vincent de Paul and Francis de Sales knew a good deal more of the royal affairs than did those whose sole knowledge of current events depended on what they read in the *Recueils*. Later that year, the embassy which brought de Sales to Paris having concluded its mission, he returned to Annecy, for the Calvinists had never permitted him to take possession of Geneva, his episcopal city. He went by Tours, for the Queen, Marie de Medici, wished to see him before he left.* 'There I came to know many prelates and especially the Bishop of Luçon [Richelieu] who vowed all friendship for me and told me that he would come to my side and busy himself with nothing but God and the salvation of souls. . . . Finally I saw Cardinal de Retz who invited me to remain in France and made me a proposition . . . which I discussed with M. de Bérulle.' The Cardinal and others wished to keep Monsieur de Genève in Paris and probably Vincent de Paul added his pleading to theirs, but Francis set out for Annecy, 'the place of our pilgrimage and exile, where we sit, weeping the memory of our Geneva'.

While the Savoy embassy was in Paris, Madame de Chantal paid a visit to the capital to establish a convent of the Visitation, the Order she and Francis de Sales had founded. Vincent de Paul had many conversations with the joint Founders and was inter-

---

* Describing the court of Marie de Medici, Francis de Sales said, 'It reminded me of nothing but a lot of wasps feeding on a dead body.'

ested to learn that the Visitation, as its name implied, had been originally intended as a company of women vowed to the visitation and service of the sick poor. The first Visitandines, wearing lay dress, had engaged in this apostolate of charity, but the day had not yet dawned when ecclesiastical authorities would approve of uncloistered nuns. The Visitation developed on other lines, becoming a congregation in which women who felt called to contemplation but whose age, health, or temperament unfitted them for austerities practised by Poor Clares, Carmelites, and other contemplatives could realize their vocation. Madame de Chantal was a widow and the Order was then open, as it still is, to widows.

Monsieur de Genève and Jeanne de Chantal agreed that Vincent de Paul was the most suitable superior and spiritual director to be found in Paris for the new foundation. 'I do not know a more worthy or a more holy priest than Monsieur Vincent,' the Bishop declared again and again to his friends and acquaintances, but it took many entreaties and an order from Cardinal de Retz to overcome Vincent's reluctance to take on this office. He finally agreed, and was faithful to the charge entrusted to him for almost forty years, always endeavouring to foster in the Visitandines not his spirit but that of the two Founders, both of whom were later canonized. In choosing Vincent as director of the Visitation, Francis de Sales, a great judge of men, must have detected in him traits that fitted him for developing along the right lines a work newly begun. Holiness and worthiness of life were a *sine qua non*. Also needed were marked qualities of discernment, penetration, sound judgment, the ability to take the long view, to make collective effort effective by suiting the discipline that held the group together to the individuals composing it. The direction of the Visitation became a great burden on Monsieur Vincent when to the cares of his own Orders, his manifold works of charity, and the public offices imposed on him was added the charge of several Visitation communities in Paris and elsewhere. 'For me it is a cross,' he said in later years, 'the heaviest cross I have to bear.' He bore it for the sake of Francis de Sales, the saint to whom he owed so much. Towards the end of his life he tried on two occasions to resign this charge but was not permitted to do so.

Vincent had been greatly struck by the affability of de Sales. He himself, he tells us, used to suffer from moodiness and fits of deep depression. Evidently he came to realize, after his meetings with Monsieur de Genève, that such a 'black humour' could be an obstacle in his work for souls. During a retreat he made in 1621 he prayed 'to overcome this dry and repellent mood and acquire a sweetness and benignity of character'. When his Bishop friend died in 1622 he must have invoked his aid and asked him to bequeath him something of his serene and attractive manner, for he writes, 'I was completely delivered from my black humour.' Madame de Gondi noticed the change in him and could say that 'Monsieur Vincent would have been the mildest man of this century if there had not been a Francis de Sales.'

He was still attached to the de Gondis, who were, in the years subsequent to 1618, in no small difficulties. Young Pierre had joined his uncle Henri, Duc de Retz, who was with the Queen-Mother's faction at Blois; with those other ex-pupils of Monsieur Vincent, the Duc d'Épernon's nephews, he was in the circle of younger nobles prominent in the conspiracy against the Crown. His father, the General, as has been stated, took the duties of his office more seriously from 1618 on. But, apart from the representations made to him on behalf of the *galériens* by Vincent de Paul, there were other reasons that made it imperative for him to show real interest in his commission as General of the Galleys. He and his, being of Italian extraction, favoured in the previous century by Catherine de Medici and since 1607 by Marie de Medici, were under a cloud. Plotters had met in de Gondi's Paris Hôtel and in his country châteaux. His youngest brother and his son had joined the rebels. It was essential that he keep above suspicion by remaining far from conspirators. It was equally essential that he display loyalty by zeal in the King's service. For the next six years, except for a couple of fleeting visits, his family saw nothing of him. His aged uncle, Cardinal de Retz, did his best to keep in the good graces of both the King and the Queen-Mother, but when that lady's supporters attempted a second, more serious, rebellion in 1620 the General and his wife and the Cardinal had reason to feel decidedly uneasy. In the only encounter between the rebels and the royal troops, Henri de Gondi, Duc de Retz, shared with the Duc de Vendôme command of the Queen-Dowager's forces.*

Despite her anxiety for husband and son and the increased responsibilities that fell on her because of their absence, Madame de Gondi was tireless in helping Monsieur Vincent in his work for the people on her own and her husband's estates. Her entreaties had moved him to preach the necessity of good confessions; from her had come the idea of preaching the first mission in Folleville early in 1617. Seeing the good that followed from the missions in country parishes Madame la Générale wished that other estates, other provinces, might share the same benefits. She set aside a large sum of money for this project and tried to interest some of the existing Orders in the idea. Monsieur Vincent, too, endeavoured to induce various Orders and Congregations to undertake the apostolate of the countryside. There was no response, so Vincent continued to labour alone, sometimes meeting initial opposition—'They jeered at me and, as I went through the streets, pointed at me with the finger'—but in the end he invariably won the parish or hamlet or village or market town. Whether he won them or not he was not the man to relinquish lightly an enterprise so visibly blessed by God. As time went on, however, he became increasingly aware of certain facts: to ensure lasting results, the missions would need to be renewed periodically; the work would have to be systematically planned and the

---

* The rebels were routed. Pierre de Gondi, hearing that his uncle the Cardinal and others were conferring with the Queen-Mother behind the lines, trying to make peace, shouted, 'I've had enough of this. Here we put ourselves in danger while those who sent us to risk our lives sue for peace,' and he galloped off with half the army. The Duc de Vendôme, seeing himself left to face King Louis and his forces, followed suit. Vendôme galloped to Marie de Medici's quarters where she waited with her ladies and threw himself at her feet crying, 'Madame, I wish I were dead! I wish I were dead!' A maid-of-honour tartly observed, 'If that is your wish, Monsieur le Duc, you should have stayed on the field.'

missions given by priests fully conversant with his aims and methods and capable of carrying them out.

Sixteen-twenty-two was a sad year for many a Frenchwoman and Madame de Gondi had her own share of grief. Though the rebellion of 1620 had ended in little more than a cross-country gallop—led by her brother-in-law—young King Louis had tasted victory and found it sweet. Advised that it would be a mistake, having got an army in readiness, not to make use of it, he decided to march south and 'convert' at sword's point the Huguenots of Béarn, his father's native province. The staunchest upholders of the Reformed religion were there occupying strong citadels at Tárbes, Lourdes, Pau, Orthez, and other points along the western Pyrenees. The conflict spread to central and western France in 1622 and the General of the Galleys moved the Mediterranean fleet into the Atlantic to bombard La Rochelle and other ports held by the Protestants. Cardinal de Retz had accompanied the King's forces. His nephew, Henri, and grand-nephew, Pierre, were still intriguing with the pro-Medici party. In August Madame de Gondi was informed that the Cardinal had died of the plague outside the walls of Béziers. In September, her second son, eleven-year-old Henri de Gondi, destined for the purple, rode out one morning for the first hunt of the autumn. He was carried home dead. A kick from a horse ended his life and left his worldly little brother heir to the See of Paris and the Cardinal's hat.

Her son dead, her uncle-in-law dead, her eldest son in dangerous company, her husband far away and in daily danger, Marguerite de Gondi might have been expected to abandon herself to her grief. Nothing, perhaps, shows more clearly the influence of Vincent de Paul's spiritual direction than the change in this *grande dame*, one of his earliest penitents. The self-willed temperamental creature who four years before spent a summer wailing because Vincent had left her for Châtillon was now a selfless, devoted woman whose one thought was to look after the needs of others. When Vincent, having given a mission in a parish, was about to set up a Charity she was there with advice and help and funds; she was the first to lead the local women to the homes of the poor to serve the sick, the aged and the destitute. As no Order showed signs of helping the country missions the obvious course seemed to be to found a society of priests. Monsieur Vincent, too humble to think of himself as Founder, was asked by Madame de Gondi to establish a religious society that would undertake the apostolate to rural France. When peace was declared and the General visited his home, his wife broached the matter to him. In the following year, 1623, he gave a munificent sum, double the amount his lady had already earmarked for the work, and negotiations for the purchase of a one-time boarding school for boys, the *Bons-Enfants*, began.

Vincent, as though he had some premonition of the shape of things to come, managed to find time to attend Paris University during 1622 and 1623, reading for and obtaining a Licentiate in Canon Law. When the purchase of the *Bons-Enfants* was completed he found himself appointed Principal of the College, a dilapidated fourteenth-century building then almost empty of boarders. Three years after his return from the mission to the *galériens* in Bordeaux and his final farewell to his family he was to resign his parish in Clichy. He did not, however, take up residence in the *Bons-Enfants*, but installed Antoine Portail there. He still had his duties to the prisoners and the galley-slaves. Someone had to continue the country missions. Branches of the Charity were multiplying. He was always faithful to his first friends in Paris, the St John of God Brothers, and continued to visit their hospital. Francis de Sales was no more, so the direction of the Visitation and Madame de Chantal had to be all the more painstakingly carried out. He was still chaplain to the de Gondis and tremendously indebted to them. He repaid his debt in a coinage not of this world, 'good measure, heaped up and running over', and had the happiness of seeing his two benefactors make great strides in virtue and holiness. Without them the contracts could never have been drawn up and signed:

for the establishment and maintenance of a number of

ecclesiastics, to be chosen by Monsieur Vincent de Paul. . . .
priests who shall relinquish benefice and office and bind
themselves to serve devotedly, completely and disinterestedly
the poor people of the country districts and work for their
salvation, going from village to village to preach, teach and
catechize, urging their hearers to make general confessions
. . . all to be done under episcopal authority and in view of
the fact that while the towns have many preachers and
priests and religious those who work the land are almost
abandoned. . . .

Another reason why Vincent did not reside in the College
from the start was because Madame de Gondi, never very robust,
had begun to decline in health. When he returned from Châtillon
she told him that though she greatly feared death, if she knew
that she could rely on his presence and prayers she would have
courage to face that last and greatest ordeal. Now that the end
was in sight he remained by her side. The General was on the
Mediterranean with the galleys when in June, 1625, Marguerite
de Gondi died, 'meeting Death as she did everyone, gently'.
When the funeral was over Vincent went to Marseilles to break
the bad news to Philippe-Emmanuel and to tell him that he wished
to resign his chaplaincy and live with his priests in the *Bons-
Enfants*. The General asked Monsieur Vincent's advice about his
own affairs. He intended to resign from the galleys and to make
over his property to Pierre de Gondi. He would join the little
company of priests in the College, if Monsieur Vincent would
have him. But Vincent de Paul did not think that this *très-
puissant* nobleman would fit in with the shy M. Portail and himself. He advised him to apply to Bérulle. De Gondi was accepted
by the Oratory and remained Vincent's lifelong friend, outliving
him by two years.

By December, 1625, Vincent had left the Hôtel de Gondi for
the ramshackle building at the end of the rue St Victor, the
Bons-Enfants. M. Portail was glad to welcome him and, no doubt,
they spent a happy Christmas doing the rounds of the prisons,

helping in the John of God Hospital, or in the house where the men destined for the galleys were detained. That house was quite near the site being cleared for the palace Cardinal Richelieu was having built for himself. The owner of the House of the Great Bear had sold willingly and at a high price and thought his neighbour at the Sign of the Three Virgins very foolish to refuse to sell. If what the ballads and pamphlets being hawked about Paris said was true, the Cardinal was a man slow to decide, but when he did it was no use opposing him. Richelieu, having at last got his hand upon the helm of State, was to hold it firmly for the next eighteen years. If his Christmas diversions included a little lute playing for Marie de Medici, a little praying for the King, a little poring over Le Mercier's plans for the reconstruction of the Louvre, the new church for the Sorbonne, and his own palace, they also included much reflection on France and its King and the moves that might be made on that chess-board—Europe.

Chapter Eight

HAND TO THE PLOUGH

By DEGREES other priests joined Monsieur Vincent and M. Portail at the *Bons-Enfants*. In April, 1626, the Congregation received official approval from the Archbishop of Paris and before the end of that year Vincent could count seven followers. They proceeded, simply and without advertisement, to accomplish their vocation of 'evangelizing the poor, after the example of Our Lord'. Beginning with Paris and the surrounding districts and the de Gondi estates, the Mission priests and their work soon became known and they were asked to travel further afield. The missions lasted from a few weeks to a few months, according to the state of religion in the various parishes to which they were invited. In some cases the people were totally ignorant of the faith and needed instruction in the rudiments before being prepared for the general confessions that Vincent and his priests preached as the first step to reform of life. Charities and confraternities had to be established to ensure that the good work begun during the mission did not end with the last sermon. Besides the public mission, a private one to the clergy was also given; sometimes the priests of a parish would go to the *Bons-Enfants* and make a retreat there while the missioners took their place as pastors. Good priests were encouraged to continue; those who lacked knowledge of the obligations of the priesthood were tutored and helped; the careless and the scandal-givers were won round. No missions were given between the end of June and November 1st, the four intervening months being the period of the various harvests when country people were too busy to attend. When the faith had been rekindled, religious practice restored, and Catholic life solidly reorganized in a parish, the priests of the Mission gathered their few belongings and moved on to begin all over again elsewhere. They worked among those to whom Vincent often referred as 'the poor people of the countryside'. He saw them as spiritually poor, a consequence of the lack of good and well-instructed priests in rural areas; but material poverty was also the lot of the French peasantry of his time. They formed the living and sombre setting for the dazzling political and literary figures of seventeenth-century France. Tenant-farmers, share-croppers, agricultural labourers or journeymen—all lived at bare subsistence level. On them fell the major portion of the taxes, the entire economic structure depending on their contribution, in toil, time, money and produce, to the national purse. Though the individual contribution might be small, the numbers of those working on the land, in comparison to the rest of the population, were so great that a modern statesman's saying, reversed, aptly describes the position: 'Never did so few owe so much to so many.' Poor, illiterate, oppressed, unorganized, it was an easy matter to fleece them. A proverb current in Vincent's time ran: 'France is a meadow that is mown three times a year.' The few peasant risings, the *Croquants** in Périgord, the *Va-nu-pieds*† in Normandy, the *Lanturlus*‡ in Burgundy, were savagely crushed; after each of these attempts at revolt the country people relapsed into duller, more hopeless misery.

Rural France also had to bear the brunt of war, civil and foreign, an evil endemic to the country in that century. Conflict between local lords and their following, or between the royal forces and the various rebel armies, meant battles and retaliatory actions in which sometimes whole villages were wiped out. Troops, whether en route to service beyond the French frontiers or some war-torn area of France, or just hanging around spoiling for a fight, were hardly ever quartered in towns. They resented this and revenged themselves on the unfortunate peasants with whom they were billeted. A contemporary document of a Champagne official stated, 'There is not a soldier in this province who does not deserve to be hanged.' To have the discontented,

---

* Clodhoppers.　　　† Barefooted.　　　‡ Stuff-and-Nonsense.

undisciplined militiamen billeted on one for three days was regarded as worse than a year's taxes. More dreaded than the material losses were the lootings and atrocities perpetrated on defenceless peasants by the badly fed, badly led militias recruited to swell the armies. The sound of distant drums denoting the approach of this rabble was enough to send villagers and field workers flying in terror to the woods and mountains.

In Périgord, the province traversed by Vincent in 1600 on his way to ordination, his one-time pupil, the Duc de la Valette, had twelve hundred country folk massacred at the barricades they erected to protect their hamlets and farms from pillage. Suicides were common in Normandy where the people on the land despaired 'because of the burdens they could no longer bear'. In other provinces, on farms where the oxen had been seized in lieu of the *taille*, men, women, and even children, might be seen yoked to the plough or hay-cart or farm wagon. 'Nevertheless the *taille* was not reduced, but increased to the point when the shirt or shift covering the nudity of a corpse was snatched away . . . and in many places women, ashamed at being unable to cover their nakedness, were constrained to remain at home from church.' There was no respect for any law, that of God or that of the land. Each province returned to its ancestral sins. In Brittany there was drunkenness. In Provence, where the ruins of pagan temples and the balmy southern air held memories of ancient rituals and deities, debauchery sprawled, the most sacred Christian rites and processions being turned into open air amusement where the seven deadly sins, especially lust and sloth, were represented by buffoonery and made a cause for public and general laughter. The principal idol in the Cévennes and the Alps was revenge, the cult of which demanded blood sacrifices. Elsewhere robbery and perjury were admired as a proof of quick-wittedness, eloquence and subtlety of thought; avarice masqueraded as paternal foresight. Everywhere vanity, suspicion, scandal-mongering and calumny had free rein.[1]

Though the soil was fertile, farming methods were primitive; land was allowed to lie fallow for long periods. Crop yields were low and transport of farm produce from one province to another difficult, so famines were frequent. A prolonged drought in the summer and autumn of 1625 meant a great scarcity in the spring and early summer of 1626, the year when Vincent's priests set out on the first missions. Their letters to their superior not only paint a true picture of the rural areas of France at that time but also indicate the main causes of the peasants' plight. Their rulers and their more prosperous fellow Christians in all grades of society were culpable. Ignorance, stemming from an unwillingness to hear or know of the neighbour's misfortune and sufferings; selfishness and avariciousness that dried up the founts of compassion, generosity and true charity; indolence and laziness that swamped every impulse to assist, to be active in relieving the wants of the needy—these were the primary sources of the miseries of the 'poor people of the countryside'.

In September, 1626, Monsieur Vincent signed a legal document making over to his brothers and sisters a few acres of the family holding he had inherited, as well as some monies owed to him by persons in Dax. He had already divested himself of his benefices, the Abbey of St Léonard de Chaumes, the Canonry at Écouis, and his parish at Châtillon-les-Dombes. As an apostle of the poor he had to prove his disinterestedness; his message demanded that he be poor, as was his Lord. As a Founder he had to give example to his little flock, to set standards for the men, a few of them rich in worldly goods, some of them not yet detached from material things, who joined him. Having himself fully grasped the implications of Christ's call to the rich young man, 'Sell . . . Give . . . Come . . . Follow', he had to demonstrate clearly to his followers that 'those who have poverty only as an interior virtue run the risk of having none at all'. So he rid himself of the superfluities he, as an individual, possessed. There remained his parish of Clichy and those 'good people', his parishioners there. Clichy, too, was resigned in 1626.

Although the Congregation grew slowly in numbers its reputation rose rapidly; too rapidly for some. Certain Paris curés, discovering that the Mission priests formed a body not of regular but of secular clerics, feared that in time, considering the good results being obtained by the missions and the high favour Monsieur Vincent enjoyed with the King and those in high places, the best benefices would be granted to the priests from the *Bons-Enfants*. It took all Vincent's tact and friendliness to make it clear that he wanted no benefices; his resignation of his own was the best proof of that. This early opposition died down and within a short time the royal approval and that of Parliament were granted to the new Congregation. The Holy See, however, withheld approbation until 1633.

> Curiously enough, it was Cardinal de Bérulle himself who was behind the opposition in Rome. Perhaps he felt that his follower's undertaking was in some way in competition with the Oratory, which was also a society of secular priests. . . . In the letters of guidance Vincent despatched to his agent (one of the Mission priests) in Rome it is wonderful to see the extent of his knowledge of the Roman court and of how to go about business *opportune et importune* in order to obtain a decision, for the Church deals in eternity and never considers time. [2]

St Francis de Sales had prevailed on Monsieur Vincent to undertake the spiritual direction of the Visitandines, a task which by 1629 involved not only the care of the two convents of the Order then in Paris but also of a Refuge for Magdalens looked after by Mère de Chantal's nuns. Vincent de Paul, then in his fiftieth year, had by that time acquired a reputation throughout the capital as a confessor and director of unusual perception, holiness and wisdom. Girls from the Refuge, priests and prelates, lay people from all classes of society, nuns, society leaders, Sorbonne professors, came to his confessional and sought his assistance in their spiritual problems.

Among the more pious of his penitents was a woman in her middle thirties, the poor relation of a family in high favour at court, Louise de Marillac. Her husband, Antoine Le Gras, had been one of Marie de Medici's secretaries. As he was only a squire his wife was not entitled to call herself 'Madame', but simply 'Mademoiselle'. With the accession of Louis XIII and the eclipse and rebellion of the Queen-Mother, Antoine lost first his secretaryship, then his health. He died in December, 1625, leaving a twelve-year-old son, a boy who today would be classed as a retarded if not a problem child. Two of Louise's uncles held important posts in the realm: Michel de Marillac, a devout nobleman, was Keeper of the Royal Seals and Minister for Finance; his brother, Louis, was a Maréchal of France just then climbing rapidly the rungs of a successful military and diplomatic career which brought him wealth, titles, and glory.

Mademoiselle Le Gras, finding herself in very reduced circumstances after her husband's death, did not ask her uncles for help. Instead she retrenched her expenditure, let her residence, and moved to a small apartment near the *Bons-Enfants*. There at least she was more easily able to consult her director, Monsieur Vincent. She had a fine mind and was better educated than most women of her time, philosophy and Latin, art and music, housecraft and court etiquette being on the curriculum of the two schools responsible for her upbringing. But an unhappy childhood, followed by a still more unhappy, uncertain adolescence and a marriage of convenience, had effects that lasted for many years. Of over-serious, fretful disposition, she was torn by scruples and inclined to melancholy. Her aversion for the world degenerated into unwarranted apprehensions and loss of tranquillity. Unduly sensitive, forever worrying about her son and her state of soul, she was on the verge of losing her bearings altogether when she came under the reassuring, steadying influence of Vincent de Paul. He urged her to simplicity, to confidence, to submissiveness in her dealings with God. He begged her to rid herself of the *tristesse* that seemed destined to overwhelm her. His letters to her are sprinkled with phrases like, ' Smile , Mademoiselle, smile!' or 'Cheer up, Mademoiselle!' If he knew St Teresa's axiom, 'A sad saint is a sorry saint', he surely quoted it for her. As in the case of Madame de Gondi, he encouraged her to look beyond herself and to take up charitable works. In

October, 1626, he writes to her from a village some fifty miles east of Paris where he is giving a mission:

Mademoiselle,

May the grace of Our Lord be always with you!

Your letter found me here at Loisy-en-Brie. . . . I did not tell you that I was leaving Paris as I had to set out earlier than I expected; besides, I might have upset you by letting you know. Now then! This little mortification will, if it pleases Him, count for something with Our Lord, and He Himself will act as your director. Yes, surely, that is what He will do, and in such a way that you will know that it is He Himself. So be His dear daughter, all humble, submissive, all full of confidence, always patiently awaiting until He shows what is His holy and adorable Will.

We are here in an area where a third of the inhabitants are Huguenots. Please pray for us, who are in need of prayers, and especially for me—unable to answer all your letters on account of not being in a position to accede to your request. [3]

In the following June, Mademoiselle Le Gras writes him a long letter in the course of which she mentions her 'fears for the future'. She tells him that her son has gone to be educated at the seminary run by the holy, if somewhat eccentric Bourdoise. Later she writes, worried because the boy has become too fond of the community at his school, then again because he hates the community. Monsieur Vincent, in Poitou and the Cévennes giving missions and sometimes pressed for time, writes scrappy notes: 'As I write it is midnight and I am a bit harassed. Excuse me for being unable to throw any more light on matters at the moment.' When he hears of young Le Gras turning against the priests in the seminary he writes at greater length:

What can I say now about your son? Only this: as you were not to bother too much about his affection for the community, neither should you now be put out because he has turned against them. Let him be and resign him completely to the Will of God in his regard. God has the right to direct these young and tender souls. He has a greater interest in the lad than you, since he belongs to Him more than to you. . . . When I have the pleasure of seeing you and more leisure than I have just now, I must tell you of a thought that struck me one day on this very subject when speaking with Madame de Chantal. By God's mercy it consoled her and freed her from a distress just like yours. . . .

We have enough work to do here [in Joigny] to keep us busy for about six weeks more. . . . Please be good enough to give charitable care to two young girls whose departure from this place seems the best course. We will send them to you eight days from now. . . . Do cheer up, Mademoiselle, and keep yourself in the disposition of wishing all things to be as God wills. [4]

Since his two years of slavery in Tunis, Vincent suffered frequently from attacks of fever, his *'fièvrette'* he called it. In the middle of one such attack he writes to console Louise who is again upset about her son, Michel. He tells her that he has had the doctor and that the Mission priests, strongly supported by the physician, are insistent that he take the waters at Forges-les-Eaux, half-way between Beauvais and Dieppe. The thought of stopping his work and of travelling in a carriage depresses him. 'Indeed, my dear daughter, it weighs more heavily on me than I can tell you, that so much must be done for one poor carcass.' By degrees he gets her to leave her son in God's hands: 'Congratulations on having stopped crying over Michel's happiness or unhappiness. If you are a spiritual woman you will rid yourself of . . . this maternal sensitiveness. I have never met a mother who was more of a mother than you. In nothing are you so truly a woman as in this.' He himself visited Michel and reported favourably, or as favourably as one could report on so listless, so doltish a boy.

Despite her excessive fears and scruples Mademoiselle Le Gras had one fundamental virtue that gave her director hopes of great things. She was obedient. No matter what he ordered or advised she obeyed at once faithfully and to the letter, without murmur or question. Vincent de Paul waited and prayed, feeling sure that God had His plans for this woman and knowing that they who have learned to obey are the fittest to rule. Suddenly Louise herself saw her way clear. She decided to dedicate her life to the service of the poor. Monsieur Vincent was delighted. In May, 1629, when she completed a spiritual retreat, he sent her to visit the one hundred and thirty Charities which had been founded throughout France.

Among the instructions to her and others he later sent on long journeys was an order never to travel by water-coach. His own experience of the waterways must have convinced him that however speedy the public packets plying to and fro on French rivers, they were not a means of transport to be recommended to women and girls. Accompanied sometimes by a servant maid, sometimes by a friend also eager to serve the poor, Louise spent the next four years travelling from one to another of the Charities in the Paris area and throughout northern and eastern France. The ceaseless activity, the constant change of scene, the meetings with so many simple, good people banded together in the name and in the cause of true charity, all helped to change the some- what neurotic lady into a calm, mature, integrated woman.

Vincent kept in touch with her all the time, giving her exact directions as to what he wished her to do and how to set about it. When she found herself in a quandary he suggested tactful methods of getting herself out of the difficulty without hurting the feelings or susceptibilities of others. At the same time her reports helped him to decide the future management of the Charities. When the work seemed too much for one of her frail constitution he sent other ladies, penitents of his in Paris, to help her: 'Mademoiselle de Fay, always ready; Madame Polaillon, always generous; and Madame Goussault, always consequential.'

The only fly in the ointment was young Le Gras. One cannot help having some sympathy for the boy, a creature of moods, whose school bored him and whose holidays, now spent mostly at the *Bons-Enfants*, were hardly very exciting. His mother was keen on seeing him become a priest. She usually got back to Paris for part of the holidays and immediately began fussing over him again. Always convinced that he was sickening for something, she had him bled and purged every other day. She was almost as keen a collector of simples and cures as was Monsieur Vincent and they both prescribed for the luckless Michel. Following a dream, Louise removed the boy from the school conducted by M. Bourdoise and sent him to read theology with the Jesuits in the famous Collège de Clermont. One day Michel wanted to be a priest, the next he wished nothing of the kind. Vincent wrote to tell her, 'He says now that he is only entering the priesthood to please you; he says that he wishes he were dead, but that because you desire it so much he will take Minor Orders. Now, I ask you, is that a vocation?' And in a postscript he advises her to meditate on Our Lord's words to the over-eager mother of the sons of Zebedee, 'You know not what you ask.'

Although he found time to write often and at length to Mademoiselle Le Gras, Vincent meanwhile had put his hand to further enterprises in Paris. A conversation with the Bishop of Beauvais in the summer of 1628 moved him to start retreats for those about to be ordained. September, 1628, was hardly the most propitious time to begin. The siege of La Rochelle, the Huguenot stronghold on the Atlantic, which had been dragging on for fourteen months, was entering on its last grim phase. Cardinal Richelieu, admiral, general, chief engineer and quartermaster all in one, was not a whit perturbed when a second English fleet, sailing to the aid of the besieged, was sighted off the coast on Michaelmas Eve. His spies had told him of the desperate straits to which the defenders were reduced: eight thousand had died of hunger in the previous six months, two thousand since the September Quarter Tense. (That doughty old dowager, the Duchesse de Rohan, who had stayed and starved with her people to set an example and whose carriage horses had long since shared the fate of all animals within the walls, was using the tooled leather of her chairs to make soup.) He had no fear of the English ships on the horizon, nor of the expeditionary force, eleven regiments strong, which they carried. His information, correct as usual, was that the men were mutinous and that the ship's officers refused to obey the commander. La Rochelle was doomed. Paris was practically empty of nobles and churchmen and wealthy burghers. All wanted to be able to say, 'I rode in with Richelieu and the King the day La Rochelle surrendered.' Even the Marie de Medici clique and the young rebels who rallied around her younger son, Gaston of Orléans, the heir apparent, galloped to the west coast, to be in time for the capitulation—and the spoils. But there were no spoils for them or for anyone. Instead there was iron discipline for both victor and vanquished. There was none of the usual cruelty that followed such a capture. There were pardons, granted coldly. There was food, wagon-loads of food, distributed with even greater coldness.[5] Those who superintended the relief centres had not the charity of Vincent de Paul.

Monsieur Vincent, in Beauvais at the request of its Bishop, was giving his first retreat to ordinands during the final weeks of the siege of La Rochelle. The results were so gratifying that the Bishop urged other bishops to try the same experiment in their dioceses. A couple of years later such retreats were made obligatory in Paris and the priests of the Mission were commanded to receive free of charge all those to be ordained in Paris each year and to prepare them by a fifteen-day retreat.

It was a beginning, but only a beginning. How could a priest learn all his office required him to know within a fortnight? Or how could he be trained to be a man of God, a man of prayer and virtue, in so brief a period? The Decrees of the Council of Trent had at last been accepted in France but it took time to put them into practice. For the formation of good priests the Council had prescribed the establishment of seminaries and given directions as to studies; already Vincent had ideas on the matter but the opportune time for putting them into practice had not yet presented itself.

Never a man to undertake anything in haste, he waited and prayed. At this time he was approached by the Canons Regular of Saint-Victor, whose Priory and lazar-house, an immense pile of buildings, was at Saint-Lazare. The community had dwindled to eight and the Prior thought that a solution of his difficulties in attracting vocations and in providing for the upkeep of his great Priory could be found in amalgamating Monsieur Vincent's Congregation with his Canons. Eventually, he told himself, the older Order would assimilate the new. Vincent opposed the proposal steadfastly. So large and fine an establishment ran counter to his concepts of poverty and humility. He feared the effect the example of the Canons, who had no intention of adopting the strict régime of the Mission priests, might have on some of his followers. Finally he was overruled, the ecclesiastical authorities of Paris ordering him to make the change. Deeds were drawn up and duly signed. The Canons got the good rooms 'looking on to the highway leading from the city to Saint-Denis'. The Mission priests moved from the *Bons-Enfants* to Saint-Lazare, Vincent's only consolation being the solitary leper in the lazar-house and the four lunatics now transferred to his care by the Prior.

It was a change that brought many trials. The Canons had to have 'free medical attention, medicines and nursing', no easy task when, shortly after the transfer, all sleeping at the highway side of the house got the plague. Every Sunday evening Monsieur Vincent had to sup with the Prior, a testy and choleric man who could not agree with his own Canons, much less tolerate the newcomers. The supper conversation was usually a recital of the faults the Prior had noticed in the Lazarists, as the Mission priests were called after they changed their headquarters. 'I must have knelt at his feet fifty times and more to acknowledge our guilt and beg his pardon for displeasing him,' Vincent said years later, 'but after all wasn't it right that I should do so? They were our benefactors who fed and lodged us and to bear with a little annoyance was a very small price to pay in return.'

The Prior, however, was not the highest authority in his

Order. Scarcely had the documents of transfer been signed when the Abbot of the Monks of Saint-Victor in Paris took legal proceedings against Monsieur Vincent and his priests, on the grounds that the Prior of Saint-Lazare had acted without permission. But the old Vincent of Toulouse was not dead; having sought the best advice, that of his professor friend in the Sorbonne, M. Du Val, he let the case take its course. On the day when the judges' decision was to be given he went to the courts and thence to the *Sainte Chapelle* where he remained prostrate in prayer, asking not that he and his win or lose but that God's will in the matter be shown. The Lazarists were allowed to remain at Saint-Lazare, though indeed the upkeep of the vast pile and the provision that had to be made for the Prior and the Canons made it something of a white elephant, and Monsieur Vincent was often at his wits' end to meet the bills. He was not one of the saints whose stores multiplied miraculously and whose flour and meal bins never emptied. He was an able administrator and while never failing to ask God to send help he himself did everything that lay in his power to provide for those to whom he was father.

In Saint-Lazare, his Congregation, now growing yearly in numbers, had space not only for the training and development of its members but for other works. Here, every Tuesday, priests from Paris spent the afternoon conferring on matters of faith, piety, morals and church discipline. Doctors from the Sorbonne met there to discuss the current heresies and the arguments to be used against them. Laymen made retreats there. Directors of the various Charities, wealthy benefactors who supported the many good causes promoted by Monsieur Vincent, people in trouble, persons in high station, all knew the way to Saint-Lazare. The buildings and grounds, which extended over a large area and incorporated farmlands and streets of houses, were in themselves worth a visit. Yet, asked one day what he would find hardest to part with if the lawsuit were lost and the splendid new headquarters of the Mission with its chapels and cloisters and residences, its courtyards and gardens and dovecotes, its fields and windmills, its stables and cattle sheds and slaughter houses, its granaries and bakeries, were taken from him, Monsieur Vincent replied, without hesitation, 'The poor lunatics in the detention house.'

Meanwhile Mademoiselle Le Gras was travelling the roads of France, forgetting herself in face of the appalling conditions of the country people, their wretched dwellings, their ignorance of fundamental principles of farming, cooking, health and hygiene, their illiteracy and their lack of religious instruction. She organized classes in the Charities, giving women and girls elementary lessons in cooking, sewing and knitting, showing them the precautions to be taken in time of plague and how to care for the sick. She wrote a simple catechism, taught it to girls, and sent them to teach others the truths of religion. She set up schools for the teaching of 'the three R's'. So successful was she as an organizer that Vincent recalled her to Paris to set up Charities there. Then, in the early 1630's, a great trial befell her.

Marie de Medici, finding that Richelieu, whom she had helped on his way to power, had no further use for her and her favourite son, Gaston, determined to destroy the Cardinal. King Louis, then ill, yielded to his mother's entreaties to dismiss his first minister. The man designated to step into Richelieu's shoes was the uncle of Mademoiselle Le Gras, Michel de Marillac. When the dismissal of the Cardinal was imminent and his jubilant enemies hurried to court to congratulate the Queen-Mother, the King took a turn for the better, and decided that Richelieu should be retained. The assembled courtiers, gathered to witness the Cardinal's downfall on that 'day of dupes', were stupefied with disappointment. Most of them hastened to make themselves scarce, not waiting to see what course Richelieu would take with those who had upheld Marie de Medici. Among the first to suffer was Michel de Marillac who was imprisoned till his death, two years later. Then came the turn of Louis de Marillac, the Maréchal, who might, Richelieu reasoned, withdraw the army he was just then efficiently commanding in Italy and march on Paris. His fellow generals, Schomberg and La Force, were ordered to arrest him and send him back to the French capital. He was tried on trumped-up charges by a packed jury and condemned to death.

We do not know if Louise was there at ten o'clock on the morning of May 10th, 1632, when a vast concourse packed the Place de Grève to see her uncle beheaded. Some had paid eight *pistoles* for a place in the windows overlooking the square. The condemned man had his confessor with him. When the sentence for his crimes was read aloud he said, 'Certainly a good case has been made against me', but he at once turned to the priest by his side remarking, 'I should not have said that. I ask pardon of God for the feeling of resentment that prompted such words.' He knelt at the block indicated by the executioner. The latter, bandaging his eyes, asked the Maréchal's pardon for the death he was about to inflict upon him. '*Mon ami,*' was the reply, 'you are not the man guilty of my death; but I forgive you the blow as I forgive my enemies who have brought me to this.' There was a silence while the executioner fixed the crucifix firmly in the hands of the condemned and fitted his neck into the groove on the block, passing the palm of his hand over and back a few times to brush the hair out of the way of the sword. When the priests finished chanting the *Salve Regina*, a chant taken up by the entire crowd, 'The sword fell and all heard the sound of the trunk falling on the scaffold, and the head as it bounced and fell on to the ground beneath. Some soldiers picked it up and threw it back to the executioner.'

Not far away Richelieu was writing the description of de Marillac he wished to leave to posterity: 'A vain and audacious man, who embezzled monies given him for the service of France. A wicked man, lacking the very beginnings of virtue. . . . There are some of whom one should make an example, so that others, overcome by fear, may be retained for the future.' From Saint-Lazare Vincent de Paul was writing to Louise de Marillac that same morning:

Mademoiselle,
The news you send me of M. le Maréchal de Marillac

seems to be a cause for great compassion and afflicts me. Let us honour therein the good Will of God and the happiness of all who honour by their own sufferings the sufferings of the Son of God. It does not matter to us how our dear ones go to God, provided that they go. Indeed, the good customs inseparable from this kind of death is one of the greatest guarantees of eternal life. Let us not therefore make any plaints; thus we shall acquiesce in the most adorable Will of God.

Then he sat down to write her a second letter concerning several matters of urgent business in connection with the Charities which he wished her to see to. Work and time were the best cures for grief. Not far from the Place de Grève, beneath the slanted roofs and Gothic towers of his new palace, Richelieu was issuing orders that the Saint-Honoré gate was to be closed. No vehicles might pass that way; signs indicating that the carriageway was being repaired were to be hung up. He did not wish that the funeral of Louis de Marillac on its way to the church of the Feuillants at the corner of the rue de Castiglione should pass beneath his window. He hoped that his favourite niece, Marie, Marquise of Combalet, would call to keep him company. Did he know then that his Marie was one of the band of ladies who had stepped forward from both sides of the political chasm to help Vincent de Paul in his work for the poor and the suffering? He certainly knew a few years later when he approved of various relief works undertaken by Monsieur Vincent and sent the Lazarists to give missions in his native place, Richelieu. As a priest closely associated with the de Gondis and the de Retz family, and in recent years with the niece of the de Marillacs, Vincent de Paul would have been *persona non grata* with the Cardinal at that time had the latter had time to consider him. As it was there were other matters demanding the great man's attention. Bassompierre, friend of the Maréchal, was clapped into the Bastille. Marie de Medici, who had fled to Brussels and the protection of the Spaniards, might be left there, penniless, for the rest of her days. That coxcomb, Gaston, also in the Low Countries, was prevailing on the Governor of Languedoc, de Montmorency, to raise the standards of rebellion in Toulouse and the south.

The Duc de Montmorency, peer and Maréchal of France, was thirty-five. Brave, generous, affable, married to a beautiful Orsini princess, he and his wife enjoyed a popularity far beyond that of the King and Queen, not merely in Provence but throughout France. The Cardinal's spies had information that Gaston and his adventurers were to ride to Toulouse, join Montmorency and rise in rebellion. He would let the plot go forward. He knew that the wretched Gaston when cornered, would fly, crying, 'I will play no more.' He could be pardoned, for he was worthless, and 'the blood royal of France must be spared'. But Montmorency must go the way of Louis de Marillac. He might be 'the first noble of France, victor by sea and by land, heir to seven centuries of fame and the last of his line', but he was ready to rebel. His very greatness and popularity with high and low marked him as one of those 'of whom one should make an example'.

The Cardinal's niece, Marie, had been married against her will in her sixteenth year to a nephew of a court favourite. His death two years later left her free to follow her own wish. She entered the Carmelite convent in Paris and in 1622 received the habit from and pronounced her first vows before de Bérulle. A year later, her inexorable uncle insisted that she leave the convent and wrote himself to Rome asking the Pope to command her to leave her Carmel. Poor Marie, weeping, obeyed. Bérulle was her director until his death in 1629. She had been attached to the court of Marie de Medici until 1630 and the Day of Dupes. In her rage against the Cardinal the Queen-Mother turned on his niece and sent her packing. She was made welcome by Richelieu who bought her a residence in Paris and made her a generous allowance. Though the hostile pens of three contemporaries and anonymous lampoons, printed in Holland forty years after the Cardinal's death, attempted a 'smear campaign' suggesting a link stronger than their actual relationship between uncle and niece, there is no evidence whatever that such was the case. The Cardinal's private life was, to all appearances, irreproachable. Her own letters and those of French society women of her time, many of whom might reasonably have been expected to be jealous of her influence in high places, show Marie de Vignerot as she was: 'Beautiful, pious, a bit self-willed, fond of money . . . an independent character; a woman who had no love affairs and sought refuge in ambition.' That was the worst that could be said of her. Her uncle later had her created Duchesse d'Aiguillon and made her one of the wealthiest women in France. She was faithful to him to the end of his days. Much of her riches went to Monsieur Vincent. She built houses for the Lazarists and a hospital for the galley-slaves at Marseilles, and obtained a great deal for him through her court influence. Few others realized the greatness of Vincent de Paul as did she. She watched over his old age like a mother, scolding his priests for letting him give a country mission in exceptionally hot weather, insisting that he ride in the carriage she supplied for his use. After his death she devoted herself wholly to the service of the poor. A contemporary could write:

> She who a short time ago was supported by her uncle in such luxury that he would not allow her to put foot to ground lest it touch the mud of Paris, may now be seen traversing the streets, no longer in her gilded coach drawn by four swift horses, but on foot, searching for the most wretched homes and the most closely hidden miseries. She prefers the sick to all others and when she hears that someone is dying hastens to be with them and to console them. . . .

Monsieur Vincent, the great director of souls, had the secret of knowing how to turn the hearts of women like the wife of the General of the Galleys and the nieces of the first men in France from self to others. He showed them that salvation for them and theirs lay in serving the poor.

Chapter Nine

CARITAS CHRISTI URGET NOS

THE WORK of the Charities continued to extend. It had taken root in Paris as well as in the provinces and by 1633 nine parishes in the capital had a branch. Vincent received frequent notes from Mademoiselle Le Gras asking for advice in the various problems encountered in the city Charities. As the rules stipulated that members should themselves prepare meals for the sick poor, carry the food to the home and serve the sick person as he ate, Louise hesitated before asking members of the Paris Charities, many of them ladies of rank, to do so. Vincent wrote to her:

> If you now relieve each one of the duty of having the food cooked, you will never be able to impose this rule in future. And if some of them undertake to pay to have it cooked elsewhere, after a while you will find them demurring at the cost. And if you yourself pay money to have it cooked, how much is it going to cost you? Then, too, after a while we will have the Ladies of Charity saying that the soup should be carried to the poor by the women they get to make it, and in this way the Charity will fail.

Again, some of the clergy took umbrage and Mademoiselle reported. Vincent answers:

> Oh, Mademoiselle, it is a difficult thing to do good without meeting stumbling blocks. But since we must, as far as we can, smooth over the grievances of others, I think you would please God very much if you were to go to M. le Curé and apologize to him for having spoken to the Ladies of the Charity without having first acquainted him.

A kind of rivalry set in between the Charities in the capital, some parishes wanting to outshine others and get the lion's share of the credit the work already enjoyed. Vincent de Paul was rather annoyed about this. He wrote to Louise:

> What spirit is it that prompts every parish in Paris to want to have something special about its Charity and to have nothing to do with the others? I must say I don't know. You would imagine by them that it almost hurt them to say, 'Others besides ourselves are doing what we are doing.'

In the great city hospital, the Hôtel-Dieu, the care of the sick was neglected. This hospital was the oldest and largest in Paris and was packed, having two or more patients to each bed and others lying on the floor near the bed of a dying person ready to be the first to scramble into it when the corpse was removed. Admissions totalled from fifty to eighty a day, and in times of plague, patients died like flies. The Canons of Notre Dame and a community of Augustinian nuns were in charge. Some of the nuns 'did nothing but raise hands and eyes to heaven', others spent their time quarrelling, some fled from the wards and remained praying in choir all day. A faithful few did their best, in the most appalling circumstances, to cope with things.

Vincent was asked to set up a Charity to care for this hospital. It was an enterprise bristling with difficulties, as the Augustinian nuns and the Canons were likely to take offence at any intrusion. To a great lady who begged him to set up a Charity in the Hôtel-Dieu he replied that he had no wish to thrust his sickle into another man's corn. Finally, when the ecclesiastical authorities ordered him to undertake the work, he consented, calling a number of ladies together and drawing up rules for them. At first the visiting of the hospital was taken up enthusiastically by the leaders of Paris society. It became the fashion to say, 'I spent the afternoon at the Hôtel-Dieu.' More than a hundred *grandes dames*, among them Duchesses, Marquises and ladies of the blood royal, vied with one another in their care for the poor patients there. Potages and milk drinks were cooked in the mornings and taken to the hospital, and in the afternoons such a variety of breads, biscuits, preserves, jellies and fruits that those who were on the recovery list were loth to be discharged. Books and games were also distributed. If the patients, seldom less than nine hundred in number, had never known such attention in their lives, their aristocratic visitors had never known that such poverty and misery existed. Even though all did not persevere in the visiting, a tradition of social service was established and when later France was threatened with famine during the Thirty Years' War, the ladies trained by Monsieur Vincent in the Hôtel-Dieu at Paris formed the core of the relief services.[1]

Corporal needs solaced, Vincent's charity, as always, proceeded to assist souls. He had a booklet printed for the use of the members of the hospital Charity giving instructions as to the most tactful way of broaching the subject of general confession. He also wished the ladies visiting the Hôtel-Dieu to look upon their work not as mere philanthropy but as a means of self-sanctification. He admonished them:

> Let each one reflect for a moment and ask herself: 'Am I helping or retarding this holy work? What is there in me that makes me unworthy to engage in it? Am I perhaps causing God to withhold His grace from it?'

Two decades later he could review what had been accomplished:

> It is now twenty years since God gave you, ladies, the grace to undertake and maintain many works: the feeding and instruction of the poor at the Hôtel-Dieu, the board and education of foundlings, the care of providing for the bodily and spiritual needs of the *galériens*, the aid you sent to remote and war-torn provinces, besides all you have contributed to the missions throughout the country. These, ladies, are the works of your society. Imagine women doing all that! . . .
> The Brother who distributes your alms said to me, 'Monsieur Vincent, the wheat sent to the far-away provinces saved many lives; many families had not a grain to sow; no one

would lend them any; the land lay fallow and the country-side was deserted because of the death or departure of the people who lived there.' In one year alone as much as 22,000 *livres* has been expended on seed corn, giving these poor country people work during summer and food for the winter. You see, ladies, by the good accomplished what a great misfortune it would be if you were to give up the work you began.

Though practically all these women were of noble birth, elegant and expensive tastes and refined manners, Vincent de Paul, reared in the little farmstead near Dax, not only never felt ill at ease in their midst but had extraordinary influence over them. His sincerity, his simple, warm-hearted manner, his unfeigned love for 'our Lords, the poor' won them. He was able to show them how to speak with kindness, gentleness and love to the poor because he himself knew the language of both those who have and those who have not.

As in all societies, individual members of the Charities were not without their idiosyncrasies. The first President of the Association, a worthy widow named Goussault, was the soul of good nature. She was also a woman of many words, and much given to blowing her own trumpet. She had wealthy and influential connections, had married her children well, and maintained a splendidly appointed household with numbers of stewards, lackeys and servants. She was one of the two ladies Monsieur Vincent had sent to assist Mademoiselle Le Gras in the visiting of the provincial Charities. Madame Goussault found it hard to stop chattering and, to counter the habit, made a rule that there should be silence while her maids attended to her *toilette*, a protracted affair. One of the maids was detailed to read a pious book while Madame contemplated her soul in silence, and her appearance in her mirror. She told everyone about this self-imposed silence, including Monsieur Vincent. He, always ready to highlight the good points of his acquaintances, used to tell Madame Goussault's friends of her particular practice of mortification, which must have caused some suppressed smiles though his hearers knew that Vincent was aware of the unfavourable impression Madame sometimes made and was probably trying to offset it. Despite her indefatigable energy and briskness in the cause of charity, her cordiality, her utter inability to dissimulate, she was extremely satisfied with herself and showed it. Her letters to Vincent de Paul reflect her character as faithfully as her mirror did her face. 'She had something of the style, the orthography, the contradictory remarks, the naive expansiveness of the sturdy wife of an Angevin farmer who, seated in her place in the parish church, rejoices . . . because she is rich, a respectable and respected woman, one who finds it easy to sell her eggs and pullets.'[2]

She wrote long letters to the patient Monsieur Vincent describing her journeys. One such epistle starts off by describing how, the moment she set off in the carriage, she recited aloud the *In viam pacis*, to which all her fellow-passengers dutifully responded. She then gave them points for meditation and said the *Angelus*. She proceeds:

> Then we talked. Sometimes we talked of the ideas that had come to us during the prayers. Sometimes, for amusement and recreation, we talked of the things that distracted us at our prayers. Sometimes we told our dreams. At other times we attacked those whose remarks had been indiscreet. Grandom [her steward] was then set to read for half an hour from *The Pilgrim of Loreto*.

More prayers followed, always of Madame Goussault's choosing. They greet the angel guardians of the villages through which they pass. Madame halts at towns to inquire if there is a hospital and if there is she drives to it and inquires how the place is run. If she meets stray children in the street she gets them to repeat the *Our Father* after her. She wears a watch that strikes the hour and thus gives the signal for more prayers. At Étampes she dismisses her carriage and goes to the hospital on foot, accompanied 'only by my maid and my lackey'.

I found a young nun there who turned out to be the Superioress, so I sat down to talk with her after having sent the lackey
out to buy something for the poor. I told her that it was very
necessary for everyone to have a spiritual director and she
looked me full in the face. I was wearing an ordinary turned-
down collar and wore no farthingale. 'Who are you?' she
asked. 'Are you married? I have heard a lot about Madame
Acarie but I don't think you can be the same lady.'

The conversation disclosed that the nuns in Étampes hospital
had not yet reformed their ways, so Madame Goussault gave the
young Superioress a little lecture stuffed with good advice. At the
inn she converses with the son of the house, assembles her travelling companions for further prayers, meditation points and an
examination of conscience. At Orléans, where she arrived
fasting, she went to Holy Communion in the Jesuit church. She
found everything ship-shape in the town, the Hôtel-Dieu wealthy,
'but the sick no better off for that. The few nuns in the hospital
depend too much on the serving maids they have there.'

I disliked Orléans. I don't know why. I was lodging with a
Huguenot family. I cleared out and went on to Cléry. . . . I
went from that to Blois, . . . my cousin thinks that God had
perhaps permitted my arrival there just to let them see that
Paris women of rank *do* visit hospitals, and perhaps that will
move them to do likewise.

But I made no delay at Blois as there was an outbreak of
measles in my uncle's house. Instead I went to dine at Veuves
and to Amboise for the night. . . . Thence to Tours . . . then
to Angers and on to Chonze. . . . The good curé there could,
I think, profit a lot by a good mission. I even thought of saying something to that effect to the Bishop. I find the children
badly instructed.

On she goes to Saumur, herself and her entourage singing the
Te Deum, while she keeps the servants busy saying rosaries. Once
in a while she stops the praying so that all can have a bit of fun

playing 'The Yes-and-No Game'. Forfeits are paid by the 'No's' in *Ave Marias*. Arriving at one of her own estates near Angers she is given such a reception that her head is quite turned. She tells Monsieur Vincent of the compliments she got after visiting the poor in the country round about Angers. She was told: 'Anyone can see by you, Madame, that you really love the poor and that it is your heart's delight to be among them. You really look twice as lovely when speaking to them.' She assures Vincent that she has no more to tell him and then rambles on for another few pages, telling him about the way priests and people hung on every word she said; about her spiritual state; about the lessons in mental prayer she is giving to one girl; about the woman who said that if Madame Goussault would only stay in Angers for a year the whole city would be converted. 'The people here like two things about me. I don't act the reformer, I laugh heartily and I go to my parish church.' Urged by the citizens to have her portrait painted she refused, out of humility; but she since thinks her refusal to have been prompted by false humility. She also played backgammon for an hour and remains Monsieur Vincent's most humble and obedient servant. [3]

Vincent's replies to her are brief and to the point. To another letter which she wrote telling him about the suitors she was considering for her daughter he replies:

> Would it not be better for you to know exactly what your daughter's intentions are? That last man who was mentioned to you is a thoroughly good fellow, with an excellent mind, and with equally excellent and sound judgment for one of his age. But bearing in mind what you know, the other seems to me the more preferable, though not so well off. But you will need a lot of tact to deal with the last person who was spoken of to you.

Madame Goussault, as prodigal of her money and time in the service of the poor as she was of her words to all, was never heard to speak ill of others. Vincent de Paul, who knew her better than most, always spoke of her with the greatest veneration. He was not narrow-minded and could make allowances for human foibles and quirks of character, especially in persons whose good qualities more than counterbalanced their little peculiarities and weaknesses. The first President of the Ladies of Charity, full of good will and generosity, was certainly dedicated, in a degree later generations could neither imagine nor emulate, to the interests of God and 'our Lords, the poor'.

But, though the Charities flourished, the close-up view Vincent had of them in Paris showed him certain aspects that called for improvement. The members working in a parish or at the hospital did not always see eye to eye on how things should be done. Each group in the capital was inclined to seek autonomy, a course which, he remarked, 'would eventually make a hotch-potch of the whole movement'. Besides, when first enthusiasm abated, only too often the obligations voluntarily assumed were lightly relinquished. One lady had to go to a ball, another to take the waters, another had to travel to her country estates to see to business or to escape the heat of the city. Some grew tired of cooking and carrying the food to the hospitals and of attending the sick. They began to send their servants in their stead and only too often the poor patients went untended, unfed, the dishes intended for them arriving at destinations other than the Hôtel-Dieu. They would have to be given reliable helpers.

Not everyone was suited to help in this work. Kind-hearted, good strong girls who could be counted upon not to exploit the poor but to devote themselves body and soul to such service were needed. After many conversations with Mademoiselle Le Gras, Monsieur Vincent decided that she should look out for and recruit suitable girls in her journeys to the provincial Charities. He himself had already been approached by the very kind of girl that was needed, a girl who came and offered herself for the hardest work in the Hôtel-Dieu. A few others came along and stayed with Louise in Paris. She trained them in the spiritual life and taught the illiterate ones to read and write. They learned home nursing, how to use lancet and tourniquet, how to poultice and bandage. At the end of November, 1633, four of them moved with Mademoiselle to a small house in the Saint-Victor quarter. The Institute of the Daughters of Charity had its beginnings there. From that time until 1964 their white cornettes, noblest emblem of France, have winged their way all over the globe. Daniel-Rops relates how Napoleon received a group of philosophers one evening in the Tuileries and listened to them praising the benefits that philanthropy and the Age of Reason had conferred on mankind in general and the French nation in particular. 'All very fine, Messieurs,' interrupted the Emperor, 'but to my mind one grey sister, one White Bonnet, is worth the lot.'*

At the time of their Foundation the Daughters of Charity of St Vincent de Paul were as great an innovation as the modern Secular Institutes . The term 'religious' then signified enclosed nuns who lived behind a grille and did not go outside their enclosure. As has been seen, St Francis de Sales originally envisaged the Visitandines as girls who would consecrate themselves to God by the usual vows of poverty, chastity and obedience, but who would live 'in the world', finding their vocation in working for Christ and the Church through serving those in need. Though he did not succeed in bringing his dream to realization he must have discussed it with his friend, Vincent de Paul, for his plan found eventual realization when Monsieur Vincent's Daughters of Charity were established. There were initial difficulties and much distrust, as Vincent and Mademoiselle Le Gras found when they sought approbation for the new Institute. When Mademoiselle went to the palace to register her Sisters, as the law required, the procurator-general of Louis XIII was decidedly put out. 'Seculars! But, Mademoiselle, that cannot be! All communities of women are regulars. All must be registered as religious.'

The first Daughter of Charity, Marguerite Naseau, was a country girl of valiant heart. Hearing that some Paris ladies were devoting themselves to the care of the sick poor in a city hospital she said to herself, 'These fine ladies are so used to being served and so little used to serving that it must be hard for them to carry

---

* The Daughters of Charity were for a long time called the 'Grey Sisters' because of the grey habit they wore. Later the grey was exchanged for blue.

out such tasks. I, too, would like to serve God in His poor. I am used to hard work. I could undertake what they cannot do: bleed the patients, do the laundering, cleanse and bandage wounds, make beds and stay up at night with the very ill and the dying.' Fearing that her lack of education might impede her efficiency she taught herself to read, leaving her cows grazing by the roadside to ask passers-by how to pronounce words in her primer. Though people laughed a little at her, she was quite indifferent to mockery. Yet she was far from being untouched by the sorrows and sufferings of the poor. When Vincent de Paul gave a mission in her native area she went to him and offered her services for the Charities. He recognized in her a girl of great heart and soul, the salt of the earth, and accepted her offer. When she died shortly after coming to Paris—of plague contracted through sharing her bed with a poor plague-stricken woman she had found lying in the street—he felt assured that he and the new Institute had a powerful advocate in heaven. He often spoke of her in his conferences to the others whom Louise was training, always concluding his eulogy of Marguerite with the words: 'Everyone loved her.'

One of her companions had preceded her to the grave: Jeanne Dalmagne. A companion Sister, describing Jeanne, said: 'She had great liberty of spirit and spoke out her mind as frankly to rich as to poor when she saw them doing wrong. On a certain occasion, hearing that some wealthy persons were getting out of paying taxes and having them surcharged on the poor she told them outright that they were sinning against justice and that God would punish them for their extortions. And when I said to her that she had spoken rather daringly she replied that when the glory of God and the good of the poor were in question, no one should fear to speak the truth.'

Up to then works of charity were, in the public mind, associated only with the clergy, with enclosed religious and with ladies of wealth and leisure. But the Daughters of Charity were of the people; they were a living proof that the traditional faith and spirituality of France, though long dormant, was experiencing a second spring. The Catholic Reform, then being preached throughout the country, could point to them as evidence that the old tree was sound and flowering anew.

Not all the Daughters of Charity were of humble origin. Girls bearing great names asked for admission, one of the first of these 'finding it hard to bear that anyone should refer to her previous high station, or that anyone should think her noble birth a reason to spare her the laborious tasks of her companions'. A Sister from near Chartres was noted for her gaiety and for her devotion to the foundlings when Monsieur Vincent added the care of those mites to his other works. Later she was one of the Daughters of Charity sent to attend the *galériens*. Vincent drew up special rules for these Sisters, knowing the special dangers to which they would be exposed. At the same time he told them that they could help the galley-slaves in ways no one else could. Each day they were to prepare meals for the convicts and carry to each his ration, getting a jailer to help them 'in case the soup-pot is too heavy'. Nothing was to be spared in the case of sick *galériens*; food was to be more tastefully prepared and served, those in danger of death were to be discreetly urged to turn to God and prepared for the Last Sacraments. The Sisters were to be prudent; they were not to appear unless actually wanted and not to remain alone with the convicts except in case of the utmost necessity. They were to be modest, reserved, cautious, deaf to any disrespectful or lewd remarks that might be made to them. If a *galérien* went too far in conversation or conduct, they were to 'reply coldly and walk away'. They were to pray daily to the Holy Spirit that their purity might be preserved in such surroundings. 'Be like the sunbeams which continually pass over filth without having their radiance soiled or dimmed in the slightest.' If they received abuse, insolence and insults, they were to repay with extra kindness.

The Sister from Chartres, Barbe Angiboust, carried out his advice to the letter. Once when a galley-slave flung the soup and meat she had brought him on the ground, abusing her roundly, she said nothing, went on her knees, picked up the meat and went her way. On five or six occasions she actually went between the jailers and the men they were flogging, making them desist. When the Duchess of Aiguillon, Cardinal Richelieu's niece, who poured into Monsieur Vincent's hands the wealth showered upon her by her uncle, built a hospital at Marseilles for the *galériens*, the Daughters of Charity went there to assist. The Chevalier de la Coste wrote to Vincent:

> You cannot imagine the joy of the poor *galériens* when they were transferred from this hell [the galleys] to what they call heaven. The mere fact of being sent to the hospital relieves them of half their maladies for on arrival they are deloused of the vermin with which they are covered. Their feet are washed and they are put into a bed, a soft rest after the hard plank on which they usually sleep. They are absolutely delighted to find themselves lying in a real bed, and attended with more charity than they ever had on the galleys. . . .

The Duchess of Aiguillon asked Vincent if she might have a Sister to live with her in her own residence. As the Duchess was the woman 'with most authority in the kingdom after the ladies of the Royal Family', and the most devoted and generous of his benefactors, it was difficult to refuse. But Vincent was not a Gascon for nothing. He picked the Daughter of Charity whose reaction he felt sure of: Barbe Angiboust. When told that she was to pack up and go to the Hôtel du Petit-Luxembourg, she wept, but she obeyed. Monsieur Vincent went himself to the Duchess's mansion to receive her, and was there when Barbe made her way through the maze of carriages that filled the courtyard. Two of the Duchess's ladies waited to bring her to her room. 'Go on, my Daughter, go on,' said Vincent, encouragingly. 'Oh, Sir,' she pleaded, 'where are you sending me?' 'Go on, child. You are entering the house of a lady who really loves the poor,' he told her and added, 'If, after a few days, you really want to come back to Mademoiselle and the others, we will send for you. Have no fear.' The Duchess was kindness itself, but poor Barbe was miserable. She wept for three days and was unable to eat any of the good things placed before her. Finally the Duchess asked her, 'Sister, why don't you like being here with me?' Quite candidly the other replied,' 'Madame, I left my dear father and all at home to serve the poor, and you are not poor but a great lady, rich and powerful. If you, Madame, were poor, I would serve you with all my heart.' Barbe was sent back to a delighted Monsieur Vincent.

Vincent de Paul gave periodic instructions to the first Daughters of Charity. He stressed how they were to go about their duties, put them on their guard against faults and by questioning them on their daily experiences drew from themselves the rule to be followed in various circumstances and contingencies. They were to beware of singularity and self-esteem. They were to be cordial to all, 'letting the face show the joy that is in the heart'. They were to put the love of the neighbour before all else: 'Charity is your first and supreme rule.' If called to the sick when at prayer or even when at Mass, 'you must leave God for God'. They were to consider themselves as 'the visible guardian angels of the sick and suffering. Yes, you must be to them a father and a mother.' If they have spare time, they must not remain idle. 'Sew! Spin! Everyone needs linen. If you work to provide it you will never be short of it for the poor or for the foundlings.' What they get for the poor must be spent on the poor; they may not even taste the dishes prepared for the sick. Once started on that road, 'it is easy to slide down into robbery'. He rebukes their little faults. One lets a curl escape from under her coif, 'perhaps from negligence, perhaps from coquetry'. Another insists on going about with her sleeves rolled up above the elbow, even when the washing is done. Some are too talkative, some inclined to have their favourites among the poor. Because the new Institute is being praised on all sides, he fears lest their heads be turned: 'Pride, you know, is quite as likely to find as good a lodging under a grey habit as under a fine silk dress.' But charity is 'the oil in the lamp'. If they have that in abundance he will have no fears for them.

Soon their numbers multiplied and so did the demands for their services. In the city and country parishes they visited the homes of the poor and organized classes for little girls. Hospitals throughout France, hearing of their work in the Hôtel-Dieu in Paris, asked for them. The first Sisters had hardly completed their training period when they were called upon to go to the battle-front to attend wounded soldiers and to districts and towns where plague raged. In 1660 when Vincent de Paul followed Louise de Marillac to the tomb, there were a hundred foundations of the Institute, thirty of them in Paris alone. Today there are over forty thousand Daughters of Charity scattered over five continents. Wars, riots, prisons, epidemics, refugee camps, shanty towns, the aged, the orphaned, the abandoned, the poor, the sick, the insane, the sinful, pagan and uncivilized peoples—all have known the Sisters in the neat head-dress and deep blue habit. As the whole world knows them, so the Sisters know the world. If they have occasionally received from it admiration, praise and honour, they have also and in far greater measure received at its hands insults, exile, persecution, imprisonment and martyrdom. 'Even their *patria*, France, has sent them to the scaffold, which they mounted without complaint, eyes cast down, hands folded within their voluminous sleeves, as though going to Holy Communion. If St Vincent de Paul were to come once more today in surplice and biretta to give his conferences to the novices in the Mother-House of the Daughters of Charity, he would still see a Marguerite Naseau, a Barbe Angiboust there among their modern counterparts; he would see the same good and faithful girls, with the same clear untroubled gaze, the same calm features, on which no passion has engraved its petulance or gloom.' [4]

One might have thought that Vincent's time was too occupied with the hundred and one cares of the various enterprises he had already undertaken to prevent him taking on further work. He had to see to Saint-Lazare and the Vincentians, the Charities in the provinces and in Paris, the *galériens*, the spiritual guidance of Mère de Chantal and her Visitandines and of Mademoiselle Le Gras, the religious and educational formation of Mademoiselle's young 'professional dispensers of charity', the Magdalens in the Refuge, the long queues at his confessional, the callers who sought his advice about their souls or who wished to interview him on business concerning one or other of his manifold charitable works. But, as has often been remarked, it is the man overburdened with work who always manages to fit yet more occupations into his already crowded days. As far back as 1619 Monsieur Vincent had established in the de Gondi estates a 'Confraternity of Charity for Men', the ancestor of the St Vincent de Paul Conferences founded by Frederick Ozanam two centuries later and now functioning in most countries. He directed the charitable works of the Confrères, handing over to them the care of poor people who were not ill, the aged, children, the feeble-minded, cripples, the blind, deaf-mutes. His early life as a farmer's son prompted him to suggest that the Confraternity put up or borrow a little money, buy sheep, and by the sale of the wool add to the funds for poor relief. New sheep were to be bought every fifth year. If they had any money left over at the end of a quarter they were to make up any deficit that the Charity run by their womenfolk might have. At the first Charity established in Châtillon, it will be remembered, as Vincent did not think it 'fitting that women should have to see to financial and business affairs', he made a rule that a virtuous *bourgeois* should be chosen to administer the funds. Later he changed this ruling. He refers to disagreements which arose because the men refused to hand out funds when requested. One wonders did some virtuous *bourgeois* decamp with purse, wool, sheep and all. The men's Confraternities in cities and towns looked after poor boys between the ages of eight and twenty. These lads, who were strictly brought up in a kind of institution, had a pretty thin time, but they were trained as apprentices to various trades and at the age of twenty an assured livelihood was found for them. Vincent de Paul was a great believer in work and recommended it to both rich and poor.

Passing through Mâcon, a Burgundian town not far from Cluny Abbey, he found there droves of beggars, all disreputable and ignorant and living like barbarians. He broke his journey to inquire what could be done for them and went to other towns which had successfully dealt with the same problem to see what solution they had found. He arranged that the more prosperous citizens and artisans should covenant with a Charity established there to supply a certain amount of wine, wheat, linen, meat and firewood when called upon. So well organized was this system that no citizen felt his contribution too burdensome and over three hundred poor people were fed, clothed, provided with fuel, and given free medical and surgical attention. At the same time work was found for those who could work and religious instructions were given weekly. Itinerant beggars, who seemed very partial to Mâcon, were given a night's lodging and sent on their way next day with a few coins jingling in their pockets to shorten the road for them. Similar measures were adopted by Charities in other country towns, all based on the Vincentian plan which the Mâconnais had found so effectual. Vincent was constantly perfecting his original plans for his various charities. He always liked to work slowly. 'Those who rush defeat the designs of God.' Writing to a priest of the Mission who complained that some of his fellow-Vincentians were content with mediocrity, the Founder agreed that there was certainly room for improvement. 'But I assure you that that is the usual thing with Companies in their early days. . . . Grace imitates nature in so many ways. That which is born a brute beast and most disagreeable, given time, grows to the perfection of its being.'

He was also associated with the Company of the Blessed Sacrament, which later became unpopular and was suppressed by Cardinal Mazarin. Within a decade of its foundation in 1628 it had organized and controlled a network of religious and charitable activities that covered the whole of France. It supported many of Monsieur Vincent's charitable enterprises and helped M. Bourdoise and his seminaries as well as M. Olier in Saint-Sulpice and Père Condren in the Oratory. It financed missions in France and missions to pagan lands, built schools and colleges, organized relief, opening food and clothing depots in time of war or famine.

When public protests were made to England about the persecution of Irish Catholics, the Company of the Blessed Sacrament was the power impelling the protest. The Companions sent Jesuits to the Hurons and the Algonquins in Canada, Vincentians to the Hebrides and Ireland. When French provinces were laid waste by war the Company rushed wheat seed, relief funds and teams of surgeons to the devastated areas. Priests and laymen were accepted as members, the laics predominating. Monsieur Vincent, like most other priests, belonged to it, but he left it some years before his death. It was suppressed by Cardinal Mazarin that same year.

It had a double programme, to do good and to suppress evil, and as time went on the stress was on the second part of the work. Though the members were bound to secrecy, their idea of resisting evil was to bring wrong-doers to justice, a process seldom accomplished without publicity. Priests who had not reformed their scandalous lives, sellers of charms and spells who did a good trade near Saint-Sulpice, butchers who sold meat on Fridays, market-gardeners who had their stalls in the space in front of Notre Dame, men and women who waited with bad intentions near the landing stages of the water-coaches to offer young country girls splendid situations, all these learned to their cost that it was the Companions who had set the King's Sergeants on their heels. The nobles, so given to duelling that the death rate in France from private combat was almost four hundred a year, were furious when the Company succeeded in discrediting duelling, something that even Richelieu with his laws and decrees against the practice had failed to do. Huguenots found that if they put forward a candidate for a public post the Company, alerted, became active in getting him turned down. The Jansenists and the nuns of Port-Royal, who vied with the Company in its heyday in the matter of strictness, fell foul of it.

Vincent de Paul, who disliked coercion in any shape or form, did not approve of all the Company's decisions. When asked by the Companions to imprison in Saint-Lazare priests who lived in vagabondage, and when he heard of beggars being rounded up and jailed in a Paris hospital, he showed the repugnance he felt for such highhanded measures. At the time when the Company urged the government to use force to suppress the Huguenots, Vincent, the friend of the gentle and peace-loving Francis de Sales and the inheritor of his spirit and methods, was writing to one of his priests living among those of other faiths: 'Set the example of true charity. Men are not converted by controversy but by charity and loving kindness. Be just. Are not they who belong to religions other than ours as deserving of justice as Catholics?' Finally he withdrew from the Company of the Blessed Sacrament. He had the excuse of old age and feeble health when he did so, but from all we know of him it is certain that he regretted the direction it took in its final years. In the end its downfall was brought about by the indiscreet zeal and interference of a few of the Companions and the enemies they earned for it among all classes and creeds, among churchmen and laymen, as well as by the satires of Molière, particularly *Tartuffe*, which made the Companions the laughing stock of Paris and later of the world. Yet, if the Company *did* harbour a few hypocrites and fanatics, on the whole it did not deserve the ridicule and obloquy heaped upon it by the playwright. In the thirty-two years of its existence it accomplished an incredible amount of good and after its suppression by Cardinal Mazarin in 1660 many good causes and many poor people throughout France were the greatest losers.

Chapter Ten

STONY GROUND AND THORNS

By 1635 Vincent de Paul was in his middle fifties. He wore his age well. The broad shoulders of the young Gascon who strode into Périgueux on that long gone September day of 1600 had borne many burdens since; yet, if each evening found them slightly bowed, each morning saw them squared again, their owner ready to face another day. His 'little fever', relic of Tunis and slavery, tormented him occasionally, as did a leg wound, the result of a kick from a horse. For this injury Mademoiselle Le Gras prescribed purges, blood lettings, and a peach blossom syrup which, she assured him, was a most soothing salve, an infallible cure. He usually went about Paris on foot and sometimes as he crossed the Pont Neuf on his way back to Saint-Lazare he must have wished that the good works he was associated with were not quite so far away or that they would transport themselves to his side of the Seine. With the exception of Mademoiselle and her Daughters of Charity, who lived near him, all his other enterprises were situated on or south of the river, which meant a lot of walking in the famous Paris mud. If he stood on the bridge to look back he could see the roofs of most of them. The Hôtel-Dieu on the parvis of Notre Dame. The *galériens'* new hospice at the Saint-Bernard Tower on the quays. The *Bons-Enfants*, now a retreat house. The Visitandines' convent in the Faubourg Saint-Antoine and their second foundation, further still from Saint-Lazare, in the Saint-Jacques quarter.

Near the Visitation convent in the Faubourg Saint-Jacques a new Abbey had been built. It was a vast pile, almost on a par with Saint-Lazare, and not unworthy of the fine buildings in the

University quarter, the Sorbonne, the Collège de Clermont, and the other Colleges that housed intellectual Paris. Its Abbess was the famous Mère Angélique whose holiness had edified Francis de Sales, whose austerity and zeal for reform exceeded even Bérulle's, and whose charity to the poor was encouragement and example to Monsieur Vincent himself as well as to his host of collaborators. The Abbey, Port-Royal, enclosed the Cistercian nuns of Port-Royal-des-Champs, an Abbey eighteen miles southwest of Paris which had to be abandoned because of its unhealthy situation. Vincent de Paul first heard of Mère Angélique in the years when he was with the de Gondis whose favourite estate and château, Dampierre, was beside Port-Royal-des-Champs. Madame de Gondi and the Marquise de Maignelay visited the Abbey and were friends of the Abbess. Bérulle, Vincent's confessor at that time, also called on Mère Angélique when in the neighbourhood. She sometimes asked that holy man for guidance, but her confessor and director until 1634 was Sebastian Zamet, Bishop of Langres, none other than *le bon Langres*, last met with perfecting his billiard-playing and winning high wagers from the courtiers of Marie de Medici in the gay days before Louis XIII's succession.*

Mère Angélique was no ordinary nun. In the springtime of 1608, the year Vincent de Paul, then an unknown abbé, came to Paris, a vagabond friar called at Port-Royal-des-Champs, asking for food and alms. It was Lent and the Abbess, then seventeen, gave him a meal and permission to preach a sermon. Sermons were few and far between in her Abbey. Most of the nuns, the Abbess included, were there against their wills, forced into religion by their parents. They had neither vocation nor any desire to know what the Cistercian vocation implied. To pass the time they drove out in carriages, all 'curled and powdered and masked', like the worldly ladies they mingled with at balls and similar amusements. They had valets and coachmen, and a

---

* Following a severe illness Zamet turned over a new leaf and became a model bishop. He was the friend of Bérulle, Condren and Vincent de Paul. The 'pious if eccentric Zamet' was also very prominent in the Company of the Blessed Sacrament and in the reform movement.

chaplain who did not know the *Our Father*. Their library boasted only one religious book, but Mère Angélique, addicted to novel reading as a means of whiling away her boredom, kept the shelves well stocked with romantic literature. Six years previously when the Abbey with its revenues was in danger of being lost to her family, the Arnaulds, she was forced in as Abbess. The last thing eleven-year-old Jacqueline Arnauld had wanted was to be a nun, but when her father issued an order he was accustomed to being obeyed. That stern and iron-willed man stood over her until she signed the documents he was having sent by fast messenger to Rome, documents which added years to her age and credited her with having made her final vows. Afterwards, recalling that hour, she said, 'I thought I should have burst with rage.'

In her seventh year as Abbess she was preparing to run away to a Huguenot aunt when the wandering friar called and, in gratitude for his Lenten herring, preached a homily on the Passion. Young Mère Angélique was converted on the spot and resolved to reform herself and her religious. Then followed a spiritual forced-march as the nuns of Port-Royal were led from the lowlands of worldliness and sin to the heights of perfection. No one was allowed to falter or fall out of step. Masks, jewel-caskets and their contents, silks, laces, perfumes and private purses were flung away. Rough serge habits were hastily sewn and donned. Hair-shirts, bare feet, disciplines, rigorous fasts and long vigils became the vogue. When Arnauld, *père*, accompanied by his wife and family, called to visit Jacqueline in 1609, bars and bolts were down and his daughter informed him through the grille that Port-Royal was now a convent of strict Cistercian observance and that the rules could not be broken for anyone, not even for the Lady Abbess's father. The Arnaulds, outraged, protested angrily and loudly. 'See!' cried Mère Angélique to her nuns, who had been assembled to watch this edifying scene; 'my parents forced me in here against my will when I was only a child. Now they wish me to damn my soul by breaking my rule. As they did not consider me then, neither will I consider them now. I shall live as a true religious, intent on my eternal salvation.'

The reform of Port-Royal proceeded until the Abbey became noted as one of exemplary regularity where the highest virtues flourished. The Abbess was regarded as a living saint, amazing all by her unflinching attendance upon a nun dying of a most repulsive form of cancer. Vincent de Paul, often at Dampierre, only a few miles away, came to know her either through Bérulle or the ladies of the de Gondi household. When Francis de Sales came to Paris in 1618 he, too, visited the much talked of Mère Angélique. She made a general confession to him and after his return to Geneva they kept up correspondence. 'Do not take up too many vigils and austerities,' he cautioned her, 'go to the royal gate—the Port-Royal—of the religious life by the highroad of love of God and neighbour, by humility and kindliness to all.' He counselled prudence, restraint, avoidance of singularity, the golden mean in all things. Less impetuosity and mettle and fire; more serenity and calmness. Less self-assurance; more trust in God. Less brooding on justice and judgment; more abandonment to the Divine Will. Less of self. More of God.

Jansenism was then only in the incipient stage. Its leading protagonists were the Dutchman, Jansen, a doctor of Louvain University who later became Bishop of Ypres, and de Hauranne —called Saint-Cyran from his Abbey near Poitiers—a Basque from Vincent de Paul's corner of France. During their student days at Paris and Louvain, Jansen and Saint-Cyran became fast friends. Both were intellectually gifted, studious, and imbued with a desire to reform the Church. Jansen aimed at achieving this by a new exposition of Catholic doctrine, based on the writings of the Fathers, particularly on the writings of St Augustine; Saint-Cyran by the example of an austere life. In 1619, Jansen, then in a professor's chair at Louvain, wrote to his friend telling him that he had made a wonderful discovery in the works of St Augustine, a writer not understood, he claimed, by anyone except himself. Saint-Cyran, risen to an important ecclesiastical post in Poitiers, then the intellectual capital, 'the Athens of France', was at the time working might and main to help his friend Richelieu on his road to power. But he was not too busy to reply to his other friend, Jansen, poring over Augustinian tomes in Louvain.

The following year Jansen informed Saint-Cyran that the complete solution to the problems of grace and justification were in St Augustine. He had found them and intended to write a book setting forth the teachings of the great Doctor of Carthage on free will and grace and predestination. He added, 'I am not going to be an ass all my life. I dare to make this claim: I have discovered enough to prove, and from immutable principles, that though Jesuits and Jacobins argue till Doomsday, continuing on the lines they have begun, they will only get more and more bogged, being both a hundred leagues from the truth.' They continued to correspond, but in code. Rome, weary of the long drawn-out Molinist-Thomist dispute,* had prohibited the kind of theological probings Jansen engaged in, and he did not want the conclusions he had arrived at to be condemned out of hand before publication.

Saint-Cyran was in Paris in 1622 and visited Port-Royal-des-Champs. He and the Abbess had much in common: lively, inquiring minds, similar temperaments, a pronounced antipathy towards regular priests in general and the Jesuits in particular, a conviction that they had been 'chosen' in preference to others to reform God's Church, an inner exaltation arising from this conviction, and a complete lack of humour and the ability to laugh at oneself. Vincent de Paul became very friendly with Saint-Cyran and thought him 'one of the most virtuous men I ever met'. They pooled their funds, took their meals together, and obliged one another in various ways. Saint-Cyran, native of the Basque

---

* He was referring to the dispute on free will and the gifts of grace which had been raging in European theological circles since the previous century, a dispute in which the Jesuits took one side and the Dominicans the other. Extremists on both sides weighted their respective ends of the seesaw so heavily that the Jesuits were accused by their opponents of being tainted with Pelagianism, while adversaries of the Dominicans charged that Order with sponsoring Calvinism!

province of Béarn which adjoined Gascony, was the same age as Vincent. Vincent's birthplace was within thirty miles of Bayonne where his friend's family were prosperous merchants. Saint-Cyran found Monsieur Vincent a good listener, but a 'good listener' from his point of view meant someone who allowed him to dogmatize, to monopolize conversations, someone who effaced himself, who liked to defer to others and ask advice, someone who showed respect for his, Saint-Cyran's, undoubted gifts of nature and grace.[1]

Neither Saint-Cyran nor Vincent appreciated the fact that few in Paris or indeed anywhere else, were as truly humble as Vincent de Paul. His habit of self-depreciation, his determination to speak of himself as seldom as possible and in a belittling manner, noted by his contemporaries, led many to take him at his word, to despise him as an uncouth, untaught Gascon. Nothing could be further from the truth. If there had been anything boorish or rude about him St Francis de Sales, himself an aristocrat, would never have entrusted him with the direction of the aristocratic Mère de Chantal. But no one mistook Monsieur Vincent's humility for condescension; no one ventured to be too familiar with him:

> Although he inspired great respect, yet this respect, instead of closing, opened men's hearts. No one equalled him for inspiring others with confidence when they went to him to manifest their most secret thoughts and those human weaknesses which are the most difficult to confess.

When saying Mass he used to say the *Confiteor*, the *Nobis quoque peccatoribus*, and the *Domine, non sum dignus*, 'as if utterly stricken with dread, as if he were a criminal who deserved to be condemned to death in the presence of his judge'. When speaking with educated men who were discussing high and abstruse matters he often excused himself as one not on their intellectual level. Yet, as has been seen, his educational attainments were considerable and he had a strong well-balanced intellect. The fourteen volumes of his writings are, says Henri Brémond, 'rich in doctrine, spark-

ling with humour, and—something unique in such a collection—
do not contain a commonplace line'. If historians of religious
thought have relegated him to secondary rank, it is mainly
because of the protestations which he in his humility uttered day
in day out, partly in self-defence against the praises his works
won, partly because he was a truly humble man in an age of
pride:

> The apostle of charity, absorbed by action, he was forced to
> take up what one may call anti-intellectual, anti-mystical
> positions. Aristocrats of the spirit dislike these attitudes which
> they see as the sign of a certain mental poverty. Therefore
> they neglect Vincent de Paul. They commit a grave error.
> Assuredly Monsieur Vincent could not be called a thinker.
> He did not renew or revigorate by original views religious
> speculation nor did he stir up as did Bérulle a doctrinal com-
> motion. But his effect on souls was just as great. More than
> any of his contemporaries he had an immense influence on
> men and events, and, by his institutions, commanded the
> future. Furthermore . . . detached by his activities from this
> literary culture which he nevertheless possessed to a very high
> degree, he hit upon a simple, direct, racy style in which to
> express his thought, which does not attain the distinction of a
> Bérulle or an Olier but which always remains matter of fact;
> so much so that he is a great writer, simply because he tries
> not to be a writer.
>
> He was no stranger to any of the preoccupations of his
> contemporaries and equal to all forms of the apostolate in
> which so many have imitated him. But, obedient to the
> indications of his temperament, he chose the activity to
> which he could give himself in fullest measure. 'The poor
> people of the countryside die of hunger and are damned.'
> That was the slogan that sprang from his heart and ruled his
> life. . . . [2]

After 1635 Vincent de Paul and Saint-Cyran saw less and less
of one another. One day the Abbé asked Monsieur Vincent,

'Tell me, Sir, do you really know what the Church is?' Vincent replied quietly that it was the congregation of all the faithful under the Vicar of Christ, the Pope. 'You know as much about it as you do about high Dutch,' said Saint-Cyran, in a disdainful and sarcastic tone. Monsieur Vincent said nothing but parted from the other as affably as though nothing had been said, and hurried off to one of the charitable works that took up his time. Saint-Cyran hurried away also, to write a treatise on the degrees of humility and to point out 'the dangers to which those engaged in employments beyond their capacity expose their virtue'. It would be laughable if it were not so tragic.

On another occasion in the course of conversation Saint-Cyran told Vincent, 'If you had done the studies I have done, I would have shown you and even taught you to work wonders. If you are willing to listen to me your Congregation will become one of the most famous in the Church.' Evidently Vincent was not willing to listen or to learn for the other then shouted angrily at him, 'You big ignoramus! I'm amazed that the priests of the Mission tolerate you as their Superior.' To which Vincent mildly replied, 'I'm even more amazed than you, for the extent of my ignorance is far greater than you imagine.'[3]

By this time a dozen and more Arnaulds were grouped around Mère Angélique in Port-Royal. Her mother and a sister, both widowed, who had 'taken the veil'; five other sisters and six nieces. The Abbess and her first director, the Bishop of Langres, had founded an institution for the special adoration of the Blessed Sacrament. As the Port-Royal community was a very large one several of the nuns were brought to the Institute so that there might always be adorers during exposition hours. The Bishop, ecclesiastical Superior of Port-Royal, since his conversion of life spent long periods in his diocese introducing the reform there. During his absences and at his request Saint-Cyran took over the direction of the Port-Royal nuns and preached daily at the Institute of the Blessed Sacrament which was in a street north of the Seine, off the present rue de Rivoli. A booklet, *The Secret Chaplet of the Blessed Sacrament*, written by a member of the community, was sent by Saint-Cyran to Louvain for approval and printed by Jansen in Ypres, where he was then Bishop. When it appeared in Paris the Sorbonne condemned it. After a longer sojourn than usual in Langres the Bishop returned to the capital, visited the Institute and got a shock:

> The nuns, who for some time past had given up going to Confession and Holy Communion, were all prostrate on the floor of the chapel, as far as possible from the Blessed Sacrament, to adore with due respect. They were weeping over the lax morals of the time, and sighing and longing for the discipline of the early Church. When the Bishop, their Superior, requested them to take up their former way of living, the Abbess was intractable. At that moment, Saint-Cyran, who had long been awaiting this encounter, made his appearance; he ordered the nuns to remain and pass verdict on the ensuing disputation, being certain of the outcome. Mère Angélique, without consulting any of her superiors, installed Mère Geneviève as Abbess . . . dashed out to the waiting carriage and drove fast to Port-Royal. She then appointed Saint-Cyran as her director and director of the community.

Saint-Cyran was master of Port-Royal, a centre ideally situated and equipped for the dissemination of Jansenist teachings. His next move was to round up some men followers and install them as recluses in cells in the Abbey grounds. They were all of irreproachable personal character and professional distinction. There were leading lawyers, including Mère Angélique's brother, a brilliant doctor of the Sorbonne; an eminent physician; a high-ranking army officer; three further Arnaulds, brothers of the Abbess and the Sorbonne doctor; a few priests and wealthy bourgeois, even a title or two. 'All of them had for Mère Angélique a sort of cult. When she went to visit the solitaries in the fields bells were rung and sometimes they lit bonfires.' Among the hermits was Père Singlin, a priest known to Monsieur Vincent who had been so attracted by Saint-Cyran that he abandoned Saint-Lazare for Port-Royal. Later he became confessor and spiritual director of Mère Angélique and her community.* Vincent was deeply grieved at this defection, but he never lost touch with Singlin and always hoped and prayed for his return. The Jansenists of the early decades of the seventeenth century did, in fact, 'practise a noble form of devotion, worthy of our respect'. Later, when their doctrines were condemned, they did not break away to form new Churches like the reformers of the sixteenth century. They insisted that they were Catholics, rather superior and select Catholics indeed, but Catholics. Perhaps this was one reason why Père Singlin, long after he had won renown as a Jansenist preacher, continued to come to Monsieur Vincent's Tuesday Conferences for the Clergy of Paris. Or perhaps he returned to old haunts because, having learned persuasive preaching from Vincent, a master in that art, he hoped always to learn a little more.

The Tuesday Conferences, usually held at Saint-Lazare, began in the summer of 1633. The priests, deacons and subdeacons who attended, formed an Association 'to honour the life of Our Lord Jesus Christ, His eternal Priesthood, His holy family, and His love for the poor'. Members undertook to perform certain daily exercises of piety and to help fellow members when they were ill or in trouble or need. At first the meetings were quite informal; when Vincent saw that the project was likely to achieve permanency he drew up rules, presided at the meetings and gave a brief homily before the gatherings broke up. Only clerics of exemplary life were admitted and the Conferences did a lot to raise the level of priestly holiness in France. Of the Associates enrolled during Vincent's lifetime twenty-two became bishops, and forty rose to fame in the Sorbonne and other Colleges. Olier, founder of Saint-Sulpice, and others responsible for similar works, were all members of this brotherhood of priests.

One black sheep managed to get admitted. He was Jean-François Paul de Gondi, youngest son of Vincent's dead bene-

---

* 'I would rather,' averred Mère Angélique, 'be canonized by Père Singlin than by the Pope.' Up to the end of her life the Abbess expected canonization for herself, but for few others. 'How imperfect you are still!' she said to a young nun whom she saw weeping by her deathbed.

factress, Madame de Gondi, and of the General of the Galleys who, since his wife's death, had become an Oratory priest. Jean-François, later to become the second Cardinal de Retz, held numerous benefices. To postpone his ordination as long as possible he led the life of a rake, outdoing his courtier friends in gallantry, gambling and duelling. He and his brother Pierre were hand in glove with every intriguer and if there was rioting in Paris a de Gondi was sure to be at the back of it. 'A dangerous genius', commented Cardinal Richelieu when in 1632 his buffoon showed him a historical work: *The Conspiracy of Jean Louis de Fiesque* written by Jean-François, then eighteen. A few years later the young abbé, whose talent for public speaking had won acclaim in the Sorbonne, decided to give some sermons. His friends, when they finished laughing at the idea of de Gondi with his well-known failings preaching to others, advised him to begin in the smaller convents. Spurning such advice, he appeared, still a layman, before the court on Ascension Day and Corpus Christi. His preaching was praised. Richelieu, informed of the excellent sermons, snorted, 'You can't judge things by that. The man's a coxcomb,' forgetting his own famous sermon to an even more exalted audience in Rome in 1607, when he too was just turned twenty.

De Gondi's aunt, the pious Marquise de Maignelay, was an indefatigable worker for the *galériens* and the Charities. She was agreeably surprised when one day her erring nephew produced twelve thousand crowns which he said he wanted to give to the poor with his own hands. He asked her to allow him to accompany her on her rounds of needy families. This was a wonderful change of heart indeed and the good lady no doubt attributed it to Monsieur Vincent and the Tuesday Conferences, little dreaming that Jean-François was just then knee-deep in conspiracy to overthrow Richelieu and that his rounds of the Paris garrets and his almsgiving were simply a means of acquiring popularity with the people who mattered in every mob. He tells us so himself:

My good aunt always charged them to pray to God for her
nephew, whose hand God had been pleased to make use of
for this charitable work. You may judge the influence this
gave me over the populace, over those who are without comparison the most considerable in all public disturbances. . . . I
devoted myself for four months to making the acquaintance
of people of this class . . . not beggars, who are only out for
plunder in a riot and do more harm than good . . . but those
of such straitened circumstances that they wish for nothing
more than a general change in public affairs to retrieve their
broken fortunes. . . . Later there was hardly a child in any
chimney corner in the garrets of the poor whom I did not
please with some small gift. I knew them by their pet names.
. . . My aunt was the cloak for all. . . . I also played the hypocrite far enough to frequent the Conferences at Saint-Lazare. [4]

Monsieur Vincent used to say of this rascally but engaging
young man: 'He is not very pious but he is not too far from the
kingdom of heaven.' Another holy man who saw potentialities
for good in de Gondi was the aged and virtuous Bishop of
Lisieux. Of humble birth and Flemish origin, this prelate was the
most outspoken and fearless man in France. 'He had the courage
of St Ambrose . . . and behaved so naturally in the King's presence
that Richelieu, who had once studied divinity under him, feared
and reverenced him.' The Bishop used to give de Gondi lectures
on the Epistles of St Paul three times each week. One day the
Cardinal took Monseigneur of Lisieux and said, 'That de Gondi
is a cordial friend of all my enemies.' 'That's true,' replied the
other, 'all the same you should esteem him. Why should you
complain of him like this when the men you refer to were all his
friends long before they became your enemies?' Remarking that
he must have been badly misinformed the Cardinal moved away.

Jean-François was ordained some time before 1643, the year
he became Coadjutor Archbishop of Paris. 'Being convinced that
the strictest morals are required in a bishop', he resolved not to
imitate his uncle, whose life had been a public scandal. He would

take care beforehand to cover up his failings while continuing in his sins. Yet, though he had no care for his own soul he determined to fulfil his duties as Archbishop faithfully, 'and exert myself to the utmost to save the souls of others'. The Tuesday Conferences and St Paul's Epistles had at least done that much good. Why did Vincent admit such a man to the Conferences and the Association? The rules stipulated that no cleric could come unless his conduct was blameless. Monsieur Vincent, who knew everything that went on in Paris, was as well aware as the next of his young friend's scandalous life. Perhaps he felt that his obligations to the parents of Jean-François required that he make an exception in his case. Or perhaps, knowing that de Gondi was sure to be the next Archbishop and second Cardinal de Retz, he thought that the only hope of reforming him in preparation for his future responsibilities lay in introducing him to the good priests who met at three every Tuesday in Saint-Lazare. In contrast to Saint-Cyran who often said in his sermons, 'Among six thousand priests there is hardly one good one to be found'—implying that he was that one and thanking God that he was not as the rest—de Gondi admitted to himself and to posterity that he was a shockingly bad priest, so bad that all he could do was to beat his breast and cry, 'God be merciful to me, a sinner.' Monsieur Vincent was not wide of the mark when he said that Jean-François was not too far from the kingdom of heaven. Cardinal de Retz spent his last years in retirement and penitence and peace and made a good end.

The success of the Conferences prompted several bishops to ask Vincent to establish seminaries. Bérulle and Condren and Bourdoise had been trying to do so for over twenty years without notable success and Vincent hesitated, not because his friends had little to show for their prodigious efforts in this direction but because he was not sure that God willed him to undertake the work. His Congregation had been founded for the missions to rural France and his followers were not yet sufficiently numerous to undertake a project like a seminary, which would need many priests and the best ones he had to give. He waited and prayed.

If God wanted a seminary He would send some sign. For the time being he established a seminary in the *Bons-Enfants* for boys who felt that they had a vocation. It had not the success of the Tuesday Conferences and the Retreats for those about to be ordained, but as will be seen it led to great things.

If most pictures and statues of St Vincent de Paul show him with an infant in his arms and toddlers clinging to his robes it is because his work for foundlings and orphans was of all his undertakings the one that most touched the hearts not only of his contemporaries but also of succeeding generations. Yet, though helpers hastened to his aid when he initiated his other charities, he found it very difficult to win assistance when he decided to do something to save abandoned children. He was rowing against the stream. In his time the miserable lot of such infants was considered as the just punishment of the men who had fathered and the women who had borne them. So widespread and persistent was this idea that attempts to save abandoned infants were regarded by many as going against the judgment of God. The puny wails coming at dead of night and at dawn from dark alleys and rubbish dumps in Paris were, in fact, so many cries of reproach against the hidden and deep-seated moral disorders of the times. 'For no society likes its habitual sins to be paraded or to have its responsibilities held up before its face. It is far easier to steer clear of difficult questions, to declare them insoluble, to hold them as problems subject to inescapable fate.' [5]

The numbers of infants abandoned each year represented, in public opinion, the barometer of prostitution. As eyes were kept steadfastly shut to the latter problem, the former had to be ignored. District commissaries, grumbling at having to do a work regarded on a par with scavenging, did rounds of their quarters daily, and took any live infants found to *La Couche*, an official institution so overcrowded and mismanaged that 'of three or four hundred children brought there each year there was not a single survivor at the end of half a century'. During the 1630's Vincent de Paul went to see for himself if *La Couche* was really what rumour said. Later he reported on conditions there:

The poor little creatures are badly looked after. . . . . They are sold to beggars for eight *sols* apiece, beggars who break their arms and legs to excite the pity of passers-by and induce them to give alms. They are left to die of hunger. Very few adopt them, hardly three or four childless couples offered to do so over the last two years. At *La Couche* they are given laudanum pills to make them sleep and even worse than that happens. Not one of those received in the last fifty years is now alive. Greatest evil of all, many of them die without Baptism. [6]

Sorcery and devil-worship were not unknown at the time and some of the babies at *La Couche* were bought to serve as human sacrifice or to be put to other diabolical uses.

In 1638 Monsieur Vincent, who had tried to interest the Ladies of Charity in this work, wrote to Mademoiselle Le Gras to inquire if she could do anything to supply cow's milk for the foundlings, or whether the Daughters of Charity could manage to take charge of a few. There was a raffle at *La Couche* and the twelve infants declared winners were carried to a house rented for them. It was wartime. Everything was dear. Milk and food were scarce in Paris. The military commandeered rooms everywhere, even in the house rented for the foundlings.

The Daughters of Charity, already overworked, did not spare themselves in the task of looking after the children. Some of them must have smiled to themselves when Monsieur Vincent produced his rules for the conduct of the Foundling House. The children, when old enough, were to be taught their prayers and their lessons, 'and after the lessons give them a slice of bread and some sweets, if you have any'. He had more difficulty in inducing the Ladies of Charity to persevere in this work than in looking after the sick and the poor and the prisoners. Old prejudices died hard. On one occasion, when they seemed determined to abandon the work once for all, he called a special meeting. Having referred to the motives for undertaking the rescue of foundlings, the means employed up to then, the objections met with, the perfect praise God receives from the mouths of babes, he poses the question: 'But are we free to grant or refuse them aid?' and he gives the answer: 'If we do not help them in the extreme need which is theirs we are in danger of eternal damnation.' He goes on to enumerate the neglect they suffer at *La Couche*, and the tortures inflicted on them by the professional beggars who buy them. 'They are the victims of crimes worse than that of Herod when he massacred the Holy Innocents. . . . We find fault with the Turks for selling men like beasts, yet here in Paris we have the same opprobrious practice—children sold for eight *sols* or thirty *livres* each.'

Did he hear some lady murmur about the circumstances of the children's birth? If he did not he forestalled such a murmur with, 'What! Have we not all the same origin? Are we not all born in original sin? Are we not all children of Adam? Had not Our Lord to redeem us from the curse our first parents drew upon us? And who knows but that some future saint is there among these foundlings: Melchisedech, Moses, Remus and Romulus, what were *they* but foundlings?' He pleads the cause of the infants well. 'They suffer for something of which they are innocent. If you protect and maintain them you may hope for wonderful blessings. You blot out your past and present sins and in some ways those of the future. . . . You put yourself in the happy position of being able to hold up your head on Judgment Day.'

Despite the generosity of the Duchess of Aiguillon, the Queen, and other individuals, it was an expensive undertaking and at the time of Vincent's death cost forty thousand *livres* a year. When war-stricken provinces appealed to Paris for help the patriotic diverted to the relief funds contributions usually given to the foundlings. It was a cause for which Monsieur Vincent had to beg until the end of his days. The painting which shows the Saint bringing in a newborn infant and laying it on the floor to touch the hearts of the Ladies of Charity was probably prompted by his best-remembered address to them, given at a moment when they seemed certain to leave the foundlings to their fate:

> Compassion and charity have moved you, Ladies, to adopt these little children as yours. Since their natural mothers have abandoned them you have, by God's grace, been their mothers. Think, now, are you too going to abandon them? Cease for a minute to be their mothers and become their judges; their lives, their deaths, are in your hands. I await your opinion and will put the matter to the vote. The time has come to pass sentence on them and to know if it is your wish no longer to show mercy to them. Should you continue your loving care of them they will live; on the other hand, if you abandon them they will most certainly perish. Experience has given you proof of that. [7]

The ladies, many of whom were reduced to straitened circumstances because of the wars that had ravaged their estates and razed their ancestral homes, rose nobly to his call. Family heirlooms and jewels saved from disaster were pawned or sold. In 1644 Monsieur Vincent housed four thousand foundlings and it was reckoned at his death in 1660 that he had saved over forty thousand infants from death through exposure in the streets or ill-treatment at *La Couche*. He often visited the homes, baptized the newly admitted, caressed the others and wept if told that a little one had died. Poor Mademoiselle Le Gras got the heavy end of this work and Vincent, as though realizing this, sends her an order couched in formal terms quite unusual with him:

> The Ladies of Charity request Mademoiselle Le Gras to please send four infants, two boys and two girls, with two Daughters of Charity, to the château of Bicêtre at one o'clock tomorrow, Sunday. The clothes, not the cradles, of the children are to be sent and all their necessities for two days. Madame Truluy will take the children, with the necessary linen, in her carriage at the hour stated. She will fetch them to Madame Romilly's where Madame la Chancelière and

other ladies will take them and bring them to Bicêtre. They have some special reason for this programme and they hope that Mademoiselle Le Gras will be agreeable to it. . . .[8]

Mademoiselle replies some days later. Even saints could show exasperation at times:

Monsieur,
In the end experience has shown us that I had good reason for apprehension concerning the boarding at Bicêtre. These ladies mean to get our Sisters to do the impossible; for the lodging [of infants and Sisters] they picked a few little rooms where the air will get stale in no time, and left the large rooms empty. But our poor Sisters daren't say a word. Also, they do not wish that Mass should be said here but that the Sisters walk to Gentilly for Mass. What are the babies to do while they are gone? Who is going to do all the work? I send you Sister Geneviève. Please have the goodness to interview her. She will tell you of all they have to put up with through the pretensions of these ladies. I very much fear that we must give up caring for these poor little infants. . . .[9]

Louise could not refrain from saying, 'I told you so!' Bicêtre, in ruins, had been a gift from the Queen, Anne of Austria. It was a big, empty shell of a château, too ramshackle to house wounded soldiers or war veterans. The moment Mademoiselle had seen it she had pointed out its disadvantages. For long it had been the haunt of highwaymen and evil doers; who knew but that they might return and evict the defenceless Sisters and children some snowy night. It was far from Paris and her Sisters had no carriage; she did not like obliging them to push the cart full of babies and baby-linen along the public roads in wartime. Poor Monsieur Vincent! He was learning to have a wholesome dread of good women. Harem ladies in Tunis or that delinquent Queen, Marguerite de Valois, held no terrors for him as did the Ladies of Charity and Mademoiselle when they came in collision on certain points. No wonder he began to give orders to the Vincentian Fathers who had farms to employ only 'a good strong boy'. At the main farm of Saint-Lazare, Orsigny, 'They had an old dame who was honest enough and fairly useful, but because she used to find fault with the brothers there we let her go. . . . And if *you* cannot give the care of the cows and the rest to some strong boy, sell them.' Women were needed for works of charity, but even holy women, his penitents and friends, disagreed at times. It was just another of those crosses sent by *le bon Dieu*, Monsieur Vincent told himself—like his *fièvrette*.

Chapter Eleven

FATHER OF THE *PATRIA*

No MATTER how overwhelmed with work, Monsieur Vincent always had time for his own Congregation, now beginning to increase rapidly. The worthy Père Portail, his first recruit and right-hand man, had one drawback—he could not be induced to overcome his nervousness sufficiently to go into a pulpit and preach. Vincent coaxed and encouraged him all to no avail. Then one day Antoine Portail suddenly had an access of bravery and gave an excellent sermon in a village where the Fathers were conducting a mission. He was so elated that he at once reported to Vincent. Congratulations came by return, 'Praise be to God, Sir, that you have mounted the pulpit. . . . You have begun late but it was the same story with St Charles.'

The reference was to St Charles Borromeo, reformer Archbishop of Milan, who for most of his life trembled from head to foot when he had to preach. Sooner than enter the pulpit and face the battery of eyes he used to preach from the altar steps. In a cathedral so immense as that of Milan he had to make such efforts to be heard that finally he plucked up courage and overcame his nerves. Père Portail was so delighted with Vincent's reply and with being compared to St Charles that he went to the other extreme and got letters from the Founder over the next few years with tactful hints about restraint in the pulpit. Père Pavillon is to do all the preaching, the other Fathers are to give the religious instructions, while Antoine Portail, 'my coadjutor', is to be Superior and direct his fellow Vincentians. It would be better if Portail did not preach but kept a check on the preacher and catechists; they may reprove the people of that district for their well-known weaknesses, drunkenness and self-ishness, but they are to be prudent and to avoid all vanity. Vincent was very fond of Père Portail, who, like Mademoiselle Le Gras, died a few months before himself.

Towards the end of his life, when the numbers of Saint-Lazare ran into a few hundred and when foreigners swelled the Vincentian ranks, Monsieur Vincent tightened discipline considerably, especially after the Saint-Cyran affair. Any Father who showed a tendency to vanity got a dressing down in the presence of the whole community, particularly if he was one who prided himself on being more learned and accomplished than others. The Brother Coadjutors, if caught in a public misdemeanour, came off better. A Brother on the kitchen staff on occasion helped himself liberally to the wine. As the community assembled for dinner one evening the Brother drew attention to his condition by lurching into the refectory and swaying by his place as he stood for Grace. Monsieur Vincent saw what all saw and found himself in a dilemma. Everyone looked utterly miserable, for the Superior always did what he regarded as his duty, and would undoubtedly humiliate the offender. Vincent knew the long hours the Brother was on his feet each day not only in the kitchen but helping on the farm, in the slaughterhouse and granaries, and in the herb garden. He left his place, went to the culprit and, throwing his arm around his shoulder, proceeded to walk him out of the refectory giving a loud running commentary excusing 'my poor Brother' and blaming himself, 'this *misérable*, this wretched sinner'. He, Monsieur Vincent, was to blame. He was the one who should blush for his remissness in not having given the Brother proper instructions and in not having foreseen such a temptation as the wine-cask. The commentary showed that he knew more than appeared from the Brother's state that evening. 'And you were so fuddled that you lay down in the kitchen, poor Brother, in front of all the others. What example for the novices! And it is I, sinner that I am, who am responsible for this disorder. O, my Brother, we are a nice pair. We may feel ashamed of ourselves, both of us.' He did his duty as Superior in reprimanding the Brother, but he did the backslider the charity of carrying most of the blame.[1]

His priests were scattered far and wide when in 1635 France was at war. There had been war in 1624 when Richelieu, 'to make the Pope less uncertain and the Spaniards more tractable', took a Swiss valley that served as a communication between Milan, then the territory of the Spanish Hapsburgs, and the Tyrol, the land of the Austrian Hapsburgs. There was war in 1629, when Richelieu, determined to extend French territory to its original limits, fought the Spaniards in Savoy and in Italy. In 1635, order and peace established in France itself and the power of the nobles curbed, the Cardinal turned his attention to the Thirty Years' War, then in its eighteenth year. He sided with the Protestant powers, Sweden, Germany and Holland. Vast numbers of Frenchmen were under arms, half of them in Germany, Italy and Switzerland. The fleet numbered a hundred ships and the call for galley-slaves was incessant. Vincent's priests were called on to act as chaplains to both land and sea forces.

The first week of August, 1636, found Paris in a panic. Croats, Poles and Hungarians, all allies of Spain, had invaded the kingdom and were across the Somme. The Cardinal was giving a fête for the Queen at Chaillot on Saturday 2nd, and crowds had gathered on the Seine banks and bridges to watch the notabilities arrive. Next morning, Sunday, rumours began filtering into the city. The Croats were watering their horses at Compiègne; a column of horsemen had been sighted sweeping towards Pontoise. Richelieu, all his life a sufferer from the ailment that finally killed him, had come home ill from the Chaillot fête but on hearing the rumours he got into his carriage and drove about the city. He bowed to the crowds on the Pont Neuf and affected not to notice the manifestoes against himself pasted on the sides of the Samaritan Fountain. The thing was to give the impression of calm, to allay the fears of the citizens.

But some had not waited to be reassured. Hundreds of families were already fleeing south, some going towards Lyons, the majority blocking all the roads across the Beauce as they made for Orléans. Why Orléans, people asked. No one knew unless it was because history had been made there. At Orléans France had been saved in 1429 when Joan the Maid raised the siege. Those who remained in Paris climbed to Montmartre anxiously scrutinizing the highways and fields to the northeast. Saint-Lazare was requisitioned as a military depot. Vincent wrote to Mademoiselle Le Gras telling her that his fever was better, that Saint-Lazare was like an armoury, 'all the soldiers are here being issued with arms'. He advised about some refugees coming in and asked her to receive them. He said nothing that might alarm her but a letter written the same week to Père Portail is in rather different vein:

> On no account send Brother Philip here. If he were here he would have to be sent elsewhere as Paris awaits a siege. The Spaniards have entered Picardy which they are ravaging with a large army. The advance guard is only about ten or twelve leagues away so all the people of the flat country [i.e., to northeast of Paris] are flying into the capital. And the Paris populace is so terror-stricken that many are flying to other towns. The King is trying, however, to make ready an army to oppose the invading one, our own armies being in other countries or at the very ends of France. And where do you think the Companies of soldiers are being assembled and drilled but here with us! . . . The slaughter-house, the stables, the halls and the cloister are full of arms, and the courtyard of troops. Even today, Assumption Day, was not free of this tumultuous upset. The drum-beating began at seven in the morning, so that by eight no less than seventy-two companies were drilling here. But, although that was the case, all our Fathers are off giving retreats with the exception of three or four. . . [2]

Abelly relates that Vincent went to the King's camp at Senlis to offer his services as chaplain. Vincent says nothing of this but in another letter he mentions that twenty Vincentians are with the army and writes to one of them congratulating him on having succeeded in getting three hundred soldiers to make general confessions. Again he refers to nine hundred soldiers going to the sacraments. On September 20th he has to refuse priests to Anthony Portail who asked for assistance because so many are with the troops: 'Already four thousand soldiers have been to Confession.' But, war or no war, Madame Goussault was in her carriage driving from Charity to Charity. She wrote to Monsieur Vincent reporting the scandalous manner in which a certain Abbess was treating her religious and her mother. Vincent replied telling her that the Abbess was being badly advised by a certain ecclesiastic who was responsible for the row between her and her mother. Days later Madame is driving dangerously near the war zone and Vincent is writing to tell Mademoiselle Le Gras how her son is faring. He makes no reference to the war, though he is sending mules, changes of linen, a hundred *livres* and other needs to a priest and Brother infirmarian ordered to ride with the cavalry. He also gives them directions on the correct protocol to be observed with the great, 'as I saw our saintly Monsieur de Genève do with the General of the Galleys'.

Meanwhile the King and the Cardinal went about Paris, giving an example of *sang-froid*; the Queen, being Spanish, did not dare appear in public. Richelieu, who when he declared war on Spain the previous year had recruited Swiss and Irish mercenaries, saying, 'You can do nothing with those French soldiers', was now working against time to save a rather desperate situation. Though many of the citizens shouted for his death, the peculiar mood that seems to grip the French when their territory is invaded, 'a mixture of terror and anger which is the most fruitful of their violent emotions', seized them and they rallied to the one man whom they knew could lead them. Thousands rushed up to Saint-Lazare and a great 'armed mob' set off, half-drilled but with good officers and with the King and the Cardinal in the vanguard, to meet the invaders. By November the enemy had been repulsed and the Picardy towns recaptured. But for the unfortunate Picards, 1636 marked the beginning of twenty-four years of frightful misery as armies of both sides advanced and retreated, plundering towns and villages, laying waste the countryside, and murdering and torturing the civilian population.

For practically the whole of the quarter-century before his death in 1660 Vincent de Paul was engaged in relieving the provinces that suffered most from the incessant wars: Lorraine, Picardy, the Ile de France and Champagne. A young priest destined to become the most famous preacher of his time, Bossuet, who was then attending the Tuesday Conferences of Monsieur Vincent, would denounce the seventeenth-century wars: 'War, the cruellest monster hell has ever vomited forth for the ruin of men. . . . I ask you, Christians, is it not a frightful thing to have soldiers billeted on a poor family? Would to God that you knew such things only from what I tell you. But, alas, our deserted fields and our villages and towns left miserably desolate inform us plainly that it is this sole terror, war, that has scattered from the one and the other all their former inhabitants.'

Vincentians living in the war-torn provinces wrote to Saint-Lazare describing the dreadful straits to which people were reduced. The Lorrainers were living on grass, and cannibalism was not unknown. Plague followed famine and in one district the population fell from fifteen hundred to one hundred and five within three years. The Vincentians at Saint-Lazare rationed themselves. 'This is a time for penance,' Monsieur Vincent said. 'Should we not fast to appease God's anger and to have something extra for our brothers' relief?' One day he went down to the Palais Richelieu, told the Cardinal Minister of the reports coming in to Saint-Lazare from his priests in Lorraine and, flinging himself on his knees before the great man, cried, 'My Lord Cardinal, have pity on us. Let us have peace. Give peace to France.' 'Monsieur Vincent, I long for peace just as much as you do,' replied Richelieu, 'but peace does not depend on me alone.' Vincent left the palace. If he thought to himself that those who make war are not the ones to suffer its miseries, he did not waste time lamenting that fact or the little success he had had, but set to work to raise relief funds and organize for their distribution.

Calling together the Ladies of Charity he appealed to them with such effect that they sold their jewels and plate; King Louis gave him 45,000 *livres* and several Vincentian Fathers set off to give what help they could in the stricken areas.

Brother Mathieu Regnard won a reputation for his ingenuity at getting large sums of money from Paris to the Fathers in charge at the various relief centres. In ten years he walked fifty-three times to Lorraine and never once did he arrive without his famous purse. Though held up by highwaymen, and by soldiers of different armies and nationalities, including his own, with his innocent air and his disguises and stratagems he always outwitted his inceptors. They nicknamed him Brother Reynard ('fox') and watched for him on the different roads, but he never failed to fling his purse into some unlikely spot before he was stopped and searched. One day a band of brigands surrounded him and took him into a wood. 'Give us fifty *pistoles* and we will let you go,' they said. 'Fifty *pistoles!*' cried the brother. 'A poor man like me who hasn't a Lorraine farthing!' They searched him and, finding nothing, beat him up. He fled from them like a terrified man, hid till they were gone and returned to the muddy pool into which he had kicked the purse. Having retrieved it he went his way. He brought 1,600,000 *livres* in all to Lorraine in his journeyings.

Among Vincent's most generous helpers were the Port-Royal community. Mère Angélique collected up to 400,000 *livres* for the relief of devastated areas. Under their new director, Saint-Cyran, the nuns were indeed 'serving God in fear and trembling'. Penances of the early Church were practised. Though Confessions were repeated over and over, absolution was deferred for long periods. As no one could ever hope to be worthy to approach Our Lord in the Blessed Sacrament—so Saint-Cyran said—the nuns did not dare receive Holy Communion, the more perfect remaining the longest away, Mère Angélique for several years. Religious were allowed to die without the sacraments, to show how perfectly detached they were, even from spiritual goods. The nuns in the Abbey and the solitaries in the cells in the grounds meditated on the points put before them by Saint-Cyran, on hell fire and the judgments of a God, terrible, formidable, remote and unapproachable. On the God of Jansen and Saint-Cyran—the God of Sinai. Never were they allowed to dwell on the thought of God as described by His Only Begotten Son on the Mount of the Beatitudes, the Father who clothes the flowers of the field and has a care for falling sparrows, who remembers when even mothers forget, and who has counted the hairs on the head of each of His children. It was disconcerting for reform workers not belonging to this select band to hear, on the one hand, condemnations of Saint-Cyran's teachings on predestination and free will, and on the other to witness the undoubtedly devout and austere lives the first Jansenists were leading. One of the solitaries wrote a beautiful paraphrase of the *Ave Maris Stella*:

O très pure, O très douce, O Vierge incomparable,
Humble, au-dessus de tous,
Romps les fers du pêche dont le poids nous accable,
Rends-nous, purs, humbles, doux.*

It was all very confusing for the outsider. Why have recourse to Our Lady if prayer was useless for one not numbered among God's elect? Why all the penitence and bodily mortifications, if God saved or damned whom He pleased and took no account of free will or personal merit? If one should always remain afar off and trembling before the Omnipotent God, why was there no fear or respect but a disdainful and sustained opposition to the Vicar of Christ, when the Pope censured a booklet written by one of the nuns? 'The Church has not existed for the past five or six centuries,' asserted Saint-Cyran. God had revealed it to him, he said. He told Monsieur Vincent that he did not believe in Councils, such as that of Trent, nor did he submit to the Pope's decisions. Vincent was deeply perturbed: 'Sir,' he remonstrated, 'you are going too far. Do you expect me to believe a single Doctor of

* O most pure, O most sweet, O peerless Virgin,
Humblest of all;
Break the heavy fetters of sin that weigh us down,
Make us gentle, humble, pure.

Theology like yourself in preference to the teaching Church, the pillar of Truth with whom Christ promised to remain until the end of time?'³

Richelieu, whom Saint-Cyran had helped to his present all-powerful position and who in other days had told people, 'The Abbé of Saint-Cyran is the most learned man in all Europe', now began to look on him with a jaundiced eye. If the Huguenots had been deprived of power, and interior peace secured in France, it was not without great cost in money and blood. It was unthinkable now, with France embroiled in the Thirty Years' War, that a new sect should be permitted to flare up in the heart of Paris, that a group resembling a cabal should, under cover of working for reform, begin again to reconstruct what the Cardinal had given the best years of his life to destroy, 'a State within the State'.

'Saint-Cyran is a visionary', he wrote in his *Mémoires* for the first months of 1638. A month or two later he was writing to the King asking to have the abbé arrested: 'The man is more dangerous than six armies.' When the royal order for arrest came, Richelieu, unperturbed as always, prepared to leave with the court for Compiègne. He remarked to a friend: 'Today I have done something that will raise a great outcry against me. I have had Saint-Cyran arrested by order of the King. The learned and the good will perhaps create a hubbub, but whether they do or not I know I have rendered a service to the State and to the Church. A lot of harm could have been avoided if Luther and Calvin had been imprisoned when they began to dogmatize.' All his actions were weighed in the measure of their usefulness to State and Church, the State always coming first. After a rather summary inquiry during which Condren, the Bishop of Langres, Vincent de Paul and others were interrogated, Saint-Cyran was imprisoned at Vincennes.⁴

A week later his friend Jansen died, 'of either the plague or anthrax', at Ypres. Friends had Jansen's work, *Augustinus*, printed secretly without submitting it to Rome. One of the first copies off the presses was sent to Saint-Cyran in his prison cell who hailed it with joy. 'With St Paul and St Augustine,' he said, 'Jansen makes the trio who speak of grace with divine inspiration. . . . It will be the devotional book of the final centuries. It will live as long as the Church.' Others who saw the book said that some of its propositions had been formally condemned. Richelieu urged the Pope to condemn the book. Mère Angélique told her nuns and the solitaries and the visitors to Port-Royal to remember 'that Saint-Cyran is in jail to teach us the true way of penitence'. The abbé was regarded by many as a martyr. The only text from the Gospels remembered and quoted by his followers was, 'Blessed are they who suffer persecution for justice' sake.' Yet, despite their reliance on St Augustine, none of the Jansenists seemed to have read that great Doctor's words, 'While other vices seem to nourish themselves on the evil deeds they make us commit, pride attaches itself even to good works, to make them lose all their merit.'

Saint-Cyran continued to direct his followers from prison. By orders of the Cardinal his comforts were provided for and his liberties not too restricted. Distinguished guests who visited the prisoner included Bishops and great ladies. Even the Duchess of Aiguillon, taking time off from her charitable work for Monsieur Vincent, came. After Richelieu's death Saint-Cyran was released but he died a few months later. Jansen's book was formally condemned by Rome that same year. Immediately another booklet appeared, entitled *Frequent Communion*. This was the work of Antoine Arnauld, 'le Grand Arnauld', Mère Angélique's Sorbonne brother. It was not prompted by any desire to see the faithful receive the sacraments with more respect. It stressed the necessity of perfect contrition as a disposition for approaching the Holy Table. But who could be sure whether his contrition was perfect or not? Therefore, for fear of the worst, the best course for a faithful soul was to abstain altogether from Holy Communion, unless perhaps at the hour of death.

Monsieur Vincent, noting the rapid depletion in the numbers of communicants in Paris, the direct consequence of the *Frequent Communion* booklet, which had had a wide sale, was deeply concerned. Writing to a Vincentian who was impressed by Arnauld's arguments, he mentioned how Saint-Sulpice had 3,000 less communicants in a year and other churches were experiencing a similar falling-off. He continued:

A perusal of Monsieur Arnauld's book, instead of giving men a love for frequent Communion, rather frightens them away. . . . Perhaps what you say about some persons in France and Italy having greatly benefited by this book may be true, but for a hundred here in Paris who may perhaps have derived some good from it in that they show greater reverence to the Blessed Sacrament, there are ten thousand who have been harmed by it, as it has caused them to stay away altogether. . . . Does the author not praise in the highest terms . . . the piety of those who postpone Communion until death, as proof that they deem themselves unworthy to receive the Body of Jesus Christ? Does he not assert that God is more pleased by humility than by all manner of good works? Then he goes to the other extreme and holds that to say we honour God by our Communions is to speak unworthily of the Heavenly King. He says that our frequent Communions only outrage and shame Our Lord. . . . Now, how can anyone who reads Monsieur Arnauld imagine that he wishes the faithful to receive? . . . I confess that if I thought as highly of his opinions as you do, not only would I renounce for ever, in a spirit of humility, Holy Mass and Communion, but I would have a dread and horror of the Sacrament. . . .

Can any man on earth be found who thinks so highly of his own virtue as to maintain that he is in a fit state to receive Holy Communion worthily? Only Monsieur Arnauld, it seems. After pushing the requisite dispositions for receiving worthily to such a height that even a St Paul would be afraid to go to Communion, he boasts, over and over in his pages, that he says Mass daily. In this we must admire his humility and esteem his charity; as also his high opinion of the many wise secular and religious spiritual guides and the many holy penitents who practise frequent Communion, all of whom he makes a point of attacking. . . .

As he means to deter the faithful from receiving so it will not be his fault if he banishes the Mass. . . . He speaks more favourably of a priest who abstains, as an act of penance, from saying Mass, than of one who celebrates, though he knows what the Venerable Bede said of the value of the Mass. [5]

Until the end of his life Monsieur Vincent was to be active in combating the opinions of the Jansenists. Still he always kept very friendly with them, and when Pope Innocent X condemned the 'Five Propositions' in 1653, Vincent, who might have rejoiced publicly at the news, did what he could to soften the blow, going to visit the leaders, 'not omitting the solitaries of Port-Royal', and having long and friendly conversations with them. The solitaries, increased in number, had moved out to Port-Royal-des-Champs, drained the unhealthy marshes there, and grew excellent fruit. One of the Arnaulds had great success as a cultivator of pear trees and sent Queen Anne 'some of these blessed fruits'. Mère Angélique, when news of the condemnation of her brother's thesis arrived, compared him to St Thomas of Canterbury, dying for the truth: 'The grace of God has always been attacked by hypocrites and cheats and defended by simple and sincere men,' she wrote, implying that the Pope and the Sacred College were in the former category and they of Port-Royal in the latter.

Monsieur Olier and Monsieur Vincent, seeing in the turn affairs were taking a repetition of the Reformation when whole nations seceded from the Church, redoubled their efforts to win back the 'simple and sincere men', the solitaries of Port-Royal-des-Champs. They laboured in vain. The Protestant historian, Jurieu, recorded: 'These gentlemen [the solitaries], under pretext of avenging the outrages committed against God, satisfied their own peculiar passions. . . . The most just reproofs became defamatory libels, made in a spirit of revenge and spread clandestinely.'

Monsieur Vincent was among those calumniated. His depositions at the inquiry following which Saint-Cyran was thrown into prison were quoted against him. The Port-Royal nuns complained bitterly to him that he had not stood by Saint-Cyran. He could have told them in detail of his two separate interrogations by Richelieu, Vincent having refused to appear before a lay judge on a matter concerning a fellow priest. Of the Cardinal's displeasure at his answering. Of the subsequent written depositions in which Vincent prefaced so many remarks with 'I am not sure', 'I do not recall', 'I cannot say'. Of his defence of his friend on all possible points and of the exculpating and conciliatory remarks he interpolated wherever he could, hoping to placate the Cardinal. Of the opinion expressed by men in Richelieu's confidence that only for Monsieur Vincent, Saint-Cyran's head would have rolled in the Place de Grève. Though he could have done so, he did not tell the nuns of Port-Royal how far he had gone to save Saint-Cyran. When they upbraided him he smiled his whimsical Gascon smile. Mère Angélique saw in that smile a secret delight at the misfortunes of her spiritual director. She saw in Vincent's efforts to procure the abbey of Saint-Cyran for the latter's nephew the outward proof of a guilt complex that could only be eased by some atoning gesture. But Monsieur Vincent, always courteous and kind, when he had smiled at their fidelity to a dead if mistaken and stubborn director, bowed and went away.

Mère Angélique, much given to making the dramatic, spectacular gesture—as when she sent a community of nuns on a journey, after making them take a vow of silence, with each one's name pinned to her sleeve—very much the daughter of that imperious, browbeating Arnauld who first thrust her into Port-Royal, always self-conscious, up in the clouds, scrupulous and unworldly, continued to send Monsieur Vincent large donations for war relief and other charities. Even his opponents knew that in no other hands would alms go so far or succour so many.

The Abbess was to die shortly after Monsieur Vincent. Her last words: 'Oh, Lord, have mercy on all. I repeat, *on all*, my

God, on *all*.' Life had brought her many disappointments, great and small.* Even her own nuns disgraced her on the day Saint-Cyran was released from prison. He came direct from Vincennes to the Abbey† where the entire community of one hundred and twenty was lined up in a double file to give him a solemn welcome. Saint-Cyran was walking slowly between the two lines of reverently bowed heads when suddenly a novice giggled. So did her neighbour, and soon all, either through overwrought nerves or the contagion a laugh at the wrong time and place can spread, burst into peals of laughter, a sound hardly ever heard in Port-Royal. Poor Mère Angélique had the mortification of having Saint-Cyran dismiss herself and her nuns, postponing the release celebrations 'until the octave day'. Even then he was decidedly distant with the subdued community and spent most of his time with the solitaries and Mr Jenkins, the exiled Englishman who was the abbey's wonderful gardener. Truly, as Henri Brémond observes: 'La vie sectaire tue l'humeur.'

Before turning to the other great works that were to fill Monsieur Vincent's last twenty years it is interesting to look at the timetable of his seventeen-hour day:[6]

A.M. 4 Rise.

4.30 Prayer.

5.30 Mass. Thanksgiving. Personal work.

10.30 Examination of Conscience and a meal.

11.30 Recreation.

---

* The wandering friar to whose sermon she attributed her conversion in 1608 later apostatized and led a scandalous life. After that she did not like friars. Once two Capuchins called at Port-Royal in Paris and were received 'coldly enough, as all regulars were received there', but the Abbess ordered the white bread and wine of the Messieurs (the solitaries) to be set before them. Hearing from whoever waited on them that they had backed up the Jesuits against Saint-Cyran, she had the white bread and wine quickly removed to be replaced by 'valets' bread and cider'.

† At the entrance a peasant was weeping and Saint-Cyran asked why he wept. The man said that his wife had given birth to a stillborn child that day. The abbé told him to go home and tell his wife that the infant was assuredly in hell, having died unbaptized. After this inhuman remark he turned to his travelling companion and said, 'I always took a great interest in the education of children and even paid for the education of children not related to me.' There seems to have been more than a touch of megalomania in him by this stage.

P.M. 12.30 Personal work.
   2   Recitation of Vespers. Personal work.
   5   Matins.
 5.45   Supper.
 7.15   Personal work.
   9   Night Prayers.

That 'personal work', besides the care of the many enterprises to which he had set his hand, also included letter writing, drafting of rules, and the running of Saint-Lazare. About three thousand letters, some of them of considerable length, have come down to us, a fraction of the correspondence that made tremendous inroads on his time, particularly as he grew older.

By the middle of the seventeenth century, as religious life, through the herculean work of the reform groups and especially leaders like Francis de Sales, Bérulle, Bourdoise, Monsieur Vincent, Père Condren and Olier, revived in France, there was a new burgeoning of the nation's devotion to Our Blessed Lady. People were reciting the beautiful prayer formulated by Condren and perfected by Olier:

O Jesus,living in Mary,come and live in Your servant in the holiness of Your spirit, in the fulness of Your Power, in the perfection of Your ways, in the truth of Your virtues, in the communion of Your divine mysteries. Rule over every adverse power by Your Spirit to the glory of the Father. Amen.

After the taking of La Rochelle in 1629 Louis XIII built Notre-Dame-des-Victoires in Paris. Nine years later Monsieur Vincent was asked to send priests to give a mission to the King, Queen and court at Saint-Germain. Louis intended to consecrate his kingdom to the Blessed Virgin Mary that year and some spiritual preparation was required. The previous year the King, who took little interest in women, least of all in his wife, seemed on the point of falling in love with a Maid of Honour, Louise de La Fayette. Richelieu determined to nip the affair in the bud.

When Mademoiselle de La Fayette, a young and rather innocent girl who wished to enter religion, suddenly realized why the King was urging her to take up residence in a secluded residence in Versailles, she fled the court and entered the novitiate of the Visitandines in the rue Saint-Antoine. The King called at the convent a few times to see her. It was perfectly innocent. The Maid of Honour was now a novice, Sister Louise-Angélique, and had a genuine vocation. The brief conversations at the grille were mostly a request for prayers on his part and a promise of prayers on hers. But the Cardinal was uneasy. The King's Jesuit confessor, blamed for allowing his royal penitent to harbour an affection, 'innocent, but which could become dangerous', was banished to Rennes and ordered not to leave that city. Richelieu decided to have the novice changed to the Mother-house of the Visitation Order in Savoy. That was outside French territory and the King could not there exercise his privilege of visiting any convent he chose.

But the Superior of the Visitandines was Vincent de Paul, not Richelieu, and 'neither fear nor interest ever obscured Monsieur Vincent's line of thought. He clearly saw his duty towards the King, towards the Cardinal Minister, towards Sister Louise-Angélique.' The novice had committed no crime for which she should be exiled, he reasoned; indeed her determination, goodness and generosity merited praise, not blame. She could not be charged with disloyalty. With the good sense and *finesse* that were second nature to him Vincent intervened. He demanded, as Superior of the Visitation, that the Cardinal permit the Sister to remain where she was. He obtained what he asked. He saw the King and won him round to voluntary renouncement of his affection for Louise, harmless though it was and undoubtedly a consolation to a rather friendless monarch. He spoke to Sister Louise-Angélique, pointing out the consecration of life she was about to make to the King of Kings, who had asked his followers to 'leave all', and the radical renunciation those words implied. But he also showed her how her undoubted influence with the King could be used to bring him, France, and herself closer to

God. She did not have to thrust Louis altogether from her life and from her thoughts; the more one did that with anything the more one became obsessed with the banished object. Her part was to be the sincere, disinterested, reliable and holy friend who, while keeping herself and the Visitation above reproach, would be turned to in times of uncertainty and trouble.

The story of the visit of Louis to the convent at the beginning of December, 1637, is well known. A terrible storm broke over Paris and Sister Louise begged the King not to ride to Vincennes, as he intended, but to go to the Queen at the Louvre palace and spend the night there. That Louis should have been residing at Saint-Germain and Vincennes, and the Queen at the Louvre, is an indication of how their marriage had failed. They were then twenty-two years married and the King's scarcely veiled aversion to his wife was common knowledge. Their childless union was a matter of national concern. The King's brother, the useless Gaston—always plotting, always betraying his fellow conspirators to save his own skin—was heir apparent and no one looked forward to the reign of a prince who seemed to have inherited all the bad points and none of the good qualities of his immediate forebears. No one but Sister Louise-Angélique could dare to ask the King to spend the night at the Louvre. No one else would have asked and been granted such a request. In September, 1638, the future Louise XIV was born.* The infant Dauphin was called the Dieudonné, the God-given, and to celebrate his birth 'good wine ran free in Paris and even the hungry got their fill'. Vincent

---

* Not so well known, perhaps, is the story of an apparition of Our Lady to Brother Fiacre, a Paris Augustinian. She showed him a painting of herself entitled 'Mother of Divine Grace' and said, 'Go to Cotignac and pray before this picture for that which France most desires—an heir to the throne.' The story of the vision spread about and the Brother and his Superior were ordered to set off for Cotignac in Provence. It was midwinter and the journey was nothing if not penitential. When they found the church and the picture the Brother said, 'But this is not the picture I was shown. Satan must have deceived me and I have deceived others, perhaps.' He was very much upset and, with the Superior, was preparing to return to Paris when the sacristan of Cotignac church arrived and explained that the real picture was in the sacristy, having the frame regilded. Brother Fiacre at once recognized this painting as the one he had been shown and the two Augustinians remained for nine days praying there. When Louis Quatorze was born Queen Anne sent the Brother south again to thank the Mother of Divine Grace.

de Paul was among the famous men, King Louis and Richelieu included, who went on pilgrimage to Our Lady of Ardilliers near Saumur in thanksgiving for the gift of a Dauphin.

In February, 1638, Louis, by a solemn and official act, consecrated France to 'la très sainte et très glorieuse Vierge Marie, protectrice spéciale de nostre Royaume'. In the May processions around the city that year, processions that delighted Monsieur Vincent, the old medieval hymn with the line, 'For ever reign as Queen o'er France', was sung, and the feast of the Assumption proclaimed as a special State holiday.

The next three years saw fighting in the north, east and south of France, a fierce peasant uprising in Normandy which was savagely crushed, similar disturbances in Burgundy, and all the time Monsieur Vincent busy about the things of God: sending relief to those who suffered from the savagery of the times; superintending the rescue and care of the foundlings, the Hôtel-Dieu, the Charities, the *galériens*, the country missions, the work for the clergy, and the direction of his priests and the Daughters of Charity. His letters go out from Saint-Lazare daily. He asks one Superior to let the Vincentians have a day off every Thursday 'with time to rest and with some pleasant amusements, within our own walls'. The Fathers sent, at the request of the Cardinal, to Richelieu, his native town, have succeeded, Vincent says, in coaxing the habitués of taverns to leave them on Sundays and feastdays at least. Hearing of a Father who has fallen ill he hastens to tell the Superior to spare nothing, but to buy everything the doctor orders and more besides, and to have the sick man transferred to a room in the suburbs of the town where they are and hire an attendant to nurse him. 'In his kind of illness patience and kindness and gentleness will do far more good than any medicine prescribed.'

He still found time to visit the friends, his fellow workers in the cause of reform. Perhaps his favourite was the disconcerting, eccentric Bourdoise, so full of zeal for the House of God and all that pertained to it. To him, more than to any other, was due the reform in liturgical practice and manners, the renewal of reverence and decorum too long missing from French altars. He would stride up the nave of some Paris church, laden with freshly laundered surplices, asperging his brethren to left and right, glaring at priests who did not know the proper times for standing and kneeling and bowing, shaming the silent into song when he boomed forth *Magnificat anima mea Dominum*, or whichever antiphon was correct for the season and the hour. One morning he saw a priest go straight into the street after finishing Mass, without making any thanksgiving. Bourdoise seized a taper from the altar and the acolyte's handbell and raced after him, ringing the bell as he went. When he caught up with his quarry he fell into step beside him and walked along, still ringing the bell and holding the taper. 'What on earth do you mean, Monsieur Bourdoise?' asked the priest. 'I am only accompanying the Blessed Sacrament,' replied the curé of Saint-Nicholas.

His friends, agreed that if Monsieur Bourdoise could curb his abrupt manners and hasty words he would achieve even more good, decided to get someone to speak to him tactfully about this. The one chosen was the man who never gave offence to anyone, the man who was Bourdoise's greatest friend, Monsieur Vincent. Poor Monsieur Vincent demurred. Bourdoise was his best friend, and a very holy man. They had a lot in common: both had herded cattle and pigs in their young days, both had known hardship, both worked for the same ends. Finally he was prevailed upon to beard Bourdoise in his presbytery. After a lot of preliminary apologizing and beating about the bush Vincent still had not come to the point when Bourdoise said sharply, 'What is it? Speak up, man, speak up! I see you have something to say. I am all ears.' 'Well,' faltered Vincent, 'your friends, my miserable self included, think you would do far more good if you moderated your zeal a little and spoke a bit more gently and did not take people quite so shortly.' Bourdoise blew up. 'You flock of wet hens!' he shouted. 'You pack of trimmers! You lot of quaking cowards, ready to abandon God and His Church to please men!' Vincent said nothing but knelt down and humbly begged his friend's pardon, at which Bourdoise, who cooled off as quickly as he heated up, also knelt and begged Monsieur Vincent's pardon. Shortly afterwards the choleric curé wrote a twenty-five page open letter to his friends: *Against the rudeness of Adrian Bourdoise*.[7]

The incident made no difference to the friendship between Vincent and Bourdoise. They were close friends until Bourdoise's death in 1655. Monsieur Vincent had a high opinion of his sanctity. 'I never visited the seminary of Saint-Nicholas,' he said, 'but I came away greatly edified. They shine like suns, the seminarists there. And Monsieur Bourdoise is a saint.'

Chapter Twelve

FEEDING THE FLOCKS OF GOD

AFTER the age of sixty most men, slowed down by the years, slacken their pace and shed their occupations one by one, conserving their flagging energies for life's final uphill climb. Not so Monsieur Vincent whose work increased at an incredible rate during the last quarter of his four-score years. How one aging priest, suffering from a foot that always ached and a recurrent fever, could cope with so many enterprises, organize such a variety of charitable and missionary activities at home and abroad, regulate, maintain and superintend all these works and direct hundreds of souls passes comprehension. He himself once said that he never took up a work of his own accord; if a task was suggested to him he thought and prayed about it and waited to make sure that God wished him to undertake it:

> God's business is done by little and little. . . . We must always be careful not to run on ahead of God's Providence. . . . It seems a paradox to say this but it is true, that they who are in a hurry delay the things of God.

As with other saints whose capacity for work seems prodigious the secret of Monsieur Vincent's diverse and manifold activity lay in his spiritual life. He wrote no book on reformation of life, no treatise on prayer or progress in virtue. His teaching on those matters is found in his letters and in the conferences he gave to his priests and to the Daughters of Charity. For the communities he guided as for the missionaries on apostolic assignments he very simply directed them to align their daily life with the Gospel precepts. Almost every letter he wrote contained the expression 'O, Saviour!' as though he always kept Our Lord before his eyes. The principal characteristic of his own intense inner life was his longing that the Will of God should be done on earth as it is in Heaven and that man, whom God created to love and serve Him, should put himself at God's disposal, always seeking to discover God's Will and to accomplish it fully and in the manner God wills:

> Perfection does not consist in ecstasies but in doing the Will of God well. Who is the most perfect man? He whose will is most perfectly conformed with God's. . . . Holy Scripture tells us that he who adheres to God is one with Him in spirit and who, I ask you, adheres to God more than he who never does his own will but always God's, whose will and joy are only found in whatever God wills? . . . . If one does God's will and takes care to form an intention of doing so at the beginning of each task and renews this intention from time to time, is not that living in the presence of God? . . . . Who is more in the presence of God than the person who from morn to night does all his actions to please God and for love of Him?[1]

These last words sum up Monsieur Vincent's own interior life. He begged the Daughters of Charity to see Christ in the sick, in the *galériens*, in the foundlings, in the houses of the poor. He urged the priests of the Mission to love God 'with the strength of our arms and the sweat of our brows'. Not to rest content with lofty thoughts and a calm exterior and fine words. Not to think that consolations in prayer are a proof that one loves God. 'No. No. The test is not even to come out from prayer speaking like angels. But to come out to work for God, to suffer, to mortify oneself, to teach the poor, to go after the scattered flocks, to love being left short of something, to rejoice at illness or some other unhappiness, that's the test. That's where many are lacking. No, no, my brothers, let us not fool ourselves.'

Like the man he took for model, Francis de Sales, he stressed the wisdom of observing the golden mean in everything. He warned seminarians who seemed to have worked up to a certain tension in the quest for fervour that even in this there must be prudence. 'Though God has commanded us to love Him with all our strength and with all our mind and with all our heart and soul, at the same time His Goodness never meant us to go so far in our exuberance that we impair or ruin our health. . . . Oh no. God doesn't ask us to kill ourselves to keep this commandment. . . . All virtue lies in the happy medium. Every virtue has two extremes which are vices. . . . We could have too little or no love for God . . . . or an over-zealous love too excessive for our natures.' He was granted no visions, at least none that he ever divulged. He made no prophecies, worked no miracles. When someone remarked to him that his ceaseless activity, his vast achievement, was nothing short of miraculous he turned the conversation aside and spoke of the rapid spread and the works of his two communities, both of such recent origin. 'You see,' he said, as though apologizing for the Vincentians and the Daughters of Charity, 'three can do more than ten when the Lord lends a hand.' The words were an echo of St Teresa's: 'Teresa alone is capable of nothing, but Teresa and Almighty God can do anything and everything.'

From 1640 to the end of his life Monsieur Vincent on his white horse was a familiar figure in the streets of Paris, greeting everybody courteously and affably as he trotted about on his multifarious errands. His letters contain no descriptions of the city or of the famous and infamous characters then to be found there; when in the country he is a little more expansive but only in reference to farmers and farming business. His days were so completely filled and so many letters awaited answering that he had to confine himself to essentials. Madame de Motteville, de Retz, and others with facile pens and with time on their hands were there to write gossip columns for posterity. He had more urgent matters in mind. By 1640, the state of Lorraine was desperate. A priest of the Mission wrote from there to Vincent:

The moment I arrived, I began to distribute alms. But there are so many poor that I have not enough for all. More than three hundred are in dire need and three hundred others in the last extremity. Oh, Sir, the truth is that there are more than a hundred like skeletons covered with skin, such a fearful sight that if God did not strengthen me I would not dare to look at them. Their skin is like tawny marble, their lips so drawn back that their teeth are showing, dry and bared, their eyes and features all frowning and scowling. In fine, it is the most dreadful sight that one could see. They grub about the fields for certain roots which they cook and eat. . . .

Another wrote:

A poor widow with three infants, all dying of hunger, flayed a grass snake and was trying to roast it when one of our Fathers arrived. He stopped her and got her something to eat. . . . Not a horse dies here, no matter of what sickness, but the people fall upon it and devour it. A few days ago a woman had her apron full of infected horseflesh which she was exchanging for morsels of bread. . . . Girls sell themselves for bread. The local priest yokes himself to a wagon, taking with his parishioners the place of the horses they have not got.

From Picardy and Champagne similar stories came:

In thirty-five villages we visited we found almost six hundred persons in dire want. So badly off are they that when wolves have eaten dogs and horses they go and eat what the wolves leave. . . . The famine in Saint-Quentin is such that the people eat clay, grass, tree-bark, the tattered rags they wear . . . and, something we would not dare to say had we not witnessed it, they gnaw their own hands and arms and die in despair. . . . [2]

Others reported cases of cannibalism; of a mother who killed her two children to eat them and strangled herself in her subsequent dementia. The infernal rhythm of war, famine and plague continued right through the last twenty years of Monsieur Vincent's life not only in the frontier provinces but in the capital itself when civil war broke out.

The amounts of money he collected and distributed to the devastated French provinces alone ran into twenty millions of present currency. Besides Brother 'Reynard' he had other trusted messengers, including an Irish Vincentian, one Père Donat Crowley who brought the money to the stricken districts. Père Crowley, accustomed to covering rough country barefoot in his native land, used to run like a hare across the flat plains of France, swimming rivers as he came to them and evading armed companies with an agility born of long practice in Ireland. Hearing one day that soldiers had driven away the cattle of some poor people in his area, he went hot-foot after them, caught up with them near a wood and spoke so eloquently of the poverty of his flock and their dependence upon their few cows that the raiders gave back all and the Father returned in triumph to his parishioners, driving the cows before him. Crowley is a name common enough in that part of Ireland where visitors go to kiss the famous Blarney Stone. When Donat had added the art of persuasive speaking, as taught by Monsieur Vincent, to the 'gift of the gab' that is the inheritance of most of his race, we may be sure that he could charm the birds off the bushes. The coaxing of a company of soldiers, some of whose officers were probably Irish *émigrés* like himself, to part with their ill-gotten cattle presented little difficulty.

Besides the money and goods in kind, wagons of seed-wheat, blankets, medicines and other provisions, Vincent sent every priest he could spare to the four provinces hardest hit to distribute the relief, look after the people, say Mass and administer the Sacraments. The Daughters of Charity followed to nurse, to establish food centres, to set up schools, and to take what hygienic precautions they could to prevent the spread of plague and other epidemics. Brother 'Reynard' managed to lead numbers of refugees to Paris where Vincent had them housed and fed. At one time fifteen thousand a day were lined up at his soup kitchens and he was watchful for 'the bashful poor', those whose shame at the destitution to which they had been reduced through no fault of their own made them reluctant to admit to their need.

Nuns whose convents had been burned were given shelter in the Visitation convents. Unfortunate wretches, too weak to stand upright, who succeeded in dragging themselves to the gates of Paris, were helped to the John of God Hospital where the Hospitaller Brothers received them or to the Hôtel-Dieu where the Ladies of Charity and the Daughters of Charity managed to cope with patients to the number of twenty-five thousand a year.

In May, 1642, France had been fighting in the Thirty Years' War for seven years and peace seemed as far away as ever. War abroad did not preclude disturbances at home. Here and there a few hundred peasants, maddened with hunger, weighed down with the extra taxes imposed to sustain the armies, rose against the local landlord and the hordes of rapacious officials, only to be crushed mercilessly. At Fontarabie, near the present international Hendaye-Irun bridge, Monsieur Vincent's one-time pupil, the Duc de la Valette, yielded to Spanish forces far inferior to his in numbers, in a battle which meant a great loss of prestige for France. It was reported that Valette led the retreat, 'chuckling in his throat as he did so, and when asked why he laughed he said he had to keep up a cheerful countenance to reassure his men'. Returned for trial on a charge of treason, he fled to England. He was condemned to death *in absentia* and executed in effigy. Hardly had the excitement of that affair died down when the King's half-brother, the Duc de Vendôme, friend of another of Vincent's past pupils, Pierre de Gondi, engineered a conspiracy which fizzled out through the sudden deaths of the leaders. The final plotter against Richelieu, Cinq-Mars, 'badly reared son of a good family', was a pettish young favourite of twenty who made the King laugh one day and annoyed him the next, as His Majesty did not understand irony and did not know how to defend himself against such pleasantries. Cinq-Mars took up where the previous conspirators left off, induced the Queen and the incorrigible Gaston of Orléans to join him, and signed a treaty of alliance with the enemy—Spain. Though the King was ill and Richelieu dying, both set out with an army to take Perpignan and force the Catalans back across the Pyrenees. At Narbonne, the Cardinal, one arm abscessed and paralysed, could go no further. He had himself taken to Arles where a spy awaited him with a copy of the treaty Cinq-Mars had signed. A fast courier was sent after the King and the favourite was arrested. Far away in Cologne, Marie de Medici, saved from destitution only by the money Richelieu sent her, died. If the Cardinal had few regrets for her, Louis had less. He was a son devoid of filial love, a man absolutely lacking in emotion. He stood, watch in hand, on the walls of Perpignan, which fell to him the day Cinq-Mars was executed at Lyons. When noon, the execution hour, came he waited a few seconds before turning to those about him to remark: 'I wonder what kind of grimaces young Cinq-Mars is making now.'

Richelieu, dying a little with each swish of the oars as his scarlet-curtained barge moved up the rivers towards Paris, wondered would he live to reach the capital. He lingered till Advent, his beloved niece, the Duchess of Aiguillon, remaining with him to the end. By his will,[3] dated May 23rd, 1642, he left 'all the money he possessed at his death, when other legacies, especially that made to the King, had been deducted, to Monsieur Vincent'.* One of his executors was the Duchess, 'that admirable woman who, after Madame de Gondi and Mademoiselle Le Gras, among the many generous ladies who sprang up in the first half of the century, contributed most to all the intentions of St Vincent de Paul'.

During the previous decade the Cardinal had taken an interest in the Tuesday Conferences and had discussed them with Vincent himself. After their first meeting Richelieu said to his niece, 'People have often told me about Monsieur Vincent. Now that I have met him myself I know that he is even holier than they say he is.' When he came to know him better he used to

---

* Having bequeathed to the King his magnificent palace, his superb golden altar plate, his tapestries, three state beds, and his best diamond; to his niece most of his estates and châteaux with their revenues, his celebrated gold dinner service, and his jewels; to his nephew his galleries of paintings and sculptures, his collections of china, uncut gems, Limoges enamels and Venetian glass; to France his library, and to friends and servants legacies, alone amounting to over two million francs, the amount Monsieur Vincent eventually received may not have amounted to much.

send for Vincent when dioceses became vacant and ask him to name priests he thought would make worthy bishops. He made ample provision for the maintenance of the Vincentians he had established in his home town of Richelieu. In his letters of December, 1642, Vincent did not mention the Cardinal's death though in the following June he signed, with the Duchess and others, a legal document concerning the foundation of a Vincentian house at Marseilles, the Duchess defraying expenses and the priests of the Mission promising to say many Masses each year in perpetuity for the repose of 'Monseigneur le grand Cardinal Duc de Richelieu'. Vincent, like so many other saints of his time, feared that Europe was in danger of losing the faith. He saw in the alliances and treaties with Germany and Sweden, in the Cardinal's foreign policy, an insurmountable obstacle to the work of Catholic Reform, an obstacle likely to block, for centuries if not for ever, the road to religious unity. Did the Duchess tell him her uncle's last words, the famous answer to the ritual demand that he should forgive his enemies: 'I have had no enemies, save those of the State'? Did de Retz retail the comment of Urban VIII, who had once been Papal Nuncio in France: 'If there be a God, Cardinal Richelieu has a lot to answer for. If there be none he certainly has had a successful career'? Did the priests on the Missions write telling of the bonfires blazing on the hills to signify the joy of the war-weary and tax-burdened people of France at the Cardinal's death? We do not know, but knowing Monsieur Vincent's devotion to the souls in Purgatory we can be certain that he said many prayers for the man who had often helped him to help the poor.

Some months before his death Richelieu sent Vincent a thousand crowns as a subscription towards the establishment of a proper seminary in the *Bons-Enfants*. It will be recalled that a college for boys who thought they had vocations was opened there in 1636, but was not a success. Monsieur Vincent, after giving a good deal of thought to the matter, decided that two seminaries, one for younger, the other for more advanced students, would be better. The 'minor' seminary already existing was transferred to Saint-Lazare. In the 'major' seminary at the *Bons-Enfants* he received older students preparing for the priesthood as well as priests whose preparation for their sacred calling had been inadequate. There a spiritual, moral and intellectual training was given to the seminarists and Monsieur Vincent, always ready to learn from others, paid many visits to Saint-Sulpice, opened by his friend, Monsieur Olier, at the same time and for the same purpose; to the seminary conducted by Bourdoise at Saint-Nicholas, and to the Oratory seminary where he met and talked with his former employer and benefactor, Père Philippe-Emmanuel de Gondi.

When Richelieu was sinking he wrote the King, 'Send for Mazarin.' Mazarin, though a Cardinal, was not a priest. He had come to France from Italy in 1630 with a Papal Legate and later became Nuncio. Now he fell into Richelieu's shoes and as he was known to be as suave and mild as his predecessor had been terrible and severe, all who had been mixed up in conspiracies or who had reason to fear Richelieu's anger, at once flocked back to court. Those whom Richelieu had imprisoned were released. Saint-Cyran hastened to Port-Royal. Bassompierre and a dozen others emerged from the Bastille. Vendôme and conspirators like him who had fled to England and elsewhere were recalled from exile. But Mazarin, sharp-witted, intelligent, unscrupulous, had been watching the great Cardinal rule for the past twelve years and had learned a lot. Though the hand now holding the reins had a silken glove it was the hand of a man who knew how to drive. In the spring the King fell ill. For several weeks he lay dying. Though he had his own confessor he asked for Monsieur Vincent. One day he said to him, 'Monsieur Vincent, if I recover, I would like to send every Bishop to Saint-Lazare for three years.' Besides his physical sufferings the King suffered remorse for having signed the death warrants of Cinq-Mars and Montmorency. Particularly Montmorency. The wails of the Toulousains massed beneath his lodging on that October day in 1632 crying 'Grâce! Grâce! Mercy for Montmorency!' now echoed across the years. It was not easy to banish his fears.

Among other matters he asked Vincent to bring him a list, written in order of merit, of priests suitable for appointment to a number of vacant sees and abbeys. He gave large sums of money to be sent to Vincentians working in the distressed areas. When the King was refusing the food his doctors urged him to take, Vincent got him to do as they asked. On Ascension Day, May 14th, 'after kissing a medal of St Fiacre',* Louis XIII died. Vincent was present and said afterwards, 'Never in all my life have I seen anyone die a more Christian death.' [4]

Anne of Austria, to whom Monsieur Vincent was already well known through his charitable works, was deeply grateful to him for the consolation and aid he gave her husband in his last hours. After the King's death she took Vincent as her spiritual director. When arranging his affairs Louis had insisted that during the Queen's Regency there should be a Council of State. He wished to put safeguards about a situation that was too like what it had been in his own early years: a child King, with a younger brother likely to grow up his mother's favourite; a widowed Queen, attractive but not very sensible; an Italian favourite who was also a Cardinal-statesman on the rise to power; and a lot of intriguing and mischievous courtiers, buzzing about ready to rebel should a likely leader present himself. One of the first acts of the Council of State was to form a 'Council of Conscience' for the administration of ecclesiastical affairs. It consisted of bishops and priests, and laymen holding prominent positions, such as the Chancellor and the Secretary of State. Cardinal Mazarin presided at the meetings. Vincent de Paul and his friend, the fearless and candid old Bishop of Lisieux, were among the ecclesiastics on this Council.

Monsieur Vincent's membership of the Council was no sine-cure, for he took his duties seriously. The Queen was usually present and most of the business at the meetings dealt with

* St Fiacre, an Irish saint of the seventh century who settled in Paris, is the patron of gardeners, florists, box-makers, brass-beaters, coppersmiths, lead-founders, needle-makers, knitters, tile-makers, potters and taxicab drivers. He is the protector of field and garden fruit and is invoked against headache, tummy-ache, tumours and other ills. His emblems are a spade and a basket of vegetables.

appointments of Bishops and Abbots and of matters connected with Church administration and reform. The meetings were held at one of the royal palaces and Vincent went there on his white horse, in his ordinary clothes, now greening with age, and his girdle, fraying a bit at the ends. Mazarin, who realized from the beginning that he and Monsieur Vincent were not going to see eye to eye on many matters, adopted a patronizing attitude to him, ridiculing him on occasion. Once he picked up the ravelling ends of Vincent's girdle and said to the others, 'See how Monsieur Vincent gets himself up to come to court!' Again he jeered at the faded black robe. 'Yes, my clothes are old,' said Vincent, with a flash of the Gascon showing, 'but they are clean and brushed and the holes are mended.' Richelieu, an autocrat to his fingertips, also a man of breeding and fine manners, would never have been guilty of such a remark as Mazarin's. Perhaps the latter, suffering from a real or imaginary inferiority complex, sought reassurances and compensation for his own humble beginnings in disparaging those whose retaliation he had no reason to expect or fear. His remark to Vincent prompted the Prince of Condé, also present, to say, 'Come and sit beside me, Monsieur Vincent.' 'Your Highness, it is enough for you to allow me, the son of a poor swineherd, to be in the same room with you,' protested Vincent, a protest Condé countered with a Latin tag that contained a barb for Mazarin as well as a tribute for Vincent: 'A man's nobility lies in his virtue. And it is not today or yesterday we learned your worth.'

Mazarin's entries in his diary show how little he cared to have Monsieur Vincent on the Council or near the Queen:

Monsieur Vincent wishes to promote Père de Gondi. . . . De Gondi, Lambert and Vincent de Paul are against me.

Some persons who pretend to love the Queen have approached Monsieur Vincent and told him that she is compromising her reputation by her flirtations. . . .

The Council of Conscience must not meet for some time.

De Noyers is here, evidently full of great plans and, under cover of advising Her Majesty on the building projects, has spoken to her of other important affairs. He claims to have the backing of the Queen's household, the Jesuits, the monasteries, the devout, and of course Monsieur Vincent.

The Madame de Maignelay crowd, with Lambert and company, see that Vincent de Paul is the channel through which everything reaches the Queen's ears.

Again he noted the frequent visits of the Ladies of Charity to the court, the donations the Queen gave to all Monsieur Vincent's charities, the fact that the Queen fasted in Lent, obeying Monsieur Vincent rather than the court physicians who always insisted on her having a dispensation. In February, 1644, a courtier wrote to a friend:

> They say that Monsieur Vincent will soon fall from favour. Some say that he has been exiled to Troyes for having attempted to take too much upon himself at the Council of Conscience. . . . B. said to the Queen the other day that he had just left Mazarin and had never seen the Cardinal in a worse temper. When the Queen asked him why he told her that Mazarin's conscience did not square with Monsieur Vincent's.

A month later the same courtier reports that Vincent's candidate for the bishopric of Narbonne, a priest from Olier's seminary in Saint-Sulpice, had been approved by the Council despite Mazarin's endeavours to have the worldly de la Rivière appointed to that See. 'Monsieur Vincent is not so powerless, after all,' he concludes.

Rumours that Vincent was to be banished from the court and from Paris reached Rome and a Vincentian there wrote to Saint-Lazare inquiring if the report had any foundation. Vincent replied that it was true, that there had been signs that he would not be allowed to remain any longer in the Council. 'Alas, God has permitted, because of my sins, that I be kept on.' But a man as astute as Mazarin found ways and means of getting his way.

Meetings of the Council were called seldom, at irregular intervals, and at times when those likely to support Monsieur Vincent's nominations would be certainly absent. In 1652 Vincent received a notice from the Cardinal informing him that he was no longer a member of the Council of Conscience.[5]

Duelling was one of the abuses condemned by the Council. During the last six years of the reign of Henri IV eight thousand French gentlemen had lost their lives in duels. Prohibited by Richelieu, it had reappeared. In the 1640's seventeen met their deaths at sword point on the parvis of Saint-Sulpice in one week. Many of the Ladies of Charity were widowed early in life because of duelling, and no doubt encouraged Vincent in his efforts to have the custom proscribed. His greatest service to the Council and the one that earned him Mazarin's lasting disfavour was the firm stand he took on the question of benefices. His requirements for a good bishop or religious superior may appear unexacting to an age like the present, accustomed for long to higher standards, but they were a great advance on customs then obtaining. In one instance when he opposed strenuously the appointment of a man of notorious life, a protégé of Mazarin, to a bishopric, the Cardinal tried to get the nomination through in an underhand way. But Vincent invoked the Council provision that doubtful decisions should be re-examined. He also went to the candidate's father, an important State official, and pointed out to him the danger to his son as well as to the souls in the diocese his son wished to rule, if the appointment went through. The official pleaded his own advanced age, his many children, none of whom were yet provided for, the losses he had suffered during the wars which left him much poorer than he was. Vincent was adamant. Better that one family be poor in material goods rather than have thousands of families perish spiritually for want of a good bishop. Despite all his zeal Mazarin triumphed in this case, the nomination being carried.

In 1644 the farm at Orsigny, which supplied most of the wants of Vincent's communities, was claimed by the heirs of those who had given it to the Canons Regular, predecessors of the Vincentians at Saint-Lazare. The case went to court and Vincent lost. It caused him no worry. 'All that God does He does well,' he told the Fathers at Saint-Lazare. 'You will see that this has happened for the best. It is a big loss but God will send something else.' A few years after the saint's death Orsigny farm was returned to them and also another valuable property adjoining it. Soon after the court case an influential man who wanted a benefice for his son took Vincent aside and told him that he could get back Orsigny for him, also other revenues of which Saint-Lazare had been deprived, if he would support his son's nomination. Although this was a time when Vincent was feeding from two to three thousand poor daily and needed all the funds he could get he replied, 'I know my duty. Even if I were offered the whole world to do otherwise I would still do what I think to be right. The Vincentians have nothing to fear from poverty; I would fear for them if I saw them with an abundance of earthly goods.'

Dismissed from the Council, Vincent continued to work, in every way he could, for the reform of the Church and society. His charitable works that had begun as little private ventures were now spread to the four corners of France. Bishops who had made retreats in Saint-Lazare or who had come under the influence of Monsieur Vincent implanted in their dioceses standards of religious observance, of morals, of education and charity that were already producing creditable results. The missions were bringing back by degrees to the countryside—where their work was not hindered by war and famine—the knowledge and practice of the faith. But France was not great enough for Monsieur Vincent's charity and zeal; his country's frontiers had to be crossed.

One day in the Lent of 1644 a Jesuit missionary home from Canada arrived at the court of Anne of Austria. The story of Isaac Jogues was already well known. A native of Orléans, he went to New France in 1638 and proceeded up the St Lawrence to the Huron tribes and later to the French settlement at Quebec. Ambushed by bands of Iroquois braves, his finger nails and hair were torn out and some of his finger-joints gnawed off. On the very day the late King Louis had been having the Feast of the Assumption celebrated with such fervour in Paris, Père Jogues and his companions were being beaten with cudgels and scourged with thorn bushes by their captors. After a fearful imprisonment the Father finally escaped, made his way to a Dutch settlement, and was smuggled to Europe by the Huguenot Captain of a Dutch trading ship. When the porter of the Jesuit house in Rennes opened the door on a January morning in 1644 and saw an apparition in tatters, with filthy rags bandaging stumps of fingers, he called the Rector. 'There's a beggar here who says he is Isaac Jogues, the Father whom the Iroquois captured and killed last year.' Lazarus had indeed risen from the dead.

Père Jogues was going back again to his mission and martyrdom, but before leaving he came to Paris. The Queen wanted to see him. 'We read romances,' she said, 'knowing them to be but fiction. Here is adventure beyond anything the writers imagine.' When he stood before her, hiding as well as he could his mutilated hands, the grand-daughter of Philip II and the great-granddaughter of the Emperor Charles made a gesture worthy of the greatest of the Hapsburgs. She descended from her throne, weeping, and kissed the maimed fingers. She was one of those who wrote the Pope begging a special dispensation for Père Jogues to celebrate Mass despite his injured hands. The reply came: 'Certainly. It would be unjust to deprive a martyr of Christ of the happiness of partaking of the Sacred Body and Blood of the same Jesus Christ.'

Vincent de Paul was just then working on the rules he was drawing up for his own priests, rules based mainly on those of the Jesuits. He had so great an admiration for St Ignatius of Loyola that he often quoted maxims and told anecdotes of that saint. He would have met Père Jogues through the Queen or through some of his Jesuit friends in Paris. Already he had Vincentians working in Italy. Soon, when one of the Ladies of Charity became Queen Marie-Louise of Poland, he would send priests from Saint-Lazare and Daughters of Charity to Warsaw. But he had seen a martyr from a pagan land and the thought of the countries where martyrs were made, the lands in which the Gospel had never been preached and those other nations whose faith was being stamped out in a welter of blood, was constantly in his mind.

A year after Père Jogues's visit to the French court Vincent was requested by the Sacred Congregation, *de Propaganda Fide*, in Rome, to send missionaries to Ireland. He already had some Irishmen in his Congregation and at the end of 1646 five Irish, three French and one English Vincentian set sail from Nantes, reaching Ireland early in the new year after a stormy voyage. Half of the group went to the Archbishop in Cashel and half to Limerick. It was a time of hope in Ireland. The Papal Nuncio, Rinuccini, had come to that downtrodden land in 1645 bringing money from the Pope and from Mazarin. In the summer of 1646 the leader of the Irish forces, Owen Roe O'Neill, had routed an English-Scottish army at Benburb. King Charles of England, defeated in his final battle against Cromwell's Roundheads, was a prisoner of the Scots. In the dreary February when the Vincentians were reporting their arrival to two Irish bishops, thirty-six carts of gold coin, the price of the head of a Stuart, were trundling from London to the Scottish border where the King of England was handed over to his enemies. Until August, 1648, the Vincentians worked in the counties of Limerick and Tipperary. Then the French Fathers returned to Paris, bearing letters for Vincent from the two Irish bishops in whose dioceses they had worked. All the Irish Fathers remained in Ireland, except Father Dermot Duggan whom Vincent wanted back to prepare a band of missionaries for the Hebrides.

The letters of the Irish bishops should have rejoiced Monsieur Vincent. Bishop Dwyer of Limerick thanked him from his heart and assured him that the Fathers had done great good. Through their example and good conduct the Catholic gentry, then few indeed, had become 'models of virtue and piety which was by no means the case before your missionaries came'. The political troubles and the armies had hindered the work of the Vincentians somewhat, but at a mission in Limerick no less than twenty thousand had received Holy Communion. Drunkenness, swearing, adultery, and other disorders had vanished. 'The whole face of this city has been changed, indeed. Our cathedral was full each time the Fathers preached or gave instructions or conducted the other mission exercises. . . . I myself owe the salvation of my soul to your sons, Father, and I beg you to write a few consoling words to them.' The Archbishop of Cashel, Thomas Walsh, wrote in similar terms. Both of these Bishops were later to be exiled for the faith and Bishop Walsh did a term in prison.

In January, 1649, the English King was beheaded and in September of that year Oliver Cromwell arrived in Ireland to leave blood and terror in the wake of his army everywhere. 'I meddle not with any man's conscience,' he declared, 'but as for liberty to exercise the Mass . . . that will not be allowed.' Limerick and Tipperary were not spared, the Mayor of Limerick, who had led the citizens earlier that year to the mission given by the Vincentians and who had placed the keys of the city in the hands of the statue of Our Lady, being executed with three of the City Fathers. In Limerick, too, Monsieur Vincent got his first martyr when Brother Thady Lee was butchered before his mother's eyes. The Cromwellians cut off his hands and feet and crushed his head to pulp. Monsieur Vincent himself gave these details in a postscript to the following letter to a Father then in Poland:

We have just got news of our dear confèrres in Ireland. We were sure they were among those killed when the English took Limerick, but thank God, Who saved them from their hands. It is certain that as far as Father Barry is concerned he has arrived at Nantes and we are expecting him here. We hope, too, that Father Brin [Bryan] has escaped, though of that we are not certain. They left Limerick together in the company of five or six score priests and religious, all disguised and mixed up through the soldiers of the city who left that city the day their enemies were to enter. Our brethren passed the night preparing for death, because ecclesiastics were given no quarter, but God did not permit that they should be recognized for what they were. After leaving Limerick, they separated, not without great sorrow, and took different roads. They thought that it was best to act thus, so that if one perished the other at least would be in a position to save himself.

Father Brin then followed the road to his native place, having with him the Vicar-General of Cashel, who has been a good friend to them, while Father Barry made for some mountains which he names.* He chanced to meet a charitable lady who sheltered him for two months at the end of which, luckily, a ship arrived from France. He boarded her without having heard any news of Father Brin. He thinks it will be difficult for him to get back to France because the English are on the sea, and also in his [Father Bryan's] native place. So he has need of prayers. 6

Father Bryan did get back eventually, the Duchess of Aiguillon defraying some of his expenses. A third Vincentian remained in Ireland, one of several fugitive priests who lived and died in hiding, a price on their heads. Father Duggan and a Father White and others had meanwhile gone, via Holland, to the Hebrides. Compton Mackenzie, in *Catholicism and Scotland*, says:

> The labours of Father Duggan to establish the Faith in the outer Islands lasted for five years, by the end of which time the people from Benbecula to Barra Head were safe under God against the basest ingenuity of men. . . . St Vincent's response to the appeal of Propaganda for missionary help entitled him to be called the Apostle of the Hebrides.

A Scot, Father Lumsden, worked in his native Highlands and moved on later to the distant Orkney Islands. Father White, a Limerick man, was arrested in the Marquis of Huntly's castle in 1655 and held in Aberdeen. Vincent was in a dilemma. If he

---

* Probably the Knockmealdown Mountains or the Galtees, the names of which, written in the seventeenth century Gaelic script, would have stumped Paris scholars more erudite than Monsieur Vincent!

wrote and asked for his release it was tantamount to admitting that Father White was a priest. Besides, he had been told that political relations between England and France were 'embroiled' at the moment. He decided to wait and pray, a policy which brought him the usual good results for the Father was released six months later. The missionaries in the islands suffered great hardship, living on one meal a day of barley or oaten farls with cheese or salted butter. They had to walk long distances 'four or five leagues on foot, on very bad roads', often in snow and rain, to say Mass.

> Sometimes we go whole days without food, especially when in waste and mountainy country where nobody lives and where we cannot get anything. As for meat we hardly ever eat it. Still it can be got in some places far from the sea in the houses of the gentry. But it is so bad and served in so dirty a manner that it revolts our stomachs. They throw it on the ground on a little straw, which serves for table, chair, table-linen, dish and plates. To buy some for ourselves, so that we might cook and serve it in the French way, we cannot, as there is no butcher in these islands and it is not sold in pieces. We would have to buy the entire sheep or bullock. . . .
>
> Those sent here should know how to speak the language well, and know better how to bear hunger, thirst and sleeping on the ground.

Most of these Fathers managed to survive, moving about between the Highlands and the islands, until one by one each died alone at his post. Father White, whom the boatmen loved, was the last to bid the Catholics of the Highlands and the islands farewell:

> West of these out to seas colder than the Hebrides
>   I must go
> Where the fleet of stars is anchored and the young
>   Star-captains glow.

Before Louis XIII died he asked Vincent to send priests to the assistance of Christian captives in Barbary and gave him ten thousand *livres* for this purpose. The Duchess of Aiguillon, when she established a Vincentian foundation in Marseilles some months after her uncle's death, stipulated that the Fathers should eventually go to Barbary to do what they could for the Christian slaves there. Monsieur Vincent had never forgotten his own experiences during his two years as a slave in Tunis. Yet, he had been fortunate in having had for most of the time a humane and kindly master from whom he had learned much and for the remainder of his captivity a compatriot who was neither unjust nor cruel. Practically the entire north African coast was ruled by the Turks. French Consuls in Tunis and Algiers represented most of the European countries and acted as ambassadors to the Sultan in Constantinople. But pirates were still as active on the Mediterranean as when Vincent had fallen into their hands in 1604. Ships were rammed, southern European coasts raided, and the prisoners taken sold in the marts of Algiers and Tunis, the Deys of these cities being the men who profited most. In 1645 Vincent sent a Père Guerin as chaplain to the French Consul at Tunis. He had a most engaging manner and the Dey allowed him to visit the slaves, speak to them and do what he could to comfort them. Later on he said Mass and heard their Confessions. The venture promised so well that Vincent sent an assistant, a young Vincentian, Jean Le Vacher, with similarly charming manners and a flair for organizing.

Back in Saint-Lazare, Vincent, a still more wonderful organizer, got a private and free postal service established between the slaves—there were more than thirty thousand of them in Africa at that time—and their families. People in any part of France where the Vincentians were could write or send money to their relatives by giving it to a priest of the Mission. The Father sent their messages to Saint-Lazare where Vincent himself saw to the sorting and addressing. The mailbag went on to Marseilles where a banking firm arranged for the money that was to go with letters for slaves in Algiers and Tunis and for the unfortunates on the galleys based at Mediterranean ports. Some of the postal lists still preserved show that Vincent managed to

redeem several prisoners; indeed the stories of particularly harrowing cases being sent daily by the Fathers made it hard to
decide which slave was in worst need of ransom. In fifteen years
he collected ransom money to the tune of a million and a quarter
livres and redeemed some twelve hundred captives.

But what was twelve hundred? One in twenty-five! Monsieur Vincent, his bad leg giving him a little more trouble, his
fever and his terrible headaches recurring a little oftener each
year, sighed as the letters from Tunis and Algiers came. 'How I
wish I were where you are,' he wrote to one of the Fathers.
'How happy I would be.' Jean Le Vacher was a man after his
own heart and when the Superior in Marseilles tried to delay his
departure for Barbary on account of his youth Vincent wrote,
'If he's too weak to walk to the ship, see that he's carried there.
And if during the crossing the sea air proves too much for him,
why, have him thrown overboard.'*

The Duchess of Aiguillon, very like her uncle in some ways,
suggested that a long-term policy was the only way to end the
horrors awaiting French slaves in North Africa. The Mediterranean would have to be cleared of pirates, thus cutting off the
supply of future slaves. When the sea was safe an expeditionary
force could be sent to shell Algiers and Tunis. These places
would then either fall to France or, in parleys with the Deys,
great numbers of Christians might be ransomed. Monsieur
Vincent, usually so peace-loving, was all for the proposal and
encouraged the good lady when she began negotiating with the
Duc de Beaufort in hopes that he would lead the expedition. But
Beaufort got cold feet and Vincent himself found a leader one
day in Mazarin's rooms, a captain with the good name of Paul.
He was Lieutenant-General of the Knights of Malta, a post he
had risen to by sheer merit and bravery in an adventurous career,
mostly in the French navy. Vincent, then in his middle seventies,
did not stop to deliberate about this enterprise. Slaves died daily

---

* Vincent de Paul was correct in his estimate of the worth of Jean Le Vacher.
In 1683, having refused to 'wear the turban', the sign of apostasy, Le Vacher was
bound to a cannon mouth by the Turks and his body shot into the Mediterranean.

and good captains were scarce. In a trice he secured agreements signed by young Louis XIV and Mazarin, found thirty thousand *livres* and sent it to Marseilles, got the Ladies of Charity and the Queen to a conference on the matter, wrote letter after letter. With all this, for him, unusual haste and impetuosity, he did not fail to keep his business head. The Fathers in Marseilles were to make sure that Captain Paul would be paid when he freed the prisoners, no sooner. And though they had thirty thousand *livres* for the purpose, they were to offer him twenty, to allow for bargaining and in case he had to make a second coast-to-coast run. This enterprise was to take up Vincent's attention to the end of his days. It was as well that he died before the Captain and the squadrons set out on what was to prove a complete fiasco.[7]

From 1644 on, Monsieur Vincent used to tell his priests that their field of work was 'all the inhabited parts of the earth'. He considered sending missionaries to Quebec, to the Indies, to Indo-China, to Persia. Lack of support and lack of sufficient mission personnel did not permit him to realize his desire to establish houses in these places. Eventually, he was asked by *Propaganda Fide* to send missionaries to the French island of Madagascar. The natives there practised a religion that was a compound of Judaism, Mohammedanism and devil-worship. They also worshipped their ancestors, obeyed Mohammed as to the number of wives they might take, and were circumcised like the Jews. The first Vincentian to go out, a great-hearted man named Nacquart, found the aborigines tractable and gentle, with the mentality of children. By contrast, he found the French colonists covetous and dissolute. The situation was practically the same as that which St Francis Xavier had encountered in the Portuguese colony of Goa a century before. Just when he had taken stock of things and reported back to Vincent in Paris, detailing his need of priests, Sisters, Brothers and money for churches, schools, a hospital and a seminary, Nacquart fell ill and died. Others made the long and terrible sea journey to take his place, but the devils worshipped in Madagascar seemed intent on destroying the Mission there. Storms and shipwrecks, the climate, and the succession of misfortunes that befell Vincent's men in the island, caused a few prudent spirits in Saint-Lazare, who thought too much was being lost and nothing gained, to murmur. Fearing that after his death some might be tempted to abandon this, the first mission to the heathen, Vincent spoke of it to the Community in one of the last Conferences he gave them:

> Some of our Fathers may say that we should give up Madagascar. They will argue that no one else should be sent there. But that is the language of flesh and blood, not of the soul. What! Will we leave our good Monsieur B. out there holding the fort alone? . . . . God led six thousand men out of Egypt, not counting women and children, to bring them into the Promised Land. Yet of all this vast multitude only two, and not even the leader, Moses, arrived there. God has called our brethren to that country and yet some died on the way and others just after they landed. . . .
>
> Will we be so weak as to leave the Lord's vineyard, the vineyard to which he called us, simply because five or six have died? I ask you what kind of army it would be which at the loss of one or two or even five thousand—as they say fell in the recent siege in Normandy—surrenders at once? A fine army, indeed; an army of chicken-livered, panic-stricken soldiers. . . . What a fine lot we are if now on account of these few deaths we give up God's work! A lot of cowards, religious attached only to flesh and blood. . . . [8]

All around him his friends were dying. Mère de Chantal and Père Condren died in 1641, several of the Vincentians and Daughters of Charity during the various plagues. Saint-Cyran had followed the King and Richelieu. The Marquise de Maignelay would visit the prisons no more. But Mère Angélique was still active at Port-Royal. When the Papal Bull condemning the Five Propositions of the Jansenists was published in 1653 Vincent called upon her. He went neither to sympathize with her nor to crow over the decision given against her party but simply on a visit of courtesy to a nun who had generously helped his Charities and exerted her influence in the cause of reform. He frequently called upon other avowed Jansenists, 'persons of condition', and quietly urged them to submit to the ruling of the Holy See. Had he lived longer he could have strengthened his appeals by pointing to noted followers of Saint-Cyran and the Arnaulds who retracted their errors. Not many years after Vincent's death Thomassin, the celebrated orator, made public submission, generously including in his retraction all whom his eloquence might have led towards Jansenism.

As he bade farewell to Mère Angélique and turned his white horse away from Port-Royal and the scent of Mr Jenkins's roses, Vincent had food for thought. The preacher who said that 'the nuns at Port-Royal were as pure as angels and as proud as demons', had been lacking in charity. Monsieur Vincent abhorred such hurtful words. Jogging along the quays on the left bank and across the Pont Neuf and past the palace that would never again know the footfall of Cardinal Richelieu or the whisper of his silken robes, Vincent de Paul pondered on Port-Royal, on the dead Cardinal, on Paris, on his missionaries scattered north, south, east and west, on life that passed quicker than the Seine in spate. 'O, Saviour!' he sighed. 'May we know the Will of God and do it. May we spend ourselves doing all things to please God. May we keep to that wonderful path—the golden mean—in all things, even in virtue.'

Chapter Thirteen

THE END IS CHARITY

AFTER A series of victories won by French generals the Thirty Years' War ended in 1648. Immediately the civil war known as the Fronde broke out in Paris. On August 26th, when the Queen-Regent, Anne of Austria, accompanied by Mazarin and the court, went to Notre Dame for the Mass of Thanksgiving, rioting on a large scale broke out in the city. Monsieur Vincent's friend, Jean-François Paul de Gondi, then Coadjutor Bishop of Paris, was, as usual, in the midst of the mobs. He rushed out of the Cathedral in full pontificals and was carried shoulder high by the people; thanks to the months he had spent accompanying his good aunt on her visits to the poor he was able to hail several by name. Within a few hours barricades were flung up all over Paris. That night bonfires were lit along the quays and citizens sat around them bawling scurrilous *Mazarinades* about the Queen and the Cardinal. The 'water-men', all those to whom the river assured a livelihood, marched on the Palais-Royal and pelted the Queen's Swiss Guard with filth, stones and offal. Monsieur le Coadjutor, 'wrapped in a Spanish cloak, flitted about from group to group'. But inside the palace there was no comedy. Queen Anne, her Spanish ideas of the respect due to royalty outraged, her Hapsburg blood on the boil, refused to parley with the leaders of the riots or to listen to reason, whether proffered by her ladies, the Guard Captains, State officials or Mazarin.

For three days the city was in an uproar. Every street was blocked, some by barricades twenty feet high. Shops were shuttered and business at a standstill. A week later Vincent de Paul wrote to Mademoiselle Le Gras:

Blessed be God, Mademoiselle, for the care he has shown your dear Daughters, and for His solicitude for me, also, in these riots. Here we all are, by God's grace safe and sound, Our Lord not considering us worthy to suffer anything for Him in the clash.

As for that other matter, be assured that there was nothing which I thought I ought to have said, that I did not say, thank God. I mentioned everything. Unhappily, God did not bless my words, although I believe that what they are saying about the person to whom you know I am referring is false. . . .

I will try to say a word to the Comte de Maure, but I fear I may make a botch of things. . . .

I am glad of the news from the Charities. O, how mortified I feel at not being able to visit them. . . .[1]

This rather mysterious letter has been thought to refer to a visit Vincent made to the Queen to ask her to be more circumspect. Her friendship with Mazarin gave rise to gossip and the rumour spread, helped on its way by the disaffected, that she and the Cardinal had been secretly married by her confessor, Monsieur Vincent. Paris talked of nothing else and a Brother in Saint-Lazare ventured to ask Vincent outright if the rumour were true. He got a short but forceful reply: 'It's as false as the very devil.' The Cardinal, not being a priest, was not bound to celibacy but he would have needed to get a dispensation from the Pope, Innocent X, who had little love for him.

The Comte de Maure was a relative of Mademoiselle Le Gras and was taking an active part in the rebellion. Louise, with memories of her uncle's execution still vivid in her mind, had evidently asked Vincent to advise him. Monsieur Vincent's mortification at being unable to visit the Charities was caused by illness, not by the barricades. *Lives* of Anne of Austria record that on September 13th she visited 'her beloved friends, the nuns in the Val de Grace, and also her confessor, ill in Saint-Lazare'.

After a lull of some weeks there were further riots. The Parliament, the Princes of the Blood, and the great nobles, champing on the bridles Richelieu had put on their respective powers and fuming at their inability to dislodge Mazarin from his position as the ruler behind the ruler, kept the populace in a continuous state of unrest. Though the people, the nobles, the Princes, and the Parliament were at loggerheads on a hundred issues they were all united in their hatred of the Cardinal, a hatred which explains the bitter ferocity of the Fronde. The Christmas of 1648 and the New Year of 1649 was intensely cold and at three o'clock on the morning of January 6th the Queen-Regent, her two sons, Mazarin and the nearest of the royal relatives drove silently to the palace of Saint-Germain-en-Laye, then about six leagues west of the city. Like other rulers before and since their time they believed that to dominate Paris one must first leave it. The Queen summoned troops to post about her forest and palace at Saint-Germain. The people of Paris, persuaded that the army was going to march on the city, flew to arms. De Gondi, who dearly loved a fight, raised eight companies, levies which—despite the verse of a Psalm included in their emblem—came in for a drubbing in their first encounter with royal troops on one of the bridges. For the next four years there was chaos. The King left Paris four times and returned three times. When the first outburst, instigated by Parliament, died down, the Princes' Fronde began. The civil war spread to the provinces, and the poor in town and country suffered atrociously.

Part of Mazarin's plan when moving to Saint-Germain was to starve out the city. Saint-Lazare, with its huge granaries where the wheat Vincent had bought and collected for despatch to the famine areas was stored, was endangered. A military escort had to be asked for when grain was being sent to any of the city Charities, to the Hôtel-Dieu, to Bicêtre, or to the provinces. The first months of 1649 were extremely cold, yet Vincent was out and about. The week after the Queen left Paris he decided to see if he could do anything to secure peace. Before daybreak on January 14th he set off on horseback, accompanied by a Brother, and made for Saint-Germain, going by Clichy, his first parish. Soldiers on guard there dashed out with pikes and guns to hold up the two riders, and if one of the 'good people of Clichy' had not recognized his former curé Vincent de Paul might have ended his days there and then. At Neuilly the Seine was in flood, but he forced the white horse across. At Saint-Germain he saw his penitent, Queen Anne, and told her plainly that the citizens of Paris faced terrible misery and that her duty was to dismiss Mazarin. From her rooms he went to those of the Cardinal-Minister and said, 'Submit to the present dreadful state of affairs. Throw yourself into the sea to calm the storm.' Mazarin, amazed at such temerity, said that he would wait to get the Council's opinion. When he had conferred with such members of the Council of State as were in Saint-Germain he told Vincent that he was unable to do as he asked. Vincent blamed himself for having spoken too severely to the Queen. The following day he remarked to a friend:

> I have never, never in all my life, succeeded when I spoke with the faintest trace of harshness or asperity. I have always noted that if one wishes to move another's mind one must be ever so careful not to embitter that person's heart.

He stayed for four days and was given a safe-conduct and an escort. But he did not at once return to the capital, though his thoughts were there in the flooded streets around the Tuileries where the bridge had been carried away and many families were homeless when their houses, undermined by the swirling waters, collapsed. No one knew better than Monsieur Vincent that Monsieur le Coadjutor was at the heart of the risings. While he was at Saint-Germain a standard-bearer of de Gondi's regiment had been taken prisoner. The very mention of de Gondi was anathema to the overwrought Queen and she gave an order that the man was to be executed. That evening the Coadjutor sent a trumpeter to say that if his standard-bearer was beheaded he would behead the prisoners from the Queen's regiments whom he held in Paris. Small wonder that Monsieur Vincent, the moment he got out of sight of Saint-Germain, galloped to Villepreux, where his old friend, Père de Gondi, the General of the Galleys who had become an Oratorian, was then living. Perhaps *he* could help to bring his volatile son, the Coadjutor, to some sense of his responsibilities. There was another reason why it was wiser to remain out of Paris for the time being. The rumour that Vincent had secretly married the Queen and Mazarin was then very strong, and as it was known he had ridden to Saint-Germain, if he returned without peace terms there was every likelihood, in the humour the citizens then were, that Monsieur Vincent would be made the scapegoat for the sins of all parties.

He stayed a week in Villepreux and was spared the ordeal the community at Saint-Lazare suffered when six hundred soldiers billeted on them sacked and pillaged the place. The woodpile was burned down, the flour and corn carried down to the city markets and sold at fancy prices. Even the keys were taken away. Vincent was on his way to Le Mans to visit a house of the Congregation there when he got the news. While he wondered if he should wait at Frenéville until more news came through, snowstorms decided the issue. It also gave him the opportunity to celebrate Candlemas as Monsieur Bourdoise would like to have seen it celebrated in every church in France, and to give a sermon 'on the best means to calm the anger of God and on the way to behave in the midst of the ruin and menaces caused by the civil war'.

He wrote to Jacques Norais, who was part-owner of some of the Saint-Lazare lands:

Mon Dieu, Sir, how distressed I am . . . at the loss you have sustained in the pillaging of your house. The losses we ourselves have had and may yet suffer are, Sir, I assure you, nothing in comparison to yours. We by our sins have deserved these losses. But you, Sir, what have you and our good lady, your wife, done that Our Lord should have added so

heavy a cross to that of her long and painful illness? He
has visited you both, in your children, in your goods,
and through this prolonged and trying malady . . . .
Really, I have no words to say to you, only those He
himself said to Job whom He afflicted in a similar triple
fashion . . . .[2]

He continues to write at length to console this sorely tried
couple, making no further mention of his own losses. He was
snowed in for a whole month at Frenéville. At least he was given
the consolation of taking up once more the task of shepherding.
A quick-thinking Vincentian had driven off a flock of two hundred and fifty sheep and two horses from Saint-Lazare when the
pillaging began and managed to get them to Frenéville. Vincent
now drove them before him on the road to Orléans. Then he set
off to visit the houses of the Mission in the northwestern provinces. Things were bad in Saint-Lazare. The wheat was gone.
They were deprived of their main source of income, the tolls
paid by the coaches passing out the road to Saint-Denis. Vincent
sent back instructions that priests and brothers were to be sent to
other houses of the Congregation. The fewer Vincentians the more
to spare for the poor who still kept coming to Saint-Lazare to
the tune of two to three thousand a day. In his letters to the
Daughters of Charity he hardly mentions the war, save in the
most general terms, but he thanks them from his heart for a piece
of black bread and a few apples.

Sixteen hundred and forty-nine was only the beginning of the
conflict. The first rounds were between the Queen and a Parliament
that had seen an English Parliament filch the sovereign's authority
while in France the monarchy was moving on to absolute power.
After six months the Parliament and the Queen-Regent made peace,
a peace of short duration. Then the younger nobles, led by Louis of
Bourbon, the Prince of Condé, who had been on the Queen's side
up to then, formed a confederacy. Condé, despite his royal blood,
was imprisoned. Other princes and nobles raised troops and
tried to drive out Mazarin. Twice the Cardinal was compelled to

flee the country. Twice Vincent de Paul approached him on behalf of the unfortunate people. On the first occasion he begged him to leave France so that the Queen-Regent and the Parliament might come to some agreement. On the second, when the Fronde was ending, he begged the Cardinal not to avenge himself on those who had opposed him during the four-year conflict and not to inflame public opinion by driving with the King and his mother when they made their triumphal entry into the capital. If he had no great hopes of obtaining what he asked, at least he satisfied his conscience as he had previously done when he approached Richelieu on a similar errand. He wrote a sorrowful letter to Pope Innocent X, setting before His Holiness 'the lamentable state of France':

The Royal Family, torn by dissensions. The people, split into factions. The cities and provinces, torn by civil war. The villages, hamlets and country towns burned and in ruins. Poor farmers unable to reap what they have sown or to sow for the following year. Soldiers delivering themselves up freely to the worst excesses. The people, suffering rape and brigandage, yea, and murder and frightful tortures. The country people, those who have not perished by the sword, dying of hunger. Their priests treated with cruelty and inhumanity, put to torture and death. Maidens dishonoured and nuns suffering likewise from the licentiousness and rage of those under arms. Churches are profaned, plundered and destroyed. Those still standing have been abandoned by their priests and the people are deprived of the Sacraments, Mass and all spiritual aid. Worst of all, and too horrible to mention, the Most Blessed Sacrament is often profaned. Even Catholics rob the sacred vessels, throw the Blessed Eucharist on the ground and trample It underfoot. [3]

Having done what he felt to be his duty Vincent de Paul turned his attention to relieving the sufferings caused by the war and doing what he could to right the abuses. It was at this time that Mazarin, annoyed at Vincent's suggestion that he should not enter the capital with the young King and Queen Anne, dismissed him from the Council of Conscience. Saint-Lazare was in a sad condition compared to what it had been. Across the Seine in Port-Royal things were even worse. Mère Angélique's cornfields had been ruined and her horses all commandeered in the early days of the Fronde. The nuns lived for a while on peas and milk. The poor people all around, to save the little they had from the soldiers, brought their poultry and goats and cows, their beans and wheat, their kettles and pans into the Abbey. Once there were forty cows, with their owners and their owners' families, all shut up in the cellar for safety. The barns were full of cripples. Refugee nuns, fleeing before the troops, crowded in from country districts and Port-Royal managed to take in three hundred of them. Black bread and cabbage water was considered a good dinner. Plague followed, claiming ten thousand a week in Paris alone. Writing to one of Vincent's Ladies of Charity who had become Queen of Poland, Mère Angélique said that the barbarity of the soldiers exceeded that of the Turks: 'It seems as though they are all possessed by the devil.' She wrote in 1652 during the final phase of the senseless conflict. Vincent was at the same time asking for prayer and penance and urging all who had any influence to request a public procession of the reliquary of St Geneviève, an act of devotion to the city's patroness always resorted to in times of public calamity. Not since the great drought of 1625 had such a procession taken place. Vincent had been present then and remembered the ancient ceremonial associated with the function. The provost and the city Fathers marched first to Notre Dame, to the Parliament, and to the abbé of Saint-Geneviève to obtain permission to take out the relics. The monks at Saint-Geneviève fasted for three days before the procession, which went from Saint-Geneviève's to Notre Dame, and thence to the Hôtel-Dieu, the Petit Pont, and the churches of the Franciscans and the Carmelites before returning to the starting point. The Parliament turned up in full strength, 'in their red robes and square hats', the 'porters of Saint-Geneviève' carried the magnificent enamelled reliquary containing the relics of the

Saint, and everything was done with decorum and piety.* Though Vincent gave a sermon on this procession to clergy at the Tuesday Conferences in June, 1652, there is no record that such a public act of penitence and devotion was renewed that year.

The Fronde was over, but at what a cost to Paris and to France, and at what a cost to those who had been working for reform. Vincent de Paul was in his seventy-third year. Much of his good work had been undone and he had to begin it all over again. The influx of over one hundred thousand beggars into the capital, the complete breakdown in morals, the bitterness and rancour that divided families high and low, all the legacy of civil war, had to be faced. Time was running out for Monsieur Vincent, and the night in which no man works was closing in. The Duchess of Aiguillon, noticing that he had difficulty in mounting his horse or in limping along sidestreets, insisted on his using a carriage and pair she gave him. He accepted it because he had to, but he used to call it 'my shame'. During the Paris heat wave of May, 1653, hearing that Monsieur Vincent was off to give a mission at Sevran, the Duchess wrote to the Vincentians at Saint-Lazare:

> I am more than amazed that Monsieur Portail and the other good Fathers of Saint-Lazare should allow Monsieur Vincent to go and work in the country in sweltering weather like the present. A man of his age having to spend such long periods out of doors under the sun! It seems to me that his life is too precious and too useful to the Church and the Vincentians to squander it in this fashion. Fathers, allow me to beseech you to stop him from throwing away his life like this. And pardon me for saying to you that are obliged in conscience to do as I request. People are complaining a lot that you have so little

---

* The shrine of St Geneviève is in the beautiful little church of St Étienne du Mont, behind the Panthéon. On the wall opposite the reliquary is a plaque recording how the city was saved in World War I when the German armies were nearing Paris 'and the citizens invoked their ancient patroness who, fifteen centuries previously, by her intercession saved Paris from Attila and his Huns'. The people flocked to the shrine and prayed for three days there, and on the third day the German armies moved back from the Marne.

care of his health. I have heard it said that you are unaware of the treasure God has given you and that only his death will make you realize his worth. I would be no friend of the Fathers if I did not tell them this. [4]

Antoine Portail forwarded the Duchess's letter to Vincent who wrote to her from Sevran:

> . . . . I am going back to Sevran to continue giving the mission, as was announced to the people . . . I doubt that I will be able to leave on Wednesday for the meeting. I beg you, Madame, to please apologize to the members for my absence. I feel that if I did not do all I could for these poor people of the countryside in this Jubilee Year I would offend God . . . . I am going to buy two ells of scarlet cloth to send the Fathers in Tunis as presents for the Dey and the Pasha there. . . . It seems that the sending of missionaries to the Indies is going ahead little by little. At the last meeting concerning this your charity was highly praised . . . . [5]

Despite the heat he finished his mission and returned to Paris. There the vast building projects initiated by Richelieu and abandoned because of wars abroad and at home were being completed. The Sorbonne, with its great domed church, had been rebuilt. Roads had been driven and gardens planted on the right bank so that the hitherto congested districts north of the river had a 'lung' reaching all the way from the Seine to Montmartre. Richelieu was before his time in providing an overcrowded capital with fresh air. His mind was on the future when he gave orders to have the Bois de Boulogne, the plain of Clichy and the Bois de Vincennes laid out and thrown open to the people.

The Saint-Denis Quarter, south of Saint-Lazare, was just beyond the old Halles, or markets, the universal stores of the city. 'There you can find ready to your hand whatsoever you need to support life and to clothe the body: victuals, clothing and furniture of all kinds, and everything dirt cheap.' There, too, stood the pillory 'on which, for three hours *per diem*, for three successive market days, debtors, defrauders, bankrupts and other persons of that ilk were exposed. Every half hour they spun around on the pillory, their heads clamped fast between two blocks of wood, while the crowds doing the rounds of the market stalls jeered at them.'

The Paris of the last seven years of Monsieur Vincent's life (1653-1660) was more crowded than ever. Constant streams of refugees from the war-devastated and famine areas in the north and east, and hordes of destitute people from the various places ruined during the Fronde, succeeded in making their way to the capital. These were wandering about living on charity or by thieving. Already Vincent had set up a home for the aged. Mademoiselle Le Gras, whose genius for organization was equal to that of Vincent, thought that the way to keep the old people happy was to supply them with some extra comforts, comforts that were best provided by including among those admitted some capable of teaching others trades or crafts. She had a silk-weaver, a cloth-weaver, shoemakers and cobblers, glove-makers, lace-makers, seamstresses and button and pin makers. So successful was the venture that Monsieur Vincent was able by 1654 to tell the generous donor who had given 100,000 *livres* to start it that it was self-supporting. This establishment was called the Hospice of the Name of Jesus and was quite near Saint-Lazare. Vincent visited it frequently, instructing the old folk and chatting with them about the days when he and they were young. No matter how many requests for admission he received he would not admit more than forty. Forty was as many as could be looked after there, he maintained. Better have forty happy old people than fifty who were all unhappy.

Boys and youths who would today be classified as mentally deficient were received at Saint-Lazare where Vincent had a special building set apart for them. He called them 'our boarders' and devoted much of his time to them. His method of dealing with them was simple: he loved them and showed that he had a real interest in them. Once he discovered that they were being given badly cooked and carelessly served food, and that leavings

223

of dinner on one evening were served up the next. He was extremely angry with those responsible:

> The parents of these lads pay us well for their keep and it is wrong and unjust to give them badly prepared food. In God's name, my brethren, do not let such a thing happen again, but serve them what is served to ourselves. It is an injustice to them, poor fellows, many of them detained here though they have done no wrong and unable to see you to complain. I assure you it is wrong.
>
> If you acted in that manner to a Vincentian, to me or to any other of our Congregation, we would be able to require you to deal fairly with us and to treat us all alike. But these poor creatures, unable to ask anything from you, do not even see you who are in charge of the cooking and the meals. Not to give them their due of your own accord is a very grave sin. . . . It is indeed matter for Confession. [6]

Mazarin, whose motto was *Time and I*, had come back to Paris. Monsieur le Coadjutor had been clapped into jail, in the hopes of preventing him taking possession of the Archdiocese when his uncle, then on the point of death, died. But de Gondi had foreseen Mazarin's move and had provided for all contingencies. He became Archbishop of Paris in 1653, and as he was reported to be still plotting, Mazarin had him transferred from the Paris prison to the Château of Nantes. One evening his valet plied the guards with 'as much brandy as they could drink', while he, always nimble and athletic, scaled a forty-foot wall and escaped. He rode wildly away until his mount fell and he himself broke a shoulder blade; then he continued in a wheelbarrow, sneezing under a pile of new-mown hay. After a triumphal progress through Spain, Majorca, Florence and Rome, Jean-François, by now the second Cardinal de Retz, arrived in Rome and stayed with the Vincentians. Mazarin was furious and ordered Monsieur Vincent's priests in Rome to close down their house and to return to France. Vincent had another meeting with the Cardinal-Minister. We have no account of what passed between them but the order to the Vincentians in Rome was countermanded. Cardinal de Retz was in Rome for the death of Innocent X and at the subsequent Papal Conclave voted for Cardinal Chigi who became Alexander VII. He returned to French territory, but Mazarin's spies found him, and he had to fly for his life. For the next five years he was a fugitive with a price on his head moving about between different cities in Switzerland, Germany and Holland, being unable to return to Paris until after Mazarin's death. Louis XIV and the Queen-Mother then insisted that he resign his Archbishopric, which he eventually did and, as has been related, turned his thoughts to repentance. It was unworthy of the young King to refuse Cardinal de Retz permission to visit his father, Père de Gondi, when the latter lay dying in the Oratory. The *Grande Monarque* was capable of very petty acts of revenge.

When Vincent de Paul was in his eightieth year, he wrote to the Cardinal, then in exile. The letter, which was probably dispatched through one of the Vincentian houses, began: 'My Lord Cardinal, I have reason to think that this is my last letter to you.' Monsieur Vincent felt the weight of the years, he said, and was suffering from an illness which might prove to be his last. He begged pardon if he had ever offended the Cardinal and assured him that if he had done so it was not with intent but unwittingly. He recommended the Congregation of the Mission, 'which you have founded, favoured and maintained', to His Eminence and assured him that while the Fathers would always pray for him and the house of Retz on earth, Vincent de Paul would never cease remembering both the one and the other in heaven—which he hoped to reach by the goodness of God.

On the very same day, January 9th, 1659, he wrote a similar letter to Père de Gondi:

My Lord,
    The state of failing health in which I find myself and a little fever I have, lead me, for fear of the worst, to take the precaution of kneeling in spirit before you. I beg you, my

Lord, to pardon me the displeasure I have given you by my uncouth ways, and to thank you most humbly for the charitable forbearance you have always shown me and the countless favours our little Congregation (and myself in particular) received from your kindness. Be assured, my Lord, that if God wills to continue giving me power to pray to Him, that I will use it in this life and the next, both for your dear self and for those who are yours. Desiring to remain, in time and eternity, your servant in the Lord. [7]

But Monsieur Vincent was not to die in 1659. It was still a marvel to all how he did so much and did it so well. The magistrates of one town had written him: 'Up to the present, no one but you, Monsieur, and your priests, took compassion on our misery. For two years the province of Champagne, and this town of Rethel especially, have been kept alive solely by the relief you have sent us.' And the Lieutenant-General of Saint-Quentin wrote a similar letter, ending: 'My official position and the gratitude I feel obliges me to beg you to continue to be the Father of your Country and to save the lives of so many poor wretches dying of hunger and want whom your priests are so valiantly assisting.'

Aid for war orphans. Rehabilitation of those who had drifted into beggary and had to be won back into respectable employment. Despatch of spinning wheels, pots and pans, ploughs and milking pails to the provincial farmers slowly recovering from twenty lean years. Conferences to the Daughters of Charity. Retreats to the priests, to the ordinands, to laymen, to those whom he directed. Attendance at the meetings of the Charities and of the committee of Ladies in charge of the Hôtel-Dieu, and the Foundlings' Homes. Visits to the prisons and the *galériens*, to the children and the old people, to the sick and to the weak-minded, to the refugees, mostly priests and regiments of soldiers coming in from Ireland, unable to speak French, some of them getting into trouble in Paris. Writing out that recipe for fever, and instructions for making soup for eighty people. Writing letters to Mademoiselle Le Gras and to the Duchess of Aiguillon and to the Daughters of Charity scattered here, there and everywhere. And writing to his Vincentians, in so many places and with so many and such varying problems. 'O, Saviour!' he sighed, a thousand times a day. 'O, Saviour!' he wrote, oftener and oftener, in his letters.

His heart-warming care and his labour for all these persons and causes continued right up to the end, the indomitable old man driving his weary body until it could go no further. Early in 1658 an accident in the street caused him to fall and hit his head with violence against the pavement. The following winter the ulcers on his legs reopened and he was unable to move. It was then he wrote to Cardinal de Retz and his father. Mademoiselle Le Gras, ill herself, sent him syrups, broth, liquorice and ointments. The Duchess of Aiguillon came daily to inquire for him. A bishop sent him two hundred pills, with instructions as to when they were to be taken.

Antoine Portail died in February. 'He died as he lived,' wrote Vincent to a friend, 'holily.' Monsieur Vincent had been able to drag himself to his first companion's bedside. He knew that Père Portail feared death as he had once feared the thought of going into the pulpit. But at the end his fears vanished. In March Mademoiselle Le Gras died. He did not go to her death-bed, nor did he write her a last note. For fear of showing the grief he felt? Because he knew she was a strong and deeply interior soul, best left to God at the last? We do not know. In May a priest who had resigned several benefices to enter the Vincentians, died on his return journey from Rome. Vincent wept a little at the news. He had been looking forward to welcoming that good friend to the novitiate at Saint-Lazare.

On September 17th Vincent wrote to a Father at Marseilles wondering if anything was being done about besieging Algiers. 'There is a rumour current in Paris that Captain Paul has laid siege to Algiers, but with what result we do not know. For God's sake, Monsieur, send us some news.' It was just as well that Monsieur Vincent did not live to the end of the year when he would have heard that the commander, though he had sailed with a squadron for Algiers, was prevented by autumn gales from putting close enough to shell the city, and finally withdrew. As his contract stipulated that he was to draw the 20,000 *livres* when the city had fallen to him, not otherwise, he probably got nothing for his pains. Twenty-three years later another French admiral bombarded the town. The slaves, however, were no better treated than before, and the slave-running and piracy continued until, in 1830, France occupied the country.

Monsieur Vincent, people said, had been ailing off and on for the last few years. Even when he took a turn for the worse in the middle of September, 1660, they remembered how he had recovered from former illnesses. His constitution was still as sound as a russet apple. Everyone said that he would weather this setback too—everyone, that is, except Monsieur Vincent himself. He knew better. He smiled at the remedies sent by his well-wishers and remarked that he was eighty, beyond the age and the stage when tisanes and pills could cure. He thanked the great of Church and State who begged him to spare himself and heed his doctors' advice. He had sat by more dying people than all the medical men in Paris. He knew the approach of death too well to be mistaken now.

He could no longer celebrate Mass. The legs he had so mercilessly driven on errands of charity failed him. He was completely immobilized and suffered intensely from suppurating ulcers and from the treatment then in use for such a condition—blood-lettings, purges and sweatings. The raging fever he apologetically called his *fièvrette* seethed in his veins. Ill and feeble though he was, he would not allow himself the privilege of having Mass and Holy Communion in his room, but insisted on being carried to the Community chapel on a chair.

Someone brought a cushat dove caught in the woods near Paris. If the bird were cut and its wound held against Monsieur Vincent's temples while the hot blood pulsed out his fever would be cooled. It was an old cure. But the patient would not hear of it. Why hurt a living creature to ease an old man's aches, he asked. He and pain were no strangers; there was worse company than suffering. The shutters had to be unhasped and the pigeon released.

Some days before the end sleep suddenly swooped upon him, his body demanding payment of the accumulated arrears of rest so long and so stringently denied it.

'It is Brother Sleep,' he explained to those around him; 'soon the sister, Death, will come.'

On the last Sunday of September he heard his last Mass. At least he was bodily present, propped in his chair, but despite his efforts to keep awake, after receiving Holy Communion he slept heavily, his head drawn in between his hunched shoulders giving him the appearance of a bird trying to keep warm on a wintry day. Back in his room, his drowsiness was so great that the physician shook him to make sure that the venerable patient understood that he was to receive Extreme Unction that evening. When the hour of anointing came poor Monsieur Vincent was shaken again and again to arouse him from his stupor.

'Do you forgive all who ever offended you?' asked the priest who administered the Last Sacraments.

Slowly the response came: 'Nobody ever . . . nobody . . . ever. . . .' and Father Vincent dozed off. The priests present were in a quandary. It seemed heartless, cruel, to try to keep him awake, but their Founder would not wish them to let him receive Extreme Unction in this comatose state. So they did all they could to jolt him into consciousness, shaking him, giving him sneezing powders, and saying the prayers for the departing in loud, clear tones.

The shrunken old man, almost lost in the folds of his cassock, was dying as he did most things, slowly and well. During the night his blessing was asked for the great works he had established. For the Fathers of the Mission. For the Daughters of Charity. For the priests at the Tuesday Conferences. For the seminarians. For the orphans, the school-children, the sick in hospitals, the aged in homes. For the poor and afflicted and for all who had helped him to help them. For the missionaries gone to

Italy, Ireland, Poland, Madagascar, North Africa, the Hebrides, the Indies and to every province in France.

He had come a long way since those childhood days when he herded his father's pigs on their little farm in Ranquine. The man whose counsel kings and cardinals had sought, whose heart was open to every human woe, whose prodigious work for charity was changing the face of France, was still, at the core of his being, the shepherd lad concerned with simple elemental things like:

> The dreamy ways the herons go
> When all the hills are withered up
> Nor any waters flow.

His contemporary, Pascal, had written, 'Christ will be in agony until the end of the world.' Vincent de Paul, seeing Christ agonizing in every human being who suffered, had spent his life trying to assuage that agony. To him, loving the poor meant *loving* the poor—putting them first, and Monsieur Vincent with his likes and dislikes, his comfort and discomfort, completely out of the picture. Charity for him was much more than mere alms-giving. He gave himself; he gave unstintedly. He took time to know people personally, to call them by their Christian names. They were important, very important, to God, so they were very important and dear to him.

As he lay dying, his thoughts we may be sure went out to those who were always in his heart. Now and again he bestirred himself to utter the Holy Name or to apologize because those about him were losing their night's rest. Outside Saint-Lazare his work for *les misérables* of Paris went on. Other hands held his lantern over rubbish dumps or shone its beam into dark alleys searching for abandoned infants. Others visited the noisome prisons, the bedlams, the hospitals, the homes of the poor. Others prepared sermons for the new seminarians or for the clergy coming to Tuesday's Conference. But the spirit that animated his followers—priests, nuns, and lay helpers—was Monsieur Vincent's.

That good Gascon had neared the end of his road. No longer could he speak to proclaim what an unprofitable servant he had been, to apologize for allowing himself to be driven in a fine carriage, to bemoan the fact that he was being waited on hand and foot while the poor, *his* poor, Christ's poor . . . he had to get up and go to them. His last agony began at half-past four on Monday morning, September 27th, 1660. Well before dawn Vincent de Paul left Paris for ever.

NOTES

BIBLIOGRAPHY

INDEX

NOTES

ABBREVIATIONS

V. de P.=*Saint Vincent de Paul*: Correspondence, Entretiens, Documents. 15 vols., edited by P. Coste, C.M. (Paris, 1920-1960)
Abelly=*La vie du vénérable serviteur de Dieu, Vincent de Paul*, by Louis Abelly (Paris, 1664)

Chapter One

1. Cf.: Coste, Pierre, C.M., *Life and Labours of St. Vincent de Paul*, 3 vols. (English trans., London, 1934), vol. 1, pp. 2ff. Also Herrera, J., C.M., y Pardo, V., C.M., *S. Vicente de Paul: Biografía y Escritos* (Madrid, 1955), pp. 35ff.

2. Ménabréa, A., *St. Vincent de Paul: Le Maître des Hommes d'État* (Paris, 1944), pp. 17-18.

3. Abelly and the early biographers of St. Vincent gave 1576 as the year of his birth; the same date was engraved on his tomb. More recent biographers opt for 1580 or 1581, basing their date on the saint's own statements. When asked his age at a public enquiry in 1628, he replied, "about forty-eight." At the enquiry concerning Saint-Cyran in 1639 he stated that he was "fifty-nine or so."

4. Lahargou, P. *Trois siècles d'enseignement à Dax: le Collège de Dax* (Paris, 1909), p. 5.

5. Cf. note 3 above; also Coste, *op. cit.*, vol. I, pp. 21ff.; also Calvet, J., *Saint Vincent de Paul* (English trans., London, 1952), pp. 19-20; also Hanotaux, G., *Histoire du Cardinal de Richelieu*, 5 vols. (Paris, 1893), vol. I, pp. 83-84; also an article by Henri de l'Épinois, quoting a letter of Cardinal de Medici to Pope Clement VIII, dated 1597 when the Cardinal was Legate to France, in *Revue des Questions Historiques*, vol. XXXIV, 1883, p. 111. The disregard of the Tridentine Decree concerning the age for

ordination was still widespread in 1609, judging by letters exchanged between the then Nuncio to France and the French Cardinal Secretary of State. A Bishop appointed to Langres complained to Rome in 1615 that he found two hundred priests in his diocese who had been ordained before attaining the required age.

6. Saragossa University was then new, scarcely twenty years in existence; its founder and munificent benefactor, de Cerbuna, a leading Spanish churchman, had been born near Tamarite. Up-to-date methods were followed there, "not minding so much," writes Vincent, "whether the students wrote down what was said as ensuring that they understood what was expounded and retained it in mind." Under its great Rector, Frailla, there was order in the halls, method in the teaching and discipline in the classes.

7. St. Vincent often said, "There are no theologians like those in Spain." Some writers say that he left Saragossa soon after his arrival because of the theological disputes then raging between the Spanish Thomists and Molinists. The protagonists, mainly Jesuit on one side and Dominican on the other, accused one another of maintaining dangerous positions, one party being charged with alleged Pelagianism, the other of sponsoring Calvinism. Father Luis de Molina, S.J., whose book on the concordance of free will and the gifts of grace triggered the first metaphysical shots in the great battle, was probably discussed and supported in the Jesuit house where Vincent lodged. A letter the young man from Dax wrote to M. de Comet suggests that he was an enthusiast for and no mean exponent of the *scientia media*. The dispute dragged on for decades. Few things are more indicative of the change that has come with the centuries than the fact that European cabinets could, and did, split on that one controversial issue; in 1600 men were still sufficiently interested in abstruse points of religion to argue about them. Though the whole affair seems, in retrospect, unnecesarily inflamed, and no finality was reached, it stimulated theologians to scientific study and ought to have convinced those who lived long enough to hear all the arguments of the truth of the à Kempis saying, "Those who scrutinize mystery are overcome by glory."

8. St. Vincent more than once spoke to the Daughters of Charity about the mortified lives of the Spanish Carmelites. He said: "Carmelites, even those who were of high rank in the world and delicately nurtured, eat only vegetable soup and bad eggs. I know that for certain; the eggs they get smell putrid—like carrion; nevertheless they eat them. . . . They live very austerely, fasting for eight months each year and going without linen underclothing; they rise each night; they pray without ceasing. . . . Their mortification is indeed very great. They go barefoot. Perhaps they wear sandals here in France; I do not know what they do here but in Spain they wear neither shoes nor stockings. . . . No matter how hard the winter they sleep on a little hay or straw. . . ." He could have known the Carmelites of Saragossa; one of St. Teresa's first companions, Mother Isabel of Santo Domingo, founded a house of the Reform there in 1588. That convent was at the height of its first fervor during the following fifteen years when Vincent came to the city, and Mother Isabel's reputation for sanctity was widespread throughout Aragon.

9. During the Fronde rebellion in France, Vincent spoke of another kingdom and its king. He said, "I once lived in a kingdom where no one ever spoke about the king. Because he is a consecrated person they hold him and all that he stands for in such respect that they never talk about him. Hence in that country all is unity; the people are one and all united to their king and will allow no one to demur at anything he says or does. . . . Here in France one will say, 'Oh, the King of France is not doing his duty as he should; if we do not do something about it he will bring ruin on us all.' Another will repeat this. . . . A third will add to it. No wonder we have rebellions. If we took a lesson from other nations we would have less war." He was hardly speaking of Tunis; nor of Italy, almost as war-torn as France. The only other foreign country he had lived in was Spain; and the description fits the case for, however much men of other nations hated Philip II, that reserved man certainly fired the imagination and held the affection of his own people.

10. The present writer has followed most of the rail and road routes between France and Spain. On one occasion, taking a car through

the Pass of Béhobie to follow a journey once done by St. Ignatius Loyola, the frontier was crossed without meeting any officials, French or Spanish, though there was some difficulty convincing the authorities further south that we had not arrived by parachute or been smuggled in, and that our intentions were honorable. Smugglers do a roaring trade in the Pyreneean area, the Basques being past masters in the art. H. V. Morton tells of them smuggling a grand piano across the mountains!

Chapter II

1. Babeau, A. *Les Voyageurs depuis le Renaissance jusqu'à la Revolution* (Paris, 1885), pp. 67ff.; also de Thou, J. A., *Mémoires de la Vie de Jacques Auguste de Thou* (Rotterdam, 1711), pp. 59ff. For further descriptions of Toulouse in late 16th and early 17th century, cf. Le Roux de Lincy, *Le Voyage de France* (Paris, 1647), Vol. I, p. 379; Duchesne, André, *Les Antiquités et Recherches des Villes de toute la France* (Paris, 1629), pp. 751ff.; also Laetius, Tallemant de Roux, Golnitz, de Varenne, Jouvin de Rochefort, etc., and the works of the geographers, Masson, des Rues and le Clerc. There are several local monographs and provincial histories which cover places in France associated with St. Vincent de Paul at various periods of his life.
2. Ménabréa, A., *op. cit.*, p. 24.
3. D'Irsay, Stephen, *Histoire des Universités Françaises et étrangères* (Paris, 1932, 2 vols.), II, pp. 61ff.; also Mariéjol in *l'Histoire de France* by de Lavisse, Vol. VI, Part II, pp. 98-99. D'Irsay gives the *Cahier général des rémonstrances du clergé aux États-Généraux de 1614*, art. CXXVI; also *Université de Toulouse* by C. Jourdain, p. 85.
4. Gadave, Réne, *Les documents pour l'histoire de l'Université de Toulouse* (Toulouse, 1910), pp. 64ff. and 196ff.
5. Dudon, Paul, S.J., *Le VII centenaire de l'Université de Toulouse, Études*, Vol. 199, June 20th, 1929, pp. 731-732.
6. De Varenes, Claude, *Le voyage de France* (Paris, 1643), pp. 122ff.

7. Dom Vaissète, O.S.B., *Histoire Générale du Languedoc* (Paris, 1645, 42 vols.), Vol. V., pp. 496ff.
8. Cf. Notes 3 and 5 in Chapter I of present book.
9. Cruppi, Jean, *Le Père Ange, Duc de Joyeuse, Maréchal de France et Capucin* (Paris, 1928), pp. 247-248. Also *Histoire Générale du Languedoc*, Vol. V, pp. 494ff.

Chapter III

1. V. de P. (I), pp. 7ff.
2. V. de P. (I), p. 7, n. 19; also (VI), p. 601.
3. V. de P. (I), p. 11.
4. V. de P. (I), p. 15.
5. Calvet, J., *op. cit.*, p. 35.

Chapter IV

1. V. de P. (I), p. 18.
2. Abelly, Vol. I, Ch. 5, pp. 2ff.
3. Brantôme, de (Pierre de Bourdeille), *Livre des Dames* (English translation, London, 1899), with elucidations on some of those ladies by Sainte-Beuve), pp. 152-213; Tallemant des Réaux, *Historiettes* (Paris, 1834-35, 6 vols.), Vol. I, pp. 165ff.; Ferrière, Hector de la, *Trois Amoureuses au XVIe Siècle* (Paris, 1860), pp. 292-293.

Chapter V

1. V. de P. (XII), p. 258.
2. Poinsenet, M.D., *France Religieuse du XVIIe Siècle* (Paris, 1958), p. 11.
3. Retz, Cardinal de, *Oeuvres* (Paris, 1870-1920, 11 vols.), Vol. I, p. 89.
4. Saint-Simon, Duc de, *Mémoires* (Paris, 1879-1930, 43 vols.), Vol. II, pp. 365-366.

5. Maynard, Ulysse, *Vie de S. Vincent de Paul* (Paris, 1861), Bk. VIII, Ch. I., pp. 415ff. (Père Coste considers that Maynard embroidered this incident.)
6. Abelly, Bk. II, Ch. II, Section 1, p. 213.
7. V. de P. (IX), p. 646.
8. V. de P. (XIII), p. 339.
9. Ménabréa, André, S. *Vincent de Paul: Le Savant* (Paris, 1948), pp. 33-35.
10. V. de P. (XIII), p. 4.

Chapter VI

1. Abelly, Bk. II, Ch. II, Section 4, p. 29.
2. V. de P. (XIII), p. 53.
3. Collet, P., *La vie de S. Vincent de Paul* (Nancy, 1748, 2 vols.), Vol. I, p. 62.
4. V. de P. (XIII), pp. 423ff.
5. Peers, E. Allison (editor and translator), *Letters of Saint Teresa of Jesus* (London, 1952, 2 vols.).
6. Abelly, Bk. I, Ch. IX, p. 53.

Chapter VII

1. Desmaze, C., *Le Châtelet de Paris* (Paris, 1870), pp. 354ff.
2. Evelyn, J., *Diary and Correspondence* (London, 1854, 4 vols.), Vol. I, pp. 80-81. Diary entry for 7th October, 1644.
3. V. de P. (XII), p. 219.
4. Calvet, J., *op. cit.*, p. 65.
5. Bedoyere, M. de la, *François de Sales* (London, 1960), p. 91.

Chapter VIII

1. Hanotaux, G., *op. cit.*, Vol. I, pp. 481-496; Ménabréa, A., S. *Vincent de Paul: Le Maître des Hommes d'État* (Paris, 1944), pp. 157-162; Lough, J., *An Introduction to Seventeenth*

Century France (London, 1955), pp. 1-25.
2. Calvet, J., *op. cit.*, pp. 82–83.
3. V. de P. (I), p. 26.
4. V. de P. (I), pp. 37-38.
5. Griffet, H., S.J., *L'Histoire du règne de Louis XIII.* . . . (Paris, 1768, 3 vols.), Vol. II, pp. 78-79; Hanotaux G., *op. cit.*, Vol. III, pp. 300-361.

Chapter IX

1. V. de P. (XIII), pp. 518-519.
2. Ménabréa, A., S. *Vincent de Paul: Le Maître des Hommes d'État* (Paris, 1944), p. 122.
3. V. de P. (I), pp. 191ff.
4. Ménabréa, A., *op. cit.*, p. 137.

Chapter X

1. Addis and Arnold (editors), *Catholic Dictionary* (London, 1951), pp. 458ff.; Mourret, Fernand, *L'Ancien Régime (XVIIe et XVIIIe Siècles)*, (Paris, 1912), pp. 345ff.; Hanotaux G., *op. cit.*, Vol. VI, 172ff.; Calvet, J., *La Littérature Religieuse de François de Sales à Fénelon* (Paris, 1956), pp. 113ff.; Knox, R. A., *Enthusiam* (Oxford, 1950), pp. 176ff.
2. Calvet, J., *op. cit.*, *La Littérature Religieuse.* . . . , pp. 92-93.
3. Lancelot, C., *Mémoires touchant la vie de M. de Saint-Cyran* (Cologne, 1738, 2 vols.), Vol. II, p. 301; Abelly, Bk. III, Ch. XIII, Section 1, p. 203.
4. De Retz, Cardinal, *op. cit.*, Vol. I, pp. 177-180.
5. Ménabréa, A., *op. cit.*, p. 174.
6. V. de P. (XIII), pp. 798-799.
7. V. de P (XIII), p. 801.
8. V. de P. (III), pp. 210-211.
9. V. de P. (III), p. 211.

Chapter XI

1. Rédier, A., *La vraie vie de Saint Vincent de Paul* (Paris, 1927), pp. 105-107.
2. V. de P. (I), pp. 339-340.
3. Abelly, Vol. II, Ch. XII, p. 411.
4. Mourret, F., *op. cit.*, pp. 363-364.
5. V. de P. (III), pp. 328ff.
6. Dodin, A., *Saint Vincent de Paul et la Charité* (Paris, 1960), p. 57.
7. Descourveaux, P., *La Vie de Monsieur Bourdoise* (Paris, 1714), pp. 55ff.

Chapter XII

1. V. de P. (XI), p. 317.
2. Abelly, Bk. II, Ch. XI, Section 1, pp. 380ff.
3. Hanotaux, G., *op. cit.*, Vol. VI, p. 195; also same page, n. 3.
4. V. de P. (II), p. 393, and (X), p. 342; Abelly, Bk. III, Ch. VIII, Section 2, p. 88.
5. V. de P. (II), pp. 500ff.
6. V. de P. (IV), 340ff.; Abelly, Bk. II, Ch. I, Section 8, pp. 140ff.
7. V. de P. (VII), pp. 130, 139, 160, 165, 171, 174, 192, 197, 211, 218, 249; also (VIII), pp. 25, 268, 439, 449.
8. V. de P. (XI), p. 422.

Chapter XIII

1. V. de P. (III), pp. 360-361.
2. V. de P. (III), pp. 406-408.
3. V. de P. (IV), pp. 455ff.
4. V. de P. (IV), p. 587.
5. V. de P. (IV), pp. 586-587.
6. V. de P. (XI), pp. 331-332.
7. V. de P. (VII), pp. 130, 139, 160, 165, 171, 174, 192, 197, 211,

BIBLIOGRAPHY

(A) ST VINCENT DE PAUL

PRIMARY SOURCES:
Saint Vincent de Paul: Correspondance, Entretiens, Documents. 15 vols. (Paris, 1920-1960). Critical edition of the saint's letters, conferences, etc., edited and annotated by Pierre Coste, C.M.
La vie du vénérable serviteur de Dieu, Vincent de Paul, by Louis Abelly (Paris, 1664). Abelly, Bishop of Rodez, was well acquainted with Vincent de Paul and met him frequently between 1635 and 1660. His *Life* was published four years after the saint's death. Written in the florid, adulatory style of 17th century hagiography it is nevertheless penetrating and detailed, and the author had an advantage later biographers lacked—long and intimate knowledge of his subject.

SECONDARY SOURCES:
Ansart, André-Joseph, *L'Esprit de Saint Vincent de Paul* (Paris, 1780).
Calvet, Mgr. Jean, *Saint Vincent de Paul* (Paris, 1947. English trans., London, 1952).
Chantelauze, R., *Saint Vincent de Paul chez les Gondi* (Paris, 1882).
Collet, Pierre, C.M., *La vie de Saint Vincent de Paul,* 2 vols. (Nancy, 1748).

Coste, Pierre, C.M., *Le Grand Saint du Grand Siècle, Monsieur Vincent,* 3 vols. (Paris, 1932. English trans. by J. Leonard, C.M., entitled *The Life and Labours of St Vincent de Paul,* London, 1934)
Dodin, André, C.M., *Saint Vincent de Paul et la Charité* (Paris, 1960).
Feillet, Alphonse, *La misère au temps de la Fronde et Saint Vincent de Paul* (Paris, 1862).
Giraud, Victor, *Saint Vincent de Paul* (Paris, 1932).
Guichard, J., *Saint Vincent de Paul esclave à Tunis* (Paris, 1937).
Herrera, J., C.M., and Pardo, V., C.M., *San Vicente de Paul: Biografía y Escritos* (Madrid, 1955).
Lavedan, Henri, *Monsieur Vincent, aumônier général des galères* (Paris, 1928).
Loth, Arthur, *Saint Vincent de Paul et sa mission sociale* (Paris, 1880).
Maynard, Theodore, *Apostle of Charity: Life of St Vincent de Paul* (London, 1940).
Maynard, Ulysse, *Saint Vincent de Paul, sa vie, son temps, son influence,* 4 vols. (Paris, 1860-1861).
Ménabréa, André, *Saint Vincent de Paul: Le Maître des hommes d'État* (Paris, 1944).
———, *Saint Vincent de Paul: Le Savant* (Paris, 1948).

SECONDARY SOURCES : (cont'd.)

Mott, M., C.M., Saint Vincent de Paul et le Sacerdoce (Paris, 1900).

Rédier, Antoine, La vraie vie de Saint Vincent de Paul (Paris, 1927).

(B) ST VINCENT'S TIMES
AND CONTEMPORARIES

Addis and Arnold (editors), Catholic Dictionary (London, 1951).

Babeau, A., Les Voyageurs depuis la Renaissance jusqu'à la Révolution (Paris, 1885).

Battifol, Louis, Richelieu et le roi Louis XIII (Paris, 1934).

Bedoyère, M. de la, François de Sales (London, 1960).

Brantôme, M. l'Abbé de, The Book of the Ladies (English trans. by K. Prescott Wormeley, London, 1899).

Brémond, Henri, Histoire Littéraire du sentiment religieux, 12 vols. (Paris, 1916-1938).

Broutin, Paul, S.J., La Réforme pastorale en France au XVIIᵉ Siècle, 2 vols. (Tournai, 1956).

Calvet, Mgr. Jean, La Littérature Religieuse de François de Sales à Fénelon (Vol. v of Histoire de la Littérature Française, Paris, 1956).

————, Portrait de Louise de Marillac (Paris, 1958).

Cruppi, Jean, Le Père Ange, Duc de Joyeuse, Maréchal de France et Capucin (Paris, 1928).

Dagens, Jean, Bérulle et les origines de la restauration catholique (Paris, 1950).

Darche, J., Le saint abbé Bourdoise (Paris, 1884).

Descourveaux, Philibert, La vie de Monsieur Bourdoise (Paris, 1714).

Desmaze, C., Le Châtelet de Paris (Paris, 1870).

d'Irsay, Stephen, see Irsay.

Duchesne, André, Les Antiquités et Récherches des Villes de toute la France (Paris, 1629).

Dudon, Paul, S.J., Le VII centenaire de l'Université de Toulouse (in Études, Vol. 199, June 20th, 1929) Paris, 1929.

Evelyn, John, Diary and Correspondence, 4 vols. (London 1854).

Ferrière, Hector de la, Trois Amoureuses au XVIᵉ Siècle (Paris, 1860).

Gadave, René, Les documents pour l'histoire de l'Université de Toulouse, 2 vols. (Toulouse, 1910).

Griffet, H., S.J., L'Histoire du règne de Louis XIII, 3 vols. (Paris, 1768).

Hamon-Gonthier, Letourneau, Vie de Saint François de Sales, 2 vols. (Paris, 1909).

Hanotaux, Gabriel, and le Duc de la Force, L'Histoire du Cardinal de Richelieu, 6 vols. (Paris, 1895-1899).

Harang, J., Bourdoise (Paris, 1947).

Houssaye, M. l'Abbé, Le Père de Bérulle et l'Oratoire (Paris, 1874).

Irsay, Stephen d', Histoire des Universités françaises et étrangères, 2 vols. (Paris, 1932).

Jourdain, C., Université de Toulouse (Toulouse, 1929).

Knox, Mgr. Ronald, Enthusiasm (Oxford 1950).

Lahargou, M., *Le Collège de Dax* (Paris, 1909).

Lancelot, C., *Mémoires touchant la vie de M. de Saint-Cyran*, 2 vols. (Cologne, 1738).

Le Roux de Lincy, *Le Voyage de France* (Toulouse, 1647).

Lough, John, *An Introduction to Seventeenth Century France* (London, 1954).

Magne, Émile, *La vie quotidienne au temps de Louis XIII* (Paris, 1946).

Mariéjol, Jean-Hippolyte, *L'Histoire de France (de Lavisse)*, Vol. VI (Paris, 1906).

Motteville, Madame de, *Mémoires*, 34 vols. (Paris, 1854).

Mourret, Fernard, *L'Ancien Régime (XVIIe et XVIIIe Siècles)* (Paris, 1912).

Pagès, G., *Naissance du Grand Siècle: La France de Henri IV à Louis XIV* (Paris, 1948).

Poinsenet, M.D., *France Religieuse du XVIIe Siècle* (Paris, 1958).

Prunel, Chanoine L., *Sebastian Zamet, évêque de Langres 1588-1655* (Paris, 1912).

———, *La Renaissance catholique en France au XVIIe Siècle* (Paris, 1928).

Retz, Cardinal de, *Œuvres*, 11 vols. (Paris, 1870-1920).

Richelieu, Cardinal de, *Mémoires* (Société d'Histoire de France edition), 10 vols. (Paris, 1908-1931).

———, *Testament Politique* (Paris, 1947).

Rochefoucauld, Gabriel de la, *Le Cardinal François de la Rochefoucauld* (Paris, 1926).

Saint-Beuve, Charles-A., *Port-Royal*, 7 vols. (Paris, 1923).

Saint-Simon, Duc de, *Mémoires*, 43 vols. (Paris, 1879-1930).

Sheedy, J. P., C.M., *Untrodden Paths: The Social Apostolate of St Louise de Marillac* (London, 1958).

Tallemant des Réaux, *Historiettes*, 8 vols. (Paris, 1932).

Tapié, Victor L., *La France de Louis XIII et de Richelieu* (Paris, 1952).

Thou, Jacques-August de, *Mémoires* (Rotterdam, 1711).

Vaissette, Dom, O.S.B., *Histoire Générale du Languedoc*, Vol. V, 42 vols. (Paris, 1645).

Vaissière, P. de, *La Conjuration de Cinq-Mars* (Paris, 1928).

Varennes, Claude de, *Le Voyage de France* (Rouen, 1611).

Zeller, B., *Louis XIII et Marie de Médicis* (Paris, 1883).

INDEX